UNDERSTANDING LEARNING

Companion Volumes

The companion volumes in this series are:
Teacher Development: Exploring our own practice
Edited by: Janet Soler, Anna Craft and Hilary Burgess
Developing Pedagogy: Researching practice
Edited by Janet Collins, Kim Insley and Janet Soler

All of these readers are part of a course: Developing Practice in Primary Education, that is itself part of the Open University MA programme.

The Open University MA in Education

The Open University MA in Education is now firmly established as the most popular postgraduate degree for education professionals in Europe, with over 3,000 students registering each year. The MA in Education is designed particularly for those with experience of teaching, the advisory service, educational administration or allied fields.

Structure of the MA

The MA is a modular degree, and students are therefore free to select from a range of options the programme which best fits in with their interests and professional goals. Specialist lines in management, applied linguistics and lifelong learning are also available. Study in the Open University's Advanced Diploma can also be counted towards the MA, and successful study in the MA programme entitles students to apply for entry into the Open University Doctorate in Education programme.

OU Supported Open Learning

The MA in Education programme provides great flexibility. Students study at their own pace, in their own time, anywhere in the European Union. They receive specially prepared study materials, supported by tutorials, thus offering the chance to work with other students.

The Doctorate in Education

The Doctorate in Education is a new part-time doctoral degree, combining taught courses, research methods and a dissertation designed to meet the needs of professionals in education and related areas who are seeking to extend and deepen their knowledge and understanding of contemporary educational issues. The Doctorate in Education builds upon successful study within the Open University MA in Education programme.

How to apply

If you would like to register for this programme, or simply to find out more information about available courses, please write for the *Professional Development in Education* prospectus to the Course Reservations Centre, PO Box 724, The Open University, Walton Hall, Milton Keynes, MK7 6ZW, UK (Telephone 0 (0 44) 1908 653231). Details can also be viewed on our web page http://www.open.ac.uk.

UNDERSTANDING LEARNING

Influences and Outcomes

edited by
Janet Collins and Deirdre Cook

P·C·P
Paul Chapman
Publishing Ltd

in association with

The Open
University

First published in 2001, Reprinted 2001

 Paul Chapman Publishing Ltd
A SAGE Publications Company
6 Bonhill Street
London EC2A 4PU

SAGE Publications Inc
2455 Teller Road
Thousand Oaks, California 91320

SAGE Publications India Pvt Ltd
32, M-Block Market
Greater Kailash - I
New Delhi 110 048

British Library Cataloguing in Publication Data
A catalogue record for this book is available from the British
Library

ISBN 0 7619 6932 2
ISBN 0 7619 6933 0 (pbk)

Library of Congress catalog record available

Typeset by Dorwyn Ltd, Rowlands Castle, Hants
Printed in Great Britain by Athenaeum Press, Gateshead

Contents

Acknowledgements

The editors and publishers wish to thank the following for permission to use copyright material:

Cambridge University Press for material from R. P. McDermott (1996) 'The acquisition of a child by a learning disability' in J. Lave and S. Shanklin, eds, *Understanding Practice: Perspectives on activity and context*, pp. 269–301;

The Continuum International Publishing Group Ltd for material from S. Tomlinson (1995) 'Home–school links' in R. Best, P. Lang, C. Lodge and C. Watkins, *Pastoral Care and Personal-Social Education*, Cassell, pp. 234–45;

Lawrence Erlbaum Associates, Inc for material from Mara Krechevsky and Steve Seidel (1998) 'Minds at Work: applying multiple intelligences in the classroom' in R. J. Sternberg and W. M. Williams, eds, *Intelligence, Instruction and Assessment: Theory into Practice*, pp. 17–38. Copyright © 1998 by Lawrence Erlbaum Associates, Inc; and C. Bereiter (1998) 'Situated cognition and how to overcome it' in D. Kirshner and J. A. Whitson, eds, *Situated Cognition: Social, Semiotic and Psychological Perspectives*, pp. 281–99. Copyright © 1998 by Lawrence Erlbaum Associates;

Kluwer Academic Publishers for material from Nimrod Aloni (1997) 'A redefinition of liberal and humanistic education', *International Review of Education*, 43:1, pp. 87–107. Copyright © 1997 UNESCO Institute for Education and Kluwer Academic Publishers;

Open University Press for Wilfred Carr and Anthony Hartnett (1996) *Education and the Struggle for Democracy*, pp. 1–16;

Sage Publications for material from Cathy Nutbrown (1996) *Respectful Educators – Capable Learners*, Paul Chapman Publishing, pp. 44–55. Copyright © 1996 Cathy Nutbrown;

Taylor & Francis Ltd for material from J. Ireson and S. Hallam (1999) 'Raising standards: Is ability grouping the answer?', *Oxford Review of*

Education, 25:3, pp. 344–60; D. Reay and D. Wiliam (1999) 'I'll Be a Nothing: structure, agency and the construction of identity through assessment', *British Educational Research Journal*, 25:3, pp. 343–54; P. Silcock (1999) *New Progressivism*, Falmer Press, pp. 135–47; M. J. Drummond (1998) 'Children yesterday, today and tomorrow' in C. Richards and P. H. Taylor, eds, *How Shall We School Our Children? Primary Education and Its Future*, Falmer Press, pp. 95–106; Carol Vincent (1996) *Parents and Teachers: Power and Participation*, Falmer Press, pp. 73–90; and Patricia Broadfoot (1996) 'Liberating the learning through assessment' in G. Claxton, T. Atkinson, M. Osborn and M. Wallace, eds, *Liberating the Learner*, Routledge, pp. 32–44.

Introduction

Deirdre Cook

The model of education that underpins this book is one in which the ideas of values and evaluation feature prominently. These are set against a background of some of the classical traditions found in education and political thought. It considers how current professional issues can be illuminated by a careful reassessment of significant themes drawing on a range of inter-linked perspectives.

As both teachers and researchers, reflection is a familiar and powerful idea through which we, as professional practitioners, explore our relationship with the world around us. We are both *in* and *of* this world and our actions affect it and ourselves, and our reflections occur both while we are engaged in some action or other and after we have completed them (Schon, 1983).

If you feel that it is not possible to disentangle oneself entirely from the world of lived experiences and that it is still important to evaluate in some way the meaningfulness of the messages which come back from it then you will find Schon's ideas useful. As reflective practitioners, we revise our beliefs and theories about teaching, researching and our roles in these continually. In carrying out these reflections, we try to be as trustworthy as possible and record as accurately as we can our observations, thoughts, feelings and perceptions about what is going on around us. These are personal and subjective activities and not ones which are about establishing objective truth or proving any specific point. This view is an attempt to recognize that the social world in which we operate is complex and what we do is affected powerfully by our beliefs, values and motivation for taking action. Politics and power relations impact on our professional world and influence what we can do in both practice and research. Since it is seldom possible to be completely objective and detached in our endeavours to improve practice, we need to be clear about the values we bring with us and to be open with ourselves about the belief systems within which we oper-ate. It is these belief systems that we use to give meaning to our reflections *in* and *on* action.

A number of the themes we are dealing with here are concerned with areas where it is not possible to establish a single model of truth. They are areas where we must make judgements about ideas, to decide if we find one good or better in some sense than another. Many of the concepts, theoreti-cal positions and themes considered, link closely with philosophical, histor-ical, psychological and social approaches to education. Sometimes this requires a multidimensional and self-questioning exploration of core and

1

central concerns: examining the purpose of education, the interrelationship between our ideas about individuals and the groups in which they find themselves in terms of cultural and cognitive dimensions, and the articulation of a personal theory of educational practice, contribute to the development of professional 'voice'. If teachers expect to be heard then they too must listen to the voices of their pupils, and to those of the parents. As many influences reach into teachers in the classroom so, too, professional beliefs, practices and decision-making affect the wider community. In a society where democracy is a valued idea, no voice should be excluded.

Notions of democracy, of a democratic society and of democratic education form a recurring theme threaded through the ideas presented here. This is sometimes explicit and on other occasions more covert, but underpinning everything lies a concern with creating a view of education which will serve society well in this the twenty-first century. Central to the idea of democracy is a belief that every individual is of value as a citizen and, as a consequence, should have certain freedoms. These will be very familiar and any list of them might include freedom of expression, free and frequent elections where real choices are available, a right of assembly and a free press, an independent judiciary and freedom of movement, religion and teaching. Today as in the past, this system of ideas is not without its critics. Some people simply feel that in such bureaucratic times as ours where multinational agencies have so much influence, then our representatives and government can no longer influence decision-making as they once did. Others feel that democratic processes are too inefficient for fast and effective decision-making, while its advocates feel it needs to be extended to involve more people in decision-making at as many levels as possible. The practicality of this aspiration is questioned by those who feel that it is not possible to do this because many of the issues are too complex. Furthermore, many people are not well practised in democratic decision-making, having had little or no experience of it. Making informed decisions demands that everyone has access to, and understands, the necessary information and this makes demands on the individual and the state which are unattainable.

The debate with regard to democracy, freedom and equality here is very real, having as a fundamental question our beliefs about 'the good life', the well-being of society, the nature of individual freedoms and the ensuing tension between inclusivity and elitism. The decisions we make about what is 'of value' to us as educators may result in our experiencing real conflict and tensions within our professional lives. A commitment to freedom and equality at either a personal, institutional or state level sits uncomfortably with ideas about education as a consumer product and the levelling effect of market forces.

The ideological conflict of recent years between aspects of liberalism and democracy in education has been both intellectual and political. The associated reforms of the curriculum and teacher education were a consequent part of a powerful offensive to impose a particular political interpretation of what constituted the 'good life' in terms of its educational prerequisites. In order to achieve this end, teaching has increasingly been presented as a value-free and 'technicist' activity having an emphasis on skills and competences (Carr and Hartnett, 1996). In consequence, there seems to have been very little time set aside to consider and reflect on the ideological assumptions, interests and power structures which support or influence our teaching. As a word, 'ideology' has increasingly taken on pejorative associations but its origins were very much less negative. In the early nineteenth century it simply referred to the 'science of ideas' which, somewhat ironically, we may now feel, aspired to show us how we ordered our thinking and acquired our prejudices.

As this term is most commonly encountered as a way of describing the ways of thinking or organizing ideas held by particular groups and since such groups have often been political or religious, the word had increasingly taken on associations with ideals, beliefs and passions. When ideas are part of a particular conviction or belief, they become tremendously important values for that group. Ideological clashes are not at all uncommon when people see the world in different ways. In fact one way of characterizing an ideology is as a 'visionary speculation' (Carr and Hartnett, Chapter 1 in this volume). The implications for education of an ideological stance such as their 'democratic vision of education' is that its systems must both lead to democratic participation and do so through practices which can be seen as clearly respecting the freedoms of individuals referred to earlier. The associated processes of empowerment and the prevention of discrimination and repression are difficult to achieve at institutional, rather than individual, levels in schools. This is because, traditionally, schools have power structures and authority patterns which do not encourage or invite alternative arrangements or suggestions from teachers, parents or pupils. When education is also closely linked to the idea of grading children and beginning to prepare them for some specified place in a world beyond the school system then, consequently, empowerment and active democratic participation become ideas of diminished importance. Reconciling a wish to 'empower' with the role we have as key players in this grading and sorting process every day as we assess, evaluate and plan for the learning of the children in care can be a source of considerable professional conflict.

Multiple ideological systems exist but the outcome is not necessarily conflict or clash. Some writers, for example Aloni (Chapter 2 in this volume), aim to ensure an integration of ideas. They believe that an open discourse conducted in goodwill between those holding different views is to be preferred. 'Ideological enemies' he claims, more commonly 'dogmatically demonize and delegitimate the other.'

Emphasizing comparability rather than points of difference is seen by a number of writers as central to re-examining ideological ideas in order to realign old and new values through informed professional dialogue. One focus for this discussion is the debate which surrounds child-centred education. This is an important ideological perspective which has had considerable influence on both the professional formation of teachers and on classroom practice. This is a specific example of a dominating ideology. As educators we should be able to outline our ideological belief systems through reasoned argument in a way which recognizes that ideologies 'need not and should not polarize' (Silcock, Chapter 3 in this volume). He further suggests, that as an essential adjunct to the business of reconciling 'the twin demands of individuals and society', we are 'pragmatic' in our decision-making. Pragmatism, from a philosophical perspective, links with the writings of Pierce, James and Dewey. These caution us to be conscious of the practical effects of our interpretation and justification of our beliefs. As Silcock points out, a more politically expedient and 'common sense' use of this term suggests that it is 'whatever works'.

The educational reforms alluded to earlier led increasingly to populist views that what education required was a return to didacticism as it was conceived of in traditional nineteenth- and early twentieth-century class-rooms. The progressivist child-centred ideology of the post-Plowden era had, prior to the introduction of the Education Reform Act 1988 (ERA), come under considerable attack. Not least because of close associations with ideas drawn from developmental psychology which had attracted crit-ical attention. Child-centredness, with its associated ideas of learner auto-nomy, ambivalence about the role of the educator and individualization of the curriculum, became associated with the supposed failure of progressiv-ism to meet the economic challenges of a rapidly changing society. Despite the immense criticism levelled against them from a variety of sources, many teachers continue to hold fast to their ideological beliefs about the value of learner-centred education. For them, outside interventions and initiatives stand in marked contrast to their belief in curriculum adaptation and innovation.

Silcock links progressivist child-centred ideologies not only with de-velopmentalism but also with constructivist theories. Constructivism has its roots in pragmatist views; it has links to both philosophical and psychologi-cal traditions. At one level constructivism offers us an explanation of the nature of knowledge. At another, it describes how cognitive processes might be acquired and developed. It is used to provide models of learning and knowledge which could be used to provide insights into teaching and the curriculum. As Terwel (1999) points out it is 'not a robust concept'. It is, however, a broad and frequently referred to ideology in which the 'overlapping' of conceptual ideas can readily be seen across many of its research findings and discussion.

What is central to constructivist explanations is the view that knowledge is not seen as fixed and existing independently outside the 'knower', ready to be collected by the learner. It rejects the traditionalist view of 'know-ledge transmission' but does not deny that learners can learn as a result of a range of methods (Von Glaserfield, in Airasian and Walsh, 1997). Rather learners are to be seen as playing an active role in 'constructing', in some way, their own meanings. 'Since individuals make their own meaning from their beliefs and experiences, all knowledge is tentative, subjective and personal' (Airasian and Walsh, 1997, p. 445). Terwel's warning about its fragility acts to remind us that despite its long history, as yet, constructivism is an epistemological description of learning and not a practical prescription for teaching. Teachers must be involved in educational research and be active in relating ideas about learning to both classroom practice and curriculum development if we are to realize what he and others see as the ideal of 'authentic learning'.

The linking of existing and new experiences in the process of learning is an essential concern of progressivist and constructivist views. For many educators this idea is most readily recognizable in the familiar framework associated with the Piagetian ideas. Constructivism here sees learning as the process by which children gradually come to acquire, through their own interactions with the empirical world, the universal forms of knowledge. There are, however, multiple theoretical and ideological extensions of this notion of constructivism, most of which have come about in response to challenges which could not be convincingly explained by existing evidence or conceptualizations. Some educators see these extensions as 'emergent' ideologies, others as versions of that very broad category 'constructivism'.

One of the challenges to the Piagetian-dominated infrastructure linking constructivism to educational practices was that which saw the creation of individual personal knowledge as being paramount. The outcomes of this are interestingly diverse. When this Piagetian-inspired idea of individual patterns of learning became associated with that of intelligence then this interesting development eventually led to a way of seeing individuals' knowledge constructions in terms of multiple intelligences within the framework of theories of mind (e.g. Krechevsky and Seidel, Chapter 4 in this volume). Meadows (1993) outlines how early in the twentieth century 'intelligence' was considered to be unchanging and established in individuals at birth. Later this view was challenged because there was dissatisfaction with the outcomes of psychometric research amongst those who felt that such approaches were not truly giving a representative picture of people's ability. This psychometric tradition, when linked to explorations and studies of Piagetian concepts, she considers, led to a radical extension of views about individual constructions of knowledge and differences in performance and rates of development. The outcome of synthesis is the view that suggests that there are different and partially independent sorts of intelligence which affect individuals and their learning (Gardner, 1993).

The other development of constructivist thinking draws attention to the fact that an emphasis on individualized knowledge construction neglects to consider sufficiently the impact of social cultural, contextual and interpersonal interactions on personal learning. This challenge resulted in renewed attention to the writings of cultural psychologists in the Vygotskian and neo-Vygotskian tradition. This notion of the discrediting of Piagetian applications to education practices is quite widespread and is also discussed by a number of other writers (e.g. Bernstein, 1993; Van de Veer and Valsiner, 1994) who suggest that this created a need for a new identity figure. For many, this came from the sociocultural or socio-historic theories of Vygotsky.

Although a significant part of Vygotsky's writings were directly about educational matters his work, like that of Piaget, has been subject to the same process of 'partial borrowing'. This results in a fluid categorization system for a web of interrelated ideas about constructivism and learning, which encompasses both social and cultural psychology. There are many points of comparability between the views of the two major theorists but there are, especially at the deeper levels of analysis, quite profound differences. For example in Piagetian theory cognitive development is seen as occurring through a single invariant sequence of stages. This is a view not shared by Vygotsky who described a very different relationship of informal and scientific concepts within the stages of development. While there is an emphasis in both theories on 'activity' there is here both a split between Vygotskian and Piagetian theories and some further divisions to be found between those who emphasize practical activity and those who consider social interaction and semiotics to be a more important focus. Methodological views about ways of researching in each model would also be quite different. As one commentator pointed out *experience* as researched in a Piagetian manner occurs in a material world where experience is physical rather than cultural or emotional (Krishner, 1997, p. 86).

Studies of this kind are sometimes categorized as being social constructivist or even as situated cognition. Some writers and theorists seek a 'reconciliation' of difference while others see such a rapprochement as undesirable or even untenable given the perceived ideological differences. Interestingly Van der Veer and Valsiner (1994, p. 4) suggest the move towards Vygotsky was required because the autonomous, individualistic nature of the curriculum derived from Piagetian ideas was seen to be a threat to 'the authority and control of the teacher'. Pollard (1993; 1996) also recognizes this potential threat and he further suggests this shift was due to the increasing recognition of the *social* nature of children's learning, and greater acknowledgement of the impact on learning of discussion and 'engagements with others'. In social constructivism, knowledge is seen in relation to individuals and the social and cultural setting in which they find themselves.

Situated cognition theorists are also involved in exploring ideas which take the same starting point as social constructivists but go somewhat further. For example, researchers such as Brown, Collins and Duguid (1989) put forward a view of learning which 'locates knowledge in particular forms of activity and not simply in mental content' (Agre, 1997, p. 71). The idea of problem-solving also features significantly in situated cognition approaches, and much of the work has involved mathematics and science and the way these subjects are dealt with in education and the real world (Lave, 1988; Walkerdine, 1988). These studies ask us to remember that the problems we encounter in our everyday world are seldom neat and tidy: they do not have clearly defined boundaries. In responding to them we cannot find clear solutions and neat 'step-wise' solutions are not useful to us. We use different kinds of knowledge in different settings with different people for different reasons to make our decisions. What we need to think about in a situated cognition approach are the complex interrelationships between the person carrying out the actions and the setting in which this takes place. Because there are so many levels and layers to think about here, situated cognition theorists draw upon a number of disciplines to help investigate their ideas.

Writers from these different disciplines present their work using the vocabulary and discourse structures which often reflect their backgrounds quite strongly and they also use the language of the emerging theory. This is an important aspect of this perspective but makes summaries and short overviews like this unrepresentative of its richness and complexity.

What this perspective is trying to achieve is a clearer recognition of the social nature of learning and cognition and to refocus attention away from the psychology of the individual mind. It sets out to challenge the individualistic and dualist ideas with which we are so familiar that they seem like common sense to us. Situated cognition theorists feel that this individualistic approach to studying learning has only recognized social and cultural influences in a very limited way. In situated cognition studies the focus is not on the individual but on the structures and interrelationships which make up the activity system being studied.

Some of the ideas within situativity are probably more familiar and more easily seen to be relevant to education than others. For example, those of 'communities of practice' and 'apprenticeship'. If we think about teachers and classrooms as communities of practice then we need to look at some complex issues in multilayered and new ways. Looking at interrelated systems means remembering that when some element of a system changes then this causes reciprocal reactions elsewhere (e.g. McDermott, Chapter 5 in this volume). Since schools traditionally work towards a view of knowledge which values decontextualization and abstraction then studies made within this framework require a radical rethink of views of learners and learning.

Constructivist views of learning are not an argument for laissez-faire attitudes to teaching: they recognize the need for teachers to be accountable. Every view of learning needs to recognize criteria for making judgements about achievement and progress. Deciding that one construction of learning is more appropriate at a certain point or in a certain place is not about controlling the learning process or imposing one specific view. The teacher's role here is to achieve a sense of balance by identifying, analysing and challenging misunderstandings in order that learners can refine their knowledge constructions. The difficulty in classrooms is that pupils quickly learn what the teacher has in mind as a preferred outcome by the way in which praise or marks are allocated. Respecting autonomy and making assessments are not easily accommodated.

Considerations of the traditions of assessment bring to the foreground again both the debate about the purpose of education and the tension in the ideas of democracy and democratic education between inclusivity and elitism. Here again it is important to look back across time and to take a multidisciplinary view so that we can better understand how current debate and the tensions within practice are the outcome of changing beliefs and expectations. At the heart of all this contestation is a desire to promote learning in the most appropriate ways. Given the intensity of the debate surrounding the purposes, practices and procedural aspects of assessment, it is no longer possible to believe that making judgements about children's ability is a straightforward thing. As practitioners we need to examine very critically the ideologies of learning which lie forgotten behind many every-day practices. We need too to look at the language and terminology which we use here to separate out that which reflects older static models from those which recognize and respect the autonomy of learners and the authenticity of the tasks we use to obtain evidence for our judgements. Some of this language is technical and complex but the way we talk about learner's ability can be 'a potentially insidious form of discrimination' (Solity, 1991).

Assessment practices are a source of tension, even of anxiety, for many who have either professional or parental involvement with Primary and Early Years education. In the latter this owes much to the ideological clash between progressivist views of what the education of young children should emphasize and the more recent grafting-on of goal-orientated achievement measures which reflect a different tradition. Numerical outcomes, achievement levels and other data to support the calculation, a 'value-added' dimension, are more accurately located in traditional interpretation of liberalism. Understanding where we stand in relation to the traditions of assessment and the different views and practices linked to its various purposes can only be helpful to us in making fair and representative judgements about standards of achievement. It is important in this debate to be clear about whether we see assessment as serving children and their learning or as serving some other wider and more political agenda.

As part of this wider debate about assessment, particular attention is given to the drive to raise standards (Qualifications and Curriculum Authority [QCA] and the Office for Standards in Education [OFSTED]). As well as reflecting on 'how' this might be achieved in practical ways we need not to lose sight of the democratic and humanistic ideals associated with educational practices. Constructivism, in its many forms, assumes that everyone has the potential to learn and that there exists also the possibility of incremental improvement. However, it also accepts that learning will be different when social, cultural and contextual variation occur. In an individualistic and elitist system not everyone can have prizes. In a democratic one everyone is of equal worth. As in our earlier reflection we need to review more than one outcome here. On the one hand we need to think about the 'fitness for purpose' of the assessment instruments we use and ask if any one can effectively serve multiple purposes. On the other hand we need to decide about the equity or 'fairness' of any of the data collected not only in the light of the professional and educational value systems we adhere to but also in terms of the reliability and validity of the evidence. In addition democratic and constructivist views of education require that the practical effects of implemented beliefs be taken into account and child-centred ones would surely insist that consideration be given to the effect upon learners of assessment practices. Self-determination and the ability to make soundly based critical judgements about oneself are part of the educational processes relating to the autonomy of learners. They, too, have a part to play in the practices to which they are subjected. The processes of categorization and consignment affects not only the children at an immediate and personal level but, as some recent research shows, it also affects the pedagogical decision-making of teachers as well as the curriculum that is offered to children. The links between testing, teaching and driving up standards are clearly visible in studies which also expose the extent of the pressure on the belief systems of the teachers and on the children's perceptions of themselves. For the children and their teachers, as their voices tell, these are testing times (Reay and Wiliam, Chapter 12 in this volume).

Other dilemmas tend to follow from rigidly individualistic assessment practices: that is, there is payoff between breadth of curriculum coverage and the achievement of high scores. One can only be achieved by sacrificing the other and these children speak meaningfully of the curriculum-narrowing which precedes formal testing. There is little place either within systems of this sort for the recognition of idiosyncratic or individualistic learning. The autonomy of both teachers and pupils is reduced to nothingness and constructivist notions of learning rapidly revert to reductionist principles. The equitable collection of evidence from a range of authentic and representative learning tasks would also seem to have fallen victim to the 'tyranny of testing'.

In our very competitive and global economy there is pressure on every state to ensure that its citizens are fully equipped to protect their interests. This pressure in turn is replicated in the socio-political and cultural life of everyone, competition produces winners and losers in a way which collaboration does not. One tension in the organizational debate here is how best to balance alienation and social exclusion against practical measures to support high achievement and reduce the complexity of the teaching role. What is central to our concern is how is the evidence we have available to us to be realistically assessed? To do this it is necessary to review not only the findings of research but also examine 'how, why, when. and for what specific purpose' it was carried out. Radical changes to practice based on soundly evaluated socio-political or cognitive grounds will produce positive improvements. Considering and debating important professional issues will make this outcome more, not less, likely.

Returning to the earlier discussion about democratic participation in education and the idea of the right to contribute to the debate, it is important not to fail to hear the voices of parents. Their views about links between themselves and the education professional are an essential element of the wider debate about learning, educational achievement, raising standards and professional practices. Parents occupy an interesting threefold position in the discussion here. One of their roles is as 'consumers' in the educational marketplace. They have been encouraged to position themselves in this way by the various education Acts of recent years. Parental rights and choices are a consideration in measurement of school and teacher accountability. It is through parents' perceptions of a school's effectiveness that popular schools remain competitive and others decline. Looked at rather differently the significance of parental roles to the successful learning of their children is increasingly being recognized. This would encompass learning in cognitive, social, cultural and emotional domains in school and out. However, parents arc workers, politicians, citizens, voters and employers and, as such, also have voices in democratic processes as well as a personal stake in the answers to the key question about the purpose of education. Without exception, parents would claim that the well-being, attainments and achievement of their children should be given high priority when decisions on educational issues are to be made. For all these reasons schools need to cultivate parents and the establishing of satisfactory home–school links becomes important.

For teachers who want to enter this debate in order to develop professional practices, it is again necessary to step back from the present and look to the past as well as to the future. The ideological clashes which could occur in linking home and school can only be avoided by giving due consideration to the complex and controversial dimensions of what *partnership* is, what purposes it serves and how it is to be established and maintained in periods of rapid changes such as ours. Positive but unquestioning and uncritical assumptions about the 'right relationship' between the partners in this relationship will not serve either party well. Any evidence we have should be considered for its validity and reliability and in doing this traditional beliefs may need to be reassessed. Schools are the crucible in which children's personalities are forged and identities confirmed. What this means for us as educators is that issues of politics, social class, gender, sexuality and racism as well as achievement will all form part of the agenda.

Education has always featured prominently on the political agenda and never more so than at times of significant change such as now as a new century unfolds. Teachers have a privileged position in the debates about essential educational issues especially when we use our 'professional voices' in an informed manner. As our contributors suggest, this is best achieved through considered and reflective involvement in researching and teaching but perhaps also through always being conscious of the implications of our beliefs and values for our work with children.

References

Agre, P. E. (1997) Living math: Lave and Walkerdine on the meaning of arithmetic, in D. Kirshner and J. A. Whitson (eds), *Situated Cognition: Social, Semiotic and Psychological Perspectives*, London: Erlbaum Associates.

Airasian, P. W. and Walsh, M. E. (1997) Constructivist cautions, *Phi Delta Kappa*, pp. 444–9.

Bernstein, B. (1993) Foreword, in H. Daniels (ed.) *Charting the Agenda*, London: Routledge.

Brown, J. S., Collins, A. and Duguid, P. (1989) Situated cognition and the culture of learning, *Educational Researcher*, **18**(1), pp. 32–42.

Carr, W. and Hartnett, A. (1997) *Education and the Struggle for Democracy*, Buckingham: Open University Press.

Gardner, H. (1983) *Frames of Mind: The Theory of Multiple Intelligences*, London: Heinemann.

Kirshner, D. (1997) The situated development of logic in infancy: a case study, in D. Kirshner and J. A. Whitson (eds), *Situated Cognition: Social, Semiotic and Psychological Perspectives*, London: Erlbaum Associates.

Lave, J. (1988) *Cognition in Practice*, Cambridge: Cambridge University Press.

Meadows, S. (1993) *The Child as Thinker*, London: Routledge.

Pollard, A. (1993) Learning in primary schools, in H. Daniels (ed.), *Charting the Agenda*, London: Routledge.

Pollard, A. (1996) *An Introduction to Primary Education*, London: Cassell.

Schon, D. (1983) *The Reflective Practitioner*, London: Temple Smith.

Solity, J. E. (1991) 'Special Needs: a discriminatory concept?' Educational Psychology in practice **7**(1) pp. 12–19 in H. Daniels (ed.) *The Practice of Assessment: Charting the Agenda*, London: Routledge.

Terwel, J. (1999) Constructivism and its implications for curriculum theory and practice, *Curriculum Studies*, **31**(2) pp. 195–9.

Van der Veer, R. and Valsiner, J. (1994) *The Vygotsky Reader*, Oxford: Blackwell.

Walkerdine, V. (1988) *The Mastery of Reason*, London: Routledge.

Section 1: Influences on Education

This section explores some of the social, political, and psychological influences on ideologies in education. Ideology here is conceived as the science of ideas which would reveal its more recent sense of ideals, beliefs, values and passions. Each chapter offers a different paradigm (or framework for argument) for consideration but all have relevance for today's practitioners, especially those striving to provide pupils with experiences which offer quality learning in both the immediate and longer terms. The chapters in this section show something of the duality of thinking with regard to education and schooling. Here education is seen as a process which both 'empowers' and yet also creates good citizens. Similarly, schools may aim to be democratic but at the same time be striving to prepare pupils for jobs in later life.

The chapters in this section introduce a number of key issues which are picked up and developed throughout this book. These include:

- democracy
- acculturation
- autonomy
- authenticity
- accountability

In Chapter 1, Wilfred Carr and Anthony Hartnett argue persuasively in favour of seeking 'a democratic vision of education'. Their vision of education involves democratic participation of teachers, parents and pupils as well as practices which can be seen as clearly respecting the freedoms of individuals. However, they recognize that traditional power structures and authority patterns mean that the processes of empowerment and the prevention of discrimination and repression are difficult to achieve at institutional levels in schools. Rather than the current 'technicist' view of teaching which emphasizes skills and competencies, Carr and Hartnett argue for time to consider and reflect on the ideological assumptions, interests and power structures which support or influence our teaching.

In Chapter 2, Nimrod Aloni develops and expands the idea of empowerment raised in the previous chapter. Taking as a starting point a time before the early eighteenth century when liberal and humanistic education were synonymous terms, Aloni puts forward a case for a redefinition of liberal and humanistic education which draws on a wide range of diverse ideological positioning. Implicit in this definition of humanism, which stresses the empowerment of human beings, is included a commitment to the enhancement of human freedom and growth, as well as philosophical, social, intellectual and pedagogic principles. It is claimed that a contemporary humanistic theory of education should assimilate the three foundational pedagogic principles of acculturation, autonomy and authenticity.

In Chapter 3, Peter Silcock adds to the ideological debate by arguing for a 'new progressivism' in education which is founded in developmental, humanistic, democratic and pragmatic ideas. He goes on to claim that there are empirical, ethical, socio-political and practical grounds for choosing to be a modern child-centred teacher and that a commitment to individualized learning and learner autonomy is not a commitment to radical politics or some sort of postmodern denial of absolutes. There is, he says, no ambiguity involved in allying diverse, self-managed curricula to socially responsible aims and industrial needs. Indeed, Silcock totally accepts the validity of teacher accountability.

1

The Politics of Educational Ideas

Wilfred Carr and Anthony Hartnett

The Deintellectualization of Educational Policy

In education, as in so much else, we are living through difficult times. Over the past two decades there has been an unprecedented level of argument about the basic purposes of education, about how schools and their curriculum ought to be organized and controlled and about how teachers ought to be educated and trained. Teachers have been criticized for their incompetence, teacher educators lambasted for their obsession with progressive educational theories, and schools blamed for a variety of social ills ranging from a deterioration in moral standards to national economic decline. Furthermore, the tasks for which teachers and schools are being held responsible have accumulated at such a rate as to destroy any hope that they can all be achieved. In these circumstances it is unsurprising to find that there is now a growing confusion in the minds of teachers about the limits of their professional responsibilities and the nature of their educational role. Nor is it surprising that schools and other educational institutions are beginning to voice serious misgivings about the adverse educational consequences of many of the new demands that are now being made on them. More tragic, however, is the way in which these confusions and demands have thoroughly demoralized the education professions and created a culture of anxiety that operates at a level and to a degree that was previously unknown.

Although this constellation of criticism, anxiety and frustration obviously reflects a deep-seated sense of unease about the present state of contemporary schooling, it is not so obvious how this unease ought to be understood or expressed. One obvious source of the current malaise is the enormous number of educational 'reforms' that were introduced in England during the 1980s and 1990s, many of which were given solid statutory status in the Educational Reform Act of 1988. These include: the imposition on all state schools of a subject-based National Curriculum; the introduction of an elaborate and compulsory national system of assessment; an increase in support for independent schools; a reduction in the powers of teachers and local education authorities; the introduction of local management of schools; an increase in parental choice concerning their children's schools; and the establishment of procedures for controlling the content and organization of teacher education. [. . .]

Things were not always so. Prior to the 1980s educational policy in Britain was largely determined through the collective deliberations of teachers, politicians, local education authorities, employers and others with a legitimate interest in education. At their best, these deliberations were based on a combination of practical experience, rational argument, theoretical insight and accumulated wisdom, and allowed the conflicting interests of different groups to be acknowledged and their legitimate disagreements to be resolved. Today all this has changed. With the educational reforms of the 1980s and 1990s now largely implemented, and with the mechanisms and procedures that allow the state to control virtually all aspects of the education system now firmly established, it has become increasingly difficult to sustain the belief that educational policy should be formed through public dialogue and collective debate. Indeed, one of the sure signs of the 1990s is the way in which any informed or enlightened educational thinking is derided as 'mere theorizing' and dismissed as utopian pie in the sky that flies in the face of ordinary common sense. In many ways we seem to be witnessing the successful attempt to deintellectualize educational discussion and debate and abandon any pretence that educational policy has to be grounded in social and political ideals.

The effects of this attempt to deintellectualize educational thinking are obvious enough. One has been to erode the self-confidence of those who have sought to establish a theoretical rationale for a set of educational and political principles which could provide a guiding strategy for education and direct its future development. Another has been – quite literally – to demoralize educational policy by treating attempts to examine the moral basis of educational policy as an 'ideological' approach that is no longer appropriate. Yet another has been to reinforce the belief that educational policy can be determined, explained and defended by a pragmatic appeal to 'ordinary common sense' and 'what everybody knows'. The attractions of basing educational policy on a comforting faith in common sense are readily apparent. Unlike 'theory', common sense is an essentially unproblematic way of thinking: an uncritical mode of thought based on beliefs, ideas and assumptions which are regarded as self-evidently true. What is commonsensical is *ipso facto* unquestionable and not in need of critical examination or justification. But what is also distinctive of common sense is that it is an inherited way of thinking that is the product of precedent, ideology and tradition and, as such, inevitably impregnated with the myths, superstitions and prejudices of the past.

From the perspective of common sense, 'theory' is seen as 'irrelevant jargon' and inevitably treated with suspicion and mistrust. 'Theory', as Terry Eagleton puts it, 'is not the kind of thing one might expect to hear on the top of a bus' and differs from common sense precisely 'because it involves rejecting what seems natural and refusing to be fobbed off with shifty answers from well meaning elders'. Educational theory, in so far as it seeks systematically to assess the validity of the central postulates of conventional educational thinking, is simply a way of thinking about education that strives to be more coherent and more adequate than ordinary common-sense thought can allow. But this does not entail abandoning common sense in favour of some purely 'theoretical' view of education. What is being abandoned is an unquestioning acceptance of established educational dogmas and creeds so that a more critical, reflective and informed attitude can be adopted towards what common sense uncritically accepts. Properly understood, educational theory does not replace common sense so much as transform it, by subjecting its beliefs and justifications to systematic criticism. In this sense, educational theorizing is always a subversive activity, self-consciously aimed at challenging the irrationality of conventional thinking in order to make educational ideas and beliefs less dependent on the myths, prejudices and ideological distortions that common sense fossilizes and preserves.

There is little reason to think that all common-sense educational beliefs are true and ample reason to suspect that many of them are false. Once it is conceded that common sense does not have any particular claim to be correct and that educational theorizing is no more than an attempt critically to reassess the validity of common-sense educational assumptions, then the basis on which the attacks on educational theory have been erected begins to crumble. For it then becomes apparent that the attempt to defend educational policy by appealing to some nebulous 'common sense' is not a way of dispelling 'theory'. On the contrary, it is simply a strategy for insulating the inadequacies of politically dominant 'educational theories' from systematic exposure and for rejecting as 'ideological' any alternative educational ideas.

This kind of blanket refusal to envisage any alternative understanding of education to that which common sense embodies is one of the most persistent features of the current educational reforms. But the hostility towards alternative educational views is never based on a detailed examination of the arguments through which they are advanced. Nor is any attempt made to answer the claim that the view of education which recent policies sustain is itself an ideological view based on an impoverished and outdated 'theory' about the role of education in society. Instead, by dismissing all progressive ideas as 'fashionable theory' and by opening up the blind alley of 'common sense', the current anti-intellectual rhetoric is simply an ideological device for closing down serious educational debate by portraying opponents to current educational reforms as dangerous 'theorists' who need to be marginalized rather than given a convincing answer. It is thus a strategy that discourages any fundamental rethinking of conventional educational ideas. It also discourages all serious attempts to develop an educational strategy for the future which takes account of intellectual advances, new economic circumstances and changing cultural conditions. It is thus unsurprising to find that progressive educational innovations – whether in curriculum, pedagogy or assessment – which seek to take account of these kinds of social change are now being treated with derision and that the validity of traditional educational practices is being ritually reasserted. Nor should it come as a surprise if one of the practical consequences of implementing recent policies will be to create an educational system that only avoids the dangers and insecurities of political, economic and cultural change by preserving the dogmas and certitudes of the past. Still less should it come as a surprise to find that the dominant discourse of education has become thoroughly infected by a rampant anti-intellectualism which makes it respectable to believe that educational theory no longer has any significant part to play in the formation of educational policy. But to the extent to which nationally prescribed policy has been detached from rationally justified theory, education has become less a *rational* enterprise fed by the resources of argument, evidence and debate and more a *rationalized* enterprise which compels teachers and schools to conform to educational ideas and 'theories' which are never officially formulated or defended and to which few would willingly subscribe.

This chapter speaks to all those who are concerned by this contemporary deintellectualization and demoralization of educational policy. A central argument of the chapter is that the difficulties now confronting education will not be resolved simply by introducing still more policies for improving the technical expertise of teachers, raising standards or increasing the effectiveness of schools. They will only be adequately resolved when fundamental moral and political questions about the role of education in promoting a desirable form of social life are openly acknowledged and more consciously addressed.

Our central claim is that the current uncertainties and confusions surrounding education can only be understood by placing recent educational reforms within a perspective which will allow these reforms to be brought into more open confrontation with critical questions about the kind of society that they help to sustain. To this end, it seeks to assess the extent to which these reforms are compatible with a vision of the role of education in promoting the core values of a democratic society. Only by articulating a vision of education grounded in democratic values will it be possible to ensure that non-technical, non-utilitarian questions about the moral and social purposes being served by recent educational changes are neither neglected or ignored. And only by doing this will it be possible to articulate a morally principled response to these changes and determine how educational policy might be redirected so that it can better serve democratic aspirations and ideals. By offering arguments for this kind of educational change and by making practical suggestions about what it entails, this chapter not only aims to challenge many of the commonsense assumptions now governing educational policy. It also seeks to contribute to the intellectual resources which will help the educational professions to resist contemporary political pressures to perpetuate schooling in its present form and devise reasonable and practical ways of bringing contemporary schooling into closer harmony with democratic values and ideals.

The Fragmentation of Educational Theory and the Depoliticization of Educational Debate

The current lack of any adequate theoretical resources for discussing the significance of recent educational reforms for the future development of democracy, is not only a measure of the success of those who have sought to discredit educational theory while simultaneously promoting their own theoretical conceptions and ideological beliefs. It also reveals a basic contradiction within modern democratic society – a contradiction between the obvious need for members of a democracy publicly to debate the social and political principles underlying its educational policies and the obvious failure of these policies to address questions about the kind of education which genuine participation in such a public debate requires. It is only in a democracy which does not take seriously the need to equip its future members with the intellectual understandings, civic virtues or social attitudes necessary for participating in public debate, that democratic discussion of recent educational reforms can be treated as irrelevant and largely ignored.

One of the inevitable results of this lack of concern with the democratic purpose of education has been to deprive educational theory of any clear understanding of its own cultural or political role. Indeed, in many ways educational theory appears, like education itself, to be fragmented, confused and quite incapable of providing any coherent view of what its purpose should be. Educational theorists often behave as if they constituted a unified intellectual community, but this simply conceals the fundamental disagreements between them about how educational theorizing ought to be conducted and understood. Sometimes it seems that there are now so many different 'educational disciplines' and so many different 'paradigms' within each of these disciplines, that whatever identity educational theory can claim to possess stems more from its institutional embodiment in conferences and journals than from any internal intellectual unity. Beleaguered from without and fragmented from within, educational theory now displays all the characteristics of an endangered species on the verge of extinction.

[. . .]

Before the end of the 1960s these disciplines – the philosophy, psychology, sociology and history 'of education' – had managed to carve up their newly conquered domain among themselves. Education departments were reorganized, courses were restructured, professional identities were changed, new journals and academic societies were established all displaying total allegiance to the image of educational theory as a form of interdisciplinary enquiry in which the 'findings' of the foundation disciplines could be integrated into principles for formulating educational policy and guiding educational practice.

[. . .]

The failure of educational theory to provide answers to the questions it was supposed to resolve has been compounded by a failure to reach any agreement about what these questions should be. To the more positivistically minded education theorists, educational questions are predominantly empirical questions about, for example, how curriculum knowledge can best be organized and taught, learning outcomes can be maximized, school effectiveness can be improved, teaching quality can be enhanced or educational standards can be raised. But because non-empirical questions about why certain kinds of knowledge are included in the curriculum, or about the justification for the evaluative criteria governing the ways in which the concepts of 'effectiveness', 'quality' or 'standards' are being used, are ignored, this form of educational theorizing often serves simply to legitimize the institutional norms and political interests that determine what is to count as 'official' curriculum knowledge and that shape the criteria governing the way in which evaluative educational concepts are being understood and applied. It is thus no accident that this kind of theorizing is always conducted from a posture of 'value neutrality' that allows educational theorists to legitimate their indifference to major political, social and moral concerns. Nor is it surprising that this kind of educational theory is so frequently used by politicians and policy-makers to confer academic legitimacy on policies and practices which fit in with the political status quo.

[. . .]

One type of educational theory that emerged in the 1970s under the general name of 'reproduction theory': a form of educational theorizing which focused on the crucial role that education plays in the process whereby a society reproduces in its new members the forms of consciousness and social relationships characteristic of contemporary social life.

Although reproduction theory has undoubtedly made an important contribution to our understanding of how education operates to maintain the ideologies and social structures of society, it has nevertheless suffered from two related limitations. First, by portraying the reproductive process as an autonomous process over which individuals have little power or control, it has tended to obscure the extent to which this process is always contested by those holding different views about the future direction that society should take and the role that education should play in its realization. Second, although reproductive theory offers the basis from which to erect a negative critique of contemporary schooling, it can only acquire this critical role by first presuming a widespread intuitive commitment to the educational values intrinsic to the liberal democratic vision of society. But to the extent that the critical force of reproduction theory relies 'upon certain key judgements and critical intentions that constitute part of the liberal frame of mind in contemporary society', it always presupposes an acceptance of the normative political philosophy within which the liberal democratic vision of society is vindicated. While the sociology of education remains separate from this kind of political philosophy, its contribution to current educational debate will remain partial and incomplete. And without a form of educational theory which interweaves 'empirical' and 'explanatory' sociology of education with 'conceptual' and 'prescriptive' political philosophy, it will remain incapable of explicating people's intuitive anxieties about current educational reforms.

[. . .]

Only by means of a theoretical framework that treats the process of educational change and the process of social change as mutually constitutive and dialectically related processes can the full significance of what is now happening in, and to, education be adequately grasped and the possibilities of more desirable forms of educational change be realistically envisaged.

Education and Democracy: a Theoretical Framework

The educational reforms introduced in Britain since the beginning of the 1980s did not, of course, appear out of a political vacuum. They were a central part of the 'Thatcher revolution': a systematic attempt to reverse the historical trend towards a more democratic and egalitarian society and to foster the progressive development of the kind of liberal society in which individual freedom and laissez-faire economics would play a decisive part. In particular, they were part of a political strategy designed to create the kind of non-interventionist state which would be deeply sceptical about any attempt to use education as a political instrument for extending democracy. In the kind of liberal society being promoted 'democracy' would be primarily valued as a political mechanism for protecting individual freedom and the future of education would be determined by the only mechanism which can safeguard and preserve individual liberty: the market.

One of the successes of this political strategy has been to create a political climate in which previously accepted educational policies and structures could be called into question. What, in particular, has been undermined is the legitimacy of those post-war educational reforms – particularly the 1944 Education Act and the comprehensive reorganization of secondary education – which were designed to promote equality of educational opportunity and so help the eradication of those social and economic inequalities that were preventing the majority of people from exercising their democratic freedoms. It has thus stimulated a renewed debate about the historical tensions within the liberal democratic tradition between the 'liberal' commitment to individual freedom and the 'democratic' commitment to a more equitable distribution of power.

Since any serious discussion of contemporary educational reforms cannot escape this tension, fundamental questions inevitably arise about the extent to which these reforms are consistent with the aspirations and ideals of a democratic society. What part will they play in the development of a more democratic society? What view of the relationship between democracy and education do they imply? Because these questions cannot be answered in a neutral way, any assessment of recent reforms cannot avoid entering into a general political debate about how the democratic role of education is to be interpreted and understood. It is only by clarifying what democracy should mean for schooling, pedagogy and curriculum that it will be possible to engage critically with questions about whether recent educational changes legitimately express and uphold democratic values and ideals.

Assessing the democratic legitimacy of recent educational change is not helped by the fact that, historically, the English educational system has never adapted to the growth of democracy. Democratic rights in England were conceded slowly and various undemocratic institutions still remain: an unelected House of Lords, a peculiar electoral system, and a hereditary monarchy with considerable symbolic power. Moreover, education, like democracy, has evolved in such a way that old aristocratic educational institutions – such as the ancient universities and the elite public schools – have not only survived but continue to provide the criteria of success for the new state educational institutions that have been created.

What this has meant is that although the educational system has expanded to meet the needs of a democratic society (by bringing schooling to more of the population for longer periods), the power of pre-democratic educational traditions and practices has continued to be felt. Clearly, if new educational institutions are always to be judged by criteria devised by and for old institutions, they are bound to fail. Any change would require a fundamental rethinking of questions concerning access to higher education and the need to develop curriculum and teaching methods that would make education appropriate to the interests of previously excluded social groups. More generally, it would require a wide-ranging political debate about how the educational system could be transformed so that it no longer served the pre-democratic purpose of excluding certain social groups, but the democratic aim of offering genuine educational opportunities to all.

While it remains the case that new educational institutions and practices are judged by the criteria established by old institutions and practices, the power of pre-democratic educational traditions to distort and constrain any rational debate about the democratic role of education will remain entrenched. New educational institutions, innovative curriculum development, progressive pedagogies and new forms of assessment will constantly be opposed by a rhetoric of traditional standards, quality and academic excellence derived from the educational traditions of the past. Over the past 20 years, as this rhetoric has increasingly become the official discourse of education, educational arguments and debates have had to be conducted in a language which embodies educational assumptions and vocabularies which speak to pre-democratic traditions and prevents fundamental concerns about the democratic role of education from being adequately expressed. The only way to widen the educational debate, therefore, is to develop a language which refuses to be restricted to the official discourse of education and allows complex issues about the role of education in the future development of a democratic society to be articulated and discussed.

Such a debate is particularly important at the present time. As recently as 20 years ago, there was still a widespread commitment to educational reforms that were underpinned by a compelling vision of the importance of education in fostering a more democratic society. Moreover, most educational policy-makers and educational theorists confidently assumed that the democratic advances and achievements that had helped to galvanize this vision in the past would remain unchallenged and unchanged into the twenty-first century. Today, this confidence has been severely undermined, the process of democratization has lost its momentum and there is a widespread feeling that the time has come openly to concede that the relationship between education and democracy needs to be radically rethought.

[. . .]

Once it is accepted that 'the process of change in which we are involved' can only be understood by grasping 'the process as a whole' then some of the main organizing principles for any discussion of recent educational changes become clear. The first, and most obvious, is that 'educational change' and 'democratic change' should not be understood as separate processes. Still less should the current educational reforms be regarded as the culminative achievement of democratic progress and educational reform. Rather, they should be seen as the latest stage in the still incomplete 'long revolution' – a revolution in which 'democratic progress' and 'educational reform' are two indivisible and intrinsically related parts. What this means is that any attempt to treat 'the history of education' and 'the history of democracy' as two separate histories must be firmly resisted. To do otherwise would be to remain blind to the possibility that the understanding of 'education' now dominant in modern democratic societies would not have taken its contemporary form unless the dominant understanding of 'democracy' had not already been radically revised and transformed. The 'history of education' and the 'history of democracy' must thus be regarded as two elements of the single historical process through which our contemporary system of education *and* our contemporary system of democracy have simultaneously evolved. Only this kind of history can ensure that an analysis of current educational change is neither confined to that particular definition of 'education' to which contemporary democracy subscribes, nor constrained by that particular view of 'democracy' that contemporary definitions of education serve to legitimate and sustain.

This first organizing principle entails another. Since the system of education in a democratic society always reflects and refracts the definition of 'democracy' which that society accepts as legitimate and true, the educational changes occurring in a democracy at any time will reveal how that democratic society has interpreted itself in the past and how it intends to interpret itself in the future. This means that any analysis of recent educational reforms will inevitably be about the past, the present and the future: about the terms in which we make sense of the past, the ways in which these affect our understanding of the present and how our understanding of the present affects the way we try to deal with the future. It will have to explore the way in which the relationship between education and democracy is now understood, examine the philosophical ideas and political theories on which this understanding is based and expose the ideological framework within which this understanding continues to be sustained. It will also have to offer a historical interpretation of the sequence of events that led to the present situation and, on this basis, suggest how in the future our understanding of the democratic role of education may be revised. Only by doing this can the analysis ensure that questions about the extent to which the educational reforms of the 1980s and 1990s are consistent with democratic values and ideals are adequately formulated and addressed.

2

A Redefinition of Liberal and Humanistic Education

Nimrod Aloni

In the following discussion I will present an alternative approach to thinking and talking about liberal and humanistic education that breaks free from what Richard Rorty (1979, p. 12) has called 'outworn vocabularies and attitudes'. I will try to integrate and reach beyond three distinct established discourses: first, the contemporary philosophical/psychological curricular discourse, [. . .] second, the historical-cultural debate over the origin and nature of liberal education, and third, the highly politicized debate between conservative and radical educational theorists.

Up until the eighteenth century, liberal education and humanistic education – *artes liberales* and *studia humanitatis* – were interchangeable synonyms. In the last two centuries, however, three other distinct forms of humanistic education made their appearance. The first to emerge was the romantic form, of which Rousseau was the founder and which currently finds its expression in humanistic psychology and progressive education. A second form evolved out of existentialist philosophy and currently draws on the rich resources of contemporary existentialist and phenomenological literature. Finally, a third form of humanistic education emerged from the appearance of the radical 'counter-culture' and neo-Marxist educational theorists and practitioners. What is common to these four theories – the classical plus the three modern ones – is a commitment to *humanize* people: to provide a kind of education that all human beings, *qua* human beings, deserve and ought to receive, so that they can actualize their human potentialities and lead full, worthy, and fulfilling human lives. Despite the obvious ideological and theoretical disagreement among these approaches, it seems that they can be considered faithful to two fundamental notions of liberal education: (a) as a general and formative education which suits free persons who have the leisure to study and cultivate their human potentialities, and (b) as the kind of education that aims to liberate the individual from the fetters of ignorance, caprice, prejudice, alienation, false consciousness, the present and the particular.

Hence I am proposing to widen the domain of liberal education beyond its classical interpretation to include also the romantic, existentialist, and radical forms of humanistic liberal education. Having this as my basic premise, I shall delineate the fundamental tenets of each tradition in order to evaluate its possible contribution to a contemporary theory of humanistic liberal education. Drawing on these traditions, I will offer an integrative model of liberal education which rests upon three major principles: acculturation, autonomy and authenticity. Besides being worthy in themselves, these principles are especially suitable for our purpose by virtue of being widely recognized and accepted as desirable educational ends. After all, a good model of liberal education should pass not only the test of theoretical tenability but also the challenges of attractiveness and practicality, without which it would remain merely theoretical and irrelevant.

[. . .]

Classical Humanistic Education

The term 'classical education' inherently implies the existence of an ideal of human perfection that should serve as a universal and objective model for regulating the education of all human beings *qua* human beings. The origin of classical humanistic education lies in fifth-century BC Athens, and is reflected in the discussions of Socrates and the Sophists concerning human virtue and the good life. [. . .]

The Romans, as early as the first century BC, established the *artes liberales* or *studia humanitatis* as a normative and formative education for free persons who have the leisure to study and cultivate their human potentialities in order to become worthy and committed citizens in possession of sound judgment and noble character.

The Renaissance might be regarded as the third major era of classical humanism; of a tradition that became conscious of itself and developed a literary and pedagogical movement of 'humanists'. These humanists were determined to emancipate themselves from the ignorance, dogmatism, and self-abnegation of the 'dark ages' towards the kind of truth, beauty, freedom, and dignity that could be produced by the human faculties if only properly cultivated and exercised – having as their model the magnificent cultures of the ancient Greeks and Romans. [. . .]

The Enlightenment constitutes the fourth stage of classical humanism. Here liberal education substitutes its elitist, tradionalist, and conservative character for an egalitarian, sceptical, and liberal character. With Kant and his contemporaries, autonomous and critical thinking were placed as a barrier against blind acceptance of traditional conventions; individualism, pluralism, and political freedoms served to limit authoritarian and dogmatic domination; and the principles of equality and respect for persons were universalized, at least theoretically, so that all humans could be considered eligible for a liberal education.

In the late nineteenth and twentieth centuries, it is difficult to single out one representative among the many theorists of classical humanistic education. [. . .] Liberal education within this tradition should consist of teaching 'what it means to be fully human . . . their rightful place in the scheme of things' and a moral obligation 'to certain enduring standards of private and public conduct' (Kirk, 1989, pp. 35–6).

Romantic humanistic education

The romantic (naturalistic) form of humanistic education makes its appearance in the eighteenth century with the writings of Rousseau, who considered his educational theory a counter-movement to orthodox education. In particular, Rousseau blamed the obsession with cultural progress and encyclopedic knowledge, unrestrained pursuit of wealth and social status, and the practice of authoritarian artificial education for the ills of his contemporaries. Rousseau introduced an alternative conception of the good life which ascribes goodness to man's natural inclinations and self-regulated development, to spontaneous and playful exercise of natural powers, and to self-directedness and personal authenticity.

With this new image of human goodness Rousseau generated a major and manifold change in educational theory and practice. He initiated a shift in emphasis from culture to nature and from philosophy to psychology; from reason to sentiment and from the community to the individual; from didactic mediated learning to experiential discovery learning and from duty that is grounded in external authority to action that springs from the inherently good nature of the individual. [. . .]

In the course of the nineteenth century, with the works of Pestalozzi and Froebel, the therapeutic notions of love, care, trust, and affective interpersonal relations became increasingly dominant, especially as conditions for promoting self-regulated growth towards 'full humanity'. In the twentieth century, it was mainly the theories of A. S. Neill (and fellow supporters of 'open education'), John Dewey (and his followers in 'progressive education'), Carl Rogers (and other humanistic psychologists) that formed the child-centred naturalistic, experiential, therapeutic and individualistic form of humanistic education.

[. . .]

In sum, the romantic form of humanistic education can be characterized by its fundamental premise that there exists in every one of us an 'inner nature' or a 'fixed self' that is fundamentally good and unique, and that pushes to unfold and actualize itself – in accordance with its built-in code – toward healthy existence and full humanity. Romantic educators, in contrast to the classical, conceive the road to human perfection as the 'turning of the soul', not to the universal and objective, but rather to the inner world and unique self of the individual.

Existentialist Humanistic Education

Existentialist educators reject the classical notion of human beings. The alternative advanced by most existentialists is that since the essence of man is freedom, in the matter of values humans can appeal to no external authority, either natural or supernatural, and are therefore destined to choose, define, and create themselves as the true – and therefore responsible – authors of their identities. [. . .]

Radical Humanistic Education

According to radicals, to consider educational issues independently of the larger cultural, social, and economic context involves either serious ignorance or cynical, if not criminal, deception. Poverty, crime, homelessness, drug addiction, wars, ecological crises, suicide, illiteracy, discrimination against women and ethnic minorities, technocratic consciousness, and the disintegration of communities and families, to name some of our most pressing problems, are facts of life that affect directly the physical, emotional, intellectual, and oral development of the great majority of children in our culture. Moreover, these disturbing features of our reality are primarily not the outcomes of some technological shortcoming but rather the very embodiments of particular ideologies which serve the interests of the dominant groups at the expense of the interests of the less dominant ones. [. . .]

The Integrative Model

A normative definition of humanism

The problem we might face in trying to put humanism to work as a unifying frame of reference for liberal education is not that people reject it; on the contrary, humanism is accepted (at least in principle) by the great majority of nations and communities as the desirable ethical code for handling political, social, and educational issues (see, for example, the United Nations 'Universal Declaration of Human Rights' and 'Declaration of the Rights of the Child'). The difficulty lies in the fact that almost everybody today professes to be a humanist, so that it has lost a definite and concrete meaning. From both egalitarians and elitists, conservatives and liberals, you can hear a commitment to humanism. The term has become so popular and amorphic that it has become vacuous and lost much of its capacity to serve as a moral and educational ideal.

I am proposing to identify humanism with a commitment to the *enhancement of human freedom and growth, to the realization and perfection of human potentialities, and to an ethical code that places the highest value on the dignity of humanity, as an end in itself, in relation to which all political, religious, economic, and ideological doctrines are regarded as means to its enhancement.*

Four fundamental principles are implicit in this definition. The first is *philisophical*: it entails a conception of man – men and women – as free creatures, responsible for their identity and destiny, as well as a commitment to set human well-being and perfection as the ultimate goal of the entire human endeavour.

The second principle pertains to the *social* domain. It takes human equality, on the ground of people's shared humanity, as the basis for universal morality and solidarity. On the interpersonal level, it involves a commitment to the cultivation of sensitivity, tolerance, care and reciprocity; and in the political sphere, it aims to establish a just, democratic, and humane social order that is committed to securing human and civil rights as well as to providing all with the resources necessary for living a decent human life.

The third principle pertains to the status and forms of *intellectual activity*. It entails a commitment to open-mindedness, broad learning, rationality, critical and creative thinking as the best basis for our knowledge of reality. The fourth principle is *pedagogical*.

A normative definition of humanistic liberal education

A normative definition of humanistic liberal education: entails *the general cultivation and empowerment of human beings, in manners that are intellectually and morally appropriate, towards the best and highest life of which they are capable, in three fundamental domains of life; as individuals, actualizing their potentialities and tendencies; as members of society, becoming involved and responsible citizens; and as human beings, enriching and perfecting themselves through active engagement with the collective achievements of human culture.* [. . .]

Foundational pedagogical principles: acculturation, autonomy, authenticity

By *acculturation* we usually understand the process of initiating people – usually the young – into the culture's esteemed or worthwhile modes of thought, feeling, action and artistic appreciation. Within the suggested framework of humanistic education, acculturation will serve as a twofold principle: foundational and qualitative. The foundational aspect is related to the fact that 'a self exists only within . . . "webs of interlocution" ', namely, that 'there is no way we could be induced into personhood except by being initiated into . . . languages of spiritual and moral discernment . . . by those who bring us up' (Taylor, 1989, p. 35). [. . .]

The importance of 'foundational acculturation', as Aristotle pointed out, cannot be exaggerated: 'It makes no small difference, then, whether we form habits of one kind or of another from our very youth; it makes very great difference, or rather *all* the difference' (Aristotle, 1980, p. 29). And from another perspective, as suggested by the title of Wayne Booth's recent book, our education also depends on *The Company We Keep*. As every parent knows, the human and literary company we keep in our childhood plays a significant role in the shaping of our identity.

Dewey stressed the importance of foundational acculturation to education. In 'My Pedagogical Creed', he addressed the social foundations of every individual, stating that 'all education proceeds by the participation of the individual in the social consciousness of the race . . . shaping the individual's powers, saturating his consciousness, forming his habits, training his ideas, and arousing his feelings and emotions' (Dewey, 1964, p. 213). [. . .] Acculturation in a qualitative sense means, a process of humanization through an ever widening exposure to the multiple and diverse modes of human experience, aiming toward a synoptic and deep understanding of what it means to be human and of the standards we should live up to in order to reach true and full humanity. [. . .] If this theme is sound, that nothing of value can be achieved without an active engagement of the will, then it should have special implication for education.

Autonomy stands in this model as the critical principle. It denotes, literally, self-legislation or determining for oneself the values and principles in accordance with which the individual wishes to lead his or her life. The element of law which is inherent in the notion of autonomy – of a relatively thoughtful and stable set of action-guiding principles – should prevent us from confusing autonomy with 'personal freedoms' such as capricious, impulsive, or even spontaneous behaviour. [. . .]

The importance of autonomy, which is primarily an intellectual virtue, cannot be overestimated. Scientific and technological developments as much as social and political progress would not have been possible without that particular disposition to think and judge for oneself, independently of what the ruler, teacher, employer, or parent holds to be true and appropriate. [. . .]

The importance of autonomous and critical thinking reaches far beyond cultural criticism into fundamental issues of life and death, human rights and social justice. [. . .]

Authenticity, unlike the concept of autonomy which alludes primarily to the cognitive dimension of human existence, is a quality that embraces the totality of one's life, and it will therefore function in this educational model as the principle of *individuality*. Authenticity means not only to 'think for oneself' but rather to 'be oneself': to assert one's existence in the world in a way that is truthful to the individual's essential and unique nature. Authenticity further entails eliciting the content of one's life by means of self-generation, self-nourishment and self-creation as well as cultivating and affirming one's unique vantage point and style. In praising someone for his or her authenticity, in other words, we wish to express our respect for that individual for not being inert, conventional, banal, artificial, fake, self-alienated, or merely a role-player.

[. . .]

In sum, education for authenticity – in both the romantic and existentialist approaches – seeks to recover the individual's sense of selfhood which is constantly endangered by pressures and temptations to succumb to a pre-ordained form of life – be it religion, state, ideology, knowledge, technology, bureaucracy, public opinion or the routines of everyday life. It requires educators not only to sensitize their students to the sense of freedom, possibility, and originality that are associated with discovering and creating oneself, but also to urge and challenge them to set forth a way of life that has something honourable or worthwhile in its particular content. Without such qualifications, we are left with the nihilistic view that anything is just as good as anything else as long as one chooses it authentically – a position that has no place within the framework and commitments of humanistic education.

[. . .] Education should be manifested not only in rational and efficient thinking but also in being committed to truth as individuals and as involved citizens; not only in sound moral judgement but also in being amiable, caring and fair in everyday life as well as in being capable of moral indignation and effective moral action. [. . .] Similarly, it should be required of any contemporary humanistic theory of education that it should assimilate the important contributions of each of the four humanistic educational positions outlined above as well as utilize the three foundational pedagogical principles of acculturation, autonomy and authenticity. The issue, again, is not whether these principles should be implemented but rather to determine – with respect to the cultural condition, nature of the individual student, stage of maturity and nature of the subject matter – the proper balance in their implementation. [. . .]

References

Aristotle (1980) *The Nichomachean Ethics*, trans. D. Ross, New York: Oxford University Press.

Dewey, J. (1964) My pedagogical creed, in G. Johnston (ed.), *Issues in Education*, Boston, MA: Houghton Mifflin.

Kirk, R. (1988) The ethical purpose of literary studies, in J. Baldacchino (ed.), *Educating for Virtue*, Washington, DC: National Humanities Institute.

Neill, A. S. (1960) *Summerhill*, New York: Hart.

Rogers, C. (1961) *On Becoming a Person*, Boston, MA: Houghton Mifflin.

Rorty, R. (1979) *Philosophy and the Mirror of Nature*, Princeton, NJ: Princeton University Press.
Rousseau, J.-J. (1979) *Emile or on Education*, trans. A. Bloom, New York: Basic Books.
Taylor, C. (1989) *Sources of the Self: The Making of the Modern Identity*, Cambridge, MA: Harvard University Press.

3

New Progressivism

Peter Silcock

If Webb and Vulliamy *et al.*'s (1997) observation that teachers' personal and professional beliefs threaten to break apart under the weight of outside intervention proves prophetic, this will not signal the end of ideological influence on education. It will mean that government-sponsored ideologies will prosper, and since governments (even left-wing ones) are instinctively traditionalist in beliefs, such an outcome could easily reverse the real progress in the democratizing of classrooms which has been discernible in primary education over many years. Such misfortune should not happen, because teachers can look to their own beliefs, not those of governments, to sustain them. And what is characteristic of child-centred beliefs is that their caring, humanitarian ethic is an engine of real power: it inspires teachers of young children with an emotional resource enabling them to continue with work which is, often, arduous and demotivating. In so far as the ideology continues to survive in schools, it will evolve, as it must, in ways which mutually invigorate both 'child-centredness' and the ongoing development of the English/Welsh National Curriculum.

There is no ambiguity involved in allying diverse, self-managed curricula to socially responsible aims and industrial need. On the contrary: it is likely that the most responsible citizens and best workers are those whose ambitions are coupled to cultural ideals through choice. Child-centred commitment to individualized learning is not a commitment to radical politics or some sort of postmodern denial of absolutes. It can guide learners in whatever directions the state decrees, while keeping a weather eye on what pupils' own choices dictate: the art of progressivist teaching is to help learners address one goal from the perspective of the other.

New progressivism embraces old values. Yet its aims are more affected by social, moral and industrial demands than was needed mid-century. Politicians ruthlessly seek to control educational outputs now, and it is unlikely that state interference will quickly disappear. So, it is desirable to reassess progressivist claims for sake of today's accountability. As Richards suggests (cited in Galton, 1989), it was probably lack of accountability which in the past led some forms of progressivism to descend into a laissez-faire free-for-all. Modern progressivists will welcome appraisals of their aims and methods, providing there are no misperceptions of their belief-systems. Teachers should avoid helping critics by falling back upon simplistic polarizations and doctrinaire stubbornness as replacements for reasoned argument. They need to be pragmatically flexible and politically astute in realizing what is essential to their philosophy and cannot be compromised, and what might be left in abeyance until political fashions change.

To remind ourselves of what progressivists should in no circumstance compromise we need to review main principles and criticisms. When making a cumulative case, it is easy to lose sight of the reasons why one idea was chosen rather than another.

Ideological Foundations

New progressivism is founded in developmental, humanistic, democratic and pragmatic ideas: there are empirical, ethical, socio-political and practical grounds for choosing to be a modern, child-centred teacher. Each theoretical pillar is structurally related to the others, rather as the pillars of a temple are planned to harmonize architecturally in order to contain a specialized set of activities. So to concede the relevance to the whole of one kind of support is to predispose oneself to seeing the relevance of the others, whereas to find weaknesses in one makes it likely that weaknesses will be found in all. This happens because new progressivism builds on an association between children and cultures which stretches beyond developmentalism into philosophy and politics, though it receives testimony, at a factual level, from constructivist and neo-Piagetian psychology. From this relationship with psychology is taken a definition of personal autonomy which humanism reinforces on a philosophical level. When asserting children's rights, humanistic writers often acknowledge the concept of proactive individuality promoted by progressivists and constructivists. Establishing their ethical justification gives additional support to progressivist teachers' aims and values.

The complementary culture concept arising from a transformational view of individual learning and development is a dynamic one providing a rationale for that mutually invigorating interaction between individuals and groups we call democratic. Since the role of a teacher is to help pupils become educated through a process of 'co-construction', modern child-centred classrooms have to be democratically organized with children given rights and properly designated roles of responsibility within them. It follows that primary school teaching's pragmatism becomes channelled into the fitting of individual needs to social opportunity, and social need to individual purposes. This interrelationship of parts to whole underwrites the structure of progressivist ideology, as is seen by briefly revisiting each area of study.

Developmentalism

Children transform their cultures and cultures transform individuals: there is a growing consensus among contributors to developmental studies about this. Where there is dispute is in the detailing of mechanisms explaining how the individual/social interaction is managed.

To throw in one's lot with neo-Piagetians and constructivists is to believe that teacher interventions have to ensure that child development occurs as a cumulative, stage-wise building of capabilities. Because we no longer think that children progress, as a matter of course, toward 'higher-order' skills, we have to become clear-minded about the sorts of educated citizens we want. If we value critical argument and self-regulation, the abilities to apply and synthesize knowledge, the understandings and academic sensitivities we have always prized, we cannot believe that these will develop in some sort of unmediated way. Such a conclusion returns us to the conviction that first-hand experience and stage-related activities are as vital to childhood education as they have ever been.

The twin principles of individual experience and culturally valued knowledge become child-centred when we employ the 'constructivist' maxim that individuals reach cultural goals through their own volitions: goals must be consciously known, reachable and structurally related to the academic subject studied. A learning context will facilitate pupils' willingness and ability to adapt their existing views to new ideas. In curricular terms, there are affective, cognitive and socio-political dimensions to constructivist learning to be catered for (commitment, control and comprehension were suggested as central 'process' characteristics). There are no short cuts which bypass such a provision.

Humanism

From developmental studies we abstract a concept of individuality which happily blends research findings with humanist philosophy. If children shape their own minds through their own actions, they can be regarded from the start as fully-fledged 'whole' persons, to be accorded full human rights like anyone else. One supposition is not implied by the other: but to recognize that children have a potential for voluntary action which will ultimately give them rationality takes us some way towards admitting into classrooms their personal views of life, and respecting these in schools as elsewhere. Educationally speaking, the humanist directive is to 'teach for autonomy' such that children take full advantage of their natural rights. No one believes that children should be given full control over their own learning, but many these days see the practical as well as ethical advantages flowing from enfranchising learners as early as possible. There is no 'bottom' limit to the recognition of human autonomy, provided we define the qualities of mind composing it within the context where it has to be expressed: no matter how young a pupil is, he or she will have some decision-making capability.

To believe that learner perspectives upon curricula should be 'transformational' means designing curricula to be understood, owned and potentially managed by pupils, in negotiation with adults whose wider perspectives allow them to guard against false allegiances and corrupting influence. Whereas we have to give regard to pupils' expanding ambitions, we have also to admit that these may not always be – strategically – in their interests. So teachers 'liberate' pupil capabilities through regulating individual purpose within constraints of social responsibility and a benevolent rule-governed system. Their success in implementing curricula will be detectable through the 'process' criteria indicating quality learning.

Democracy

School communities are places where teachers, as well as pupils, have rightful views, informed by the opinions of politicians, parents, OFSTED inspectors, educational advisers, technical advisers, industrialists looking for a workforce, peers and other professionals and welfare workers, etc. etc. Intrinsic to the conceptualizing of a child–culture relationship as transformational is a culture concept equally dynamic. Cultures are webs of influence to which we attach our own personal contributions; they are treasure-houses of habits and attitudes from which we steal. As Dewey tells us: individuals and societies, children and cultures are complementary not competing agencies within the educational system.

If learners are to make their own ways in the world, they can only do so by reference to the choices of others. Which does not imply that a rough-hewn individual aspiration must, somehow, become smoothed out through social encounters. Sometimes, it is a whole culture which is altered by the ideas of a Freud or a Darwin, a Rousseau or an Einstein. Often enough we have to live with compromises respecting the integrity of opposing views, and leaving, as an accompaniment of an 'open' forum of teaching, a conflict of purposes, unreconciled for the time being but providing some stimulus for further inventions. This is the nature of a pluralist, diversely populated democratic state. Encouraging disputes, fostering peaceful argument and reconciling views without diminishing them are the food and drink of any democracy, including primary school democracies. And to state that the perspectives taken from individual and cultural purpose are both transformational is to state that each will seek to challenge the other by nature, and that this bi-transformation (or co-construction) is not only legitimate but is the only way each one of us can carve out his or her own cultural niche.

Pragmatism

Reconciling the twin demands of individuals and society is seldom a balanced job in the way educational dilemmas have to be resolved. Situations always fluctuate between one pole and another. Teachers may no sooner have sorted out someone's emotional difficulties than they have to rejig a task to make it acceptable to the learner without coming off track with regard to their objectives. One cannot prescribe for this sort of pragmatically flexible application of skill, except to realize, as Dewey did, that the two poles of attention are not opposed to each other unless we believe that they are. It is possible to give all one's time to designing a perfect curriculum without taking the trouble to match it to individual need, and it is just as possible to become preoccupied with keeping individual learners content without taking cognizance of broader aims. The art of child-centred teaching is to maintain a balanced requirement within those terms of reference (neo-Piagetian or whatever) which separate progressivism from other ideologies.

[. . .]

The Critics of Progressivism

There are three standard types of criticism made of progressivist thinking. First, there are the criticisms of those who see ideological theorizing as either unnecessary or biased. Second, there are objections stemming from those empirical research conclusions meant to test out progressivist claims. Third, there are the critiques written by those who, while conceding the validity of ideological debate, nonetheless find progressivist beliefs wanting in some way or other.

First, politicians, pragmatists, postmodernists, those philosophers of education and sociologists who stigmatize ideologies as by definition one-sided, warn us against ideological decision-making. Robin Alexander's hostility towards the detrimental effects on education of progressivist rhetoric bows suitably towards a recognition that much achievement in primary schools is owed to child-centred ideals (e.g. 1994). What he is concerned to spell out are the dangers of teachers feeling so pressurized by orthodoxies that they adopt inflexible classroom policies. Such a false polarization and dichotomizing of aims and methods shore up many attacks.

Ideologies need not and should not polarize. If they do, it is probable that the teachers concerned do not fully understand their own beliefs and demonstrate in their mediocre teaching or biased discourse not just the problem with ideologies as the problem with any form of behaviour relying on poorly known principles. If we believe teachers should be able to justify what they do, they must come to some understanding of theoretically framed justifications, whether these are ideologically charged or ideologically neutral. When we do engage in ideological study, we discover that progressivism and traditionalism, as the two easiest ways to group differences, split from each other at the level of values, but need not polarize at the level of practice or belief.

Teachers do need the guidance of beliefs, for these are questions bound up with professional educators' practices which cannot be answered factually. Questions of fact and value interweave in educational affairs, and we have to disentangle them in order to answer theoretical questions. But in a teacher's daily work, pragmatic considerations always, somewhere, serve more fundamental values, and to pretend that this is not so is tacitly to adhere to those pragmatic ideologies which can only lead us into a confusion of ends and means, and the likelihood of designing school curricula which try to achieve too much and end up achieving very little.

[. . .]

Second, Alexander's 'discussion document' (1992) was meant to move primary school teachers forward away from their entrenched positions. To achieve this, a host of research findings informed it; many meant to show that progressivist methods did not work, did not exist or were flawed in conception. The lengthy trail of such findings winds back to the immediate post-Plowden era when erratically achieved formal skills were blamed for Britain's unsatisfactory trade and industrial performance worldwide. The year 1976 was that of Callaghan's Ruskin speech, and the year Neville Bennett's comparisons of progressivist and tradionalist teaching styles were published in the wake of the William Tyndale affair (Ellis *et al.*, 1976) and 'Black Paper' attacks (Cox and Dyson, 1960; 1971). Some were even questioning whether primary school teachers were really implementing 'Plowden' policies at all (Sharp and Green, 1975), a view which has become accepted wisdom (e.g., Galton, 1989). The Bennett research and the influential ORACLE studies (Galton, Simon and Croll, 1980), trying to draw together teaching styles, pupil behaviour and outcomes in order to test out the efficacy of the former, purported to show that child-centredness – as the researchers defined it – was not producing the quality outcomes it was supposed to produce.

But any unambiguous classification of styles risks missing that very mix of techniques and strategies which works, because they have combined pragmatically to achieve their ends. Bennett (1976) noticed that the most effective teacher met during his research used a mix of methods, implying that she was neither child-centred nor traditionalist in orientation. Yet to mix methodologies says little about ideology. It is not methods but the values justifying them which create child-centredness. This is not to deny that methodologies become grouped under ideological umbrellas – it would be surprising if child-centred teachers sought at all costs to avoid contact with individual learners! But any teacher who seeks solely to work with individuals and small groups is raising these forms of organization themselves to the status of value, not the interests of children as individuals.

[. . .]

The interpretation of research findings is no hard and fast business: researchers select and interpret from their findings what suits their own purposes. This is not to be cynical, simply to notice the different agendas of educationalists who are testing hypotheses belonging to distinct belief systems. Politicians make, similarly, their own selections from research to justify policy aims and political strategies. Only, when one looks at the circumstances giving rise to the interpretation made, one sees that even contradictory conclusions live together within broader verities. In applying Piagetian or Vygotskian theory to modern classrooms for example, the question is not (and never has been) which of the two psychologists is correct or of whether individual and social action both have a place in educational success. It is a question of which perspective serves our best interests regarding educational policies, and of how, ultimately, both sets of perspectives might be harnessed to facilitate our practices.

Third, traditionalists (such as O'Hear, 1987) look to the weaknesses of progressivist thinking as inhering in the ideology's very diversity and pluralist pretensions. 'Black Paper' writers (Cox and Dyson, 1960; 1971) and neo-right-wing critics (e.g., Lawlor, 1990) similarly fear or feared that the dilution of a traditional culture by attempts to widen access to it threatens established modes of academic achievement, such as the ability to exercise formally acquired skills and memorize well-loved texts. Critics more to the left of the political spectrum (e.g., Lawton, 1989) attack progressivism for the opposite reason: they surmise that its individuality diverts it from socially responsible ends. Again, these are not contradictory criticisms. For the former group regrets that child-centred teachers embrace diversity of outcome and sees this as problematic in itself, while the latter desire in learners a particular attitude towards diversity – i.e., a pre-specified attitude of social responsibility, tolerating differences and recognizing issues of prejudice and discrimination.

Neo-progressivism's developmentalism, redefining individuals and cultures in relationship with each other, while insisting that it is pupils who construct their minds for their own purposes, conceives as part of that construction process a dynamic notion of culture itself. This notion makes possible the articulating of a role for teachers and structured curricula in both educational and developmental schemes. All developmental-stage theories, as all educational systems which relate somewhere to them, are value driven. So there is no conflict between an education which gives succour to personal ambition while insisting that developments must be guided. This is to acquiesce with the second sort of criticism above, while redrawing the line between progressivism and the traditionalist ideology sponsored by the first. Traditional values, depending on a 'transmission' hypothesis, have their place within a community wishing to maintain a homogeneity of aim, a commonality of lifestyles and a consensus on values, but not, it is suggested, within a society fluctuating in what it takes to be appropriate lifestyles and achievements and highly patterned in terms of values and ideals, as western societies are likely to stay for the foreseeable future.

[. . .]

Modern Progressivists

Progressivism's unfashionable image owes much to every educationist's and politician's desire to improve on past ideas. Only when critiques are shown to be based on misconceptions, misinterpretations, risky speculations or dogma dangerously unsuited to a modern-day society might we move forward to a more balanced assessment and, hopefully, a situation where those preferring child-centred forms of teaching will not be shamelessly harassed or scapegoated. It is sad that most writings about progressivism over the past couple of decades have been critical of it, and the success of critics has been to fragment and divide the British movement. [. . .]

Teaching is a conservative business given its practical preoccupations. Sutherland (1992) finds, on visiting schools, 'no awareness whatsoever of constructivist ideas' (p. 81). Galton periodically wonders why innovatory schemes in education flop fairly disastrously (Galton and Williamson, 1992). Teachers on INSET courses may find ORACLE enlightening, but they take little heed of its research conclusions in classrooms. Yet many teachers remain child-centred, despite media batterings and political censure. It could be that academics' and politicians' belief that, in order to raise standards, teacher attitudes must change is actually wrong. If we trusted teachers to improve through refining their own skills in the confidence that their professional ideologies were soundly based, educational standards might rise more quickly than through a 'top-down' attempt to wrench improvements out of a profession through unwelcomed reforms.

Primary school teachers whose values have survived the past decades and are unabashed in advertising their ideas about the 'whole child', integrated topic-based teaching and 'informal approaches' are already new progressivists. Their child-centred commitment may not be as it was because standardized curricula are not always immediately attractive to learners and they have had to look for newer ways of applying their beliefs.

It should be more not less possible for modern primary school teachers to reach the quite sophisticated ends at which progressivists aim, providing we do not underestimate the time needed to do so. What modern teachers might insist on is that any assessments made of their methods must be more sensitive to cognitive gains than popular 'pencil and paper' tasks which always understate comprehension in favour of accuracy of reproduction and rote capacity. If we want rational, autonomous learners who will pursue learning through life for the sake of public welfare as much as for their own satisfaction, it is not good enough to use tests which measure very limited skills. If we want high standards in education, we have to devise ways of assessing a quality process.

The benefits which should follow from liberating the professional energies of teachers so that they, in turn, can liberate the drive towards learning springing out of every child's native endowment ought to be self-evident. What is new about neo-progressivism are its adjusted theoretical reformulations to bring it within the value orbit of a modern industrial society, hungry for growth, social peace and multicultural richness. It is old in its platform of beliefs that individual teachers and pupils will perform their roles most effectively when freed from unwanted bureaucratic interference. There are enormous powers of achievement hidden within even the youngest human beings. Modern progressivist theory reminds us of this without diminishing the role of teachers, analysing their cultural backdrop as a more dynamic and kaleidoscopic tapestry than is often supposed. It is the dualism of responsibilities distributed between teacher and taught, and the friction sparked by these, hinting at the disputatious nature of free bargaining within all democratic states, which distinguishes the new ideology and makes its embodiment in future classroom practices an exciting prospect.

References

Alexander, R. J. (1992) *Policy and Practice in Primary Education*, London: Routledge.

Alexander, R. J. (1994) *Innocence and Experience: Reconstructing Primary Education*, Stoke-on-Trent: ASPE/Trentham Books.

Bennett, S. N. (1976) *Teaching Styles and Pupil Progress*, London: Open Books.

Cox, C. B. and Dyson, A. E. (1960) *Fight for Education: A Black Paper*, London: Critical Quarterly Society.

Cox, C. B. and Dyson, A. E. (eds) (1971) *The Black Papers*, London: Davis-Poynter.

Ellis, T., McWhirter, J., McColgan, D. and Haddow, B. (1976) *William Tyndale: The Teachers' Story*, London: Writers and Readers Publishers Co-operative.

Galton, M. (1989) *Teaching in the Primary School*, London: Fulton.

Galton, M. and Williamson, J. (1992) *Group Work in the Primary Classroom*, London: Routledge.

Galton, M., Simon, B. and Croll, P. (1980) *Inside the Primary School Classroom*, London: Routledge and Kegan Paul.

Lawlor, S. (1990) *Teachers Mistaught*, London: Centre for Policy Studies.

Lawton, D. (1989) *Education, Culture and the National Curriculum*, London: Hodder and Stoughton.

O'Hear, A. (1987) The importance of traditional learning, *British Journal of Educational Studies*, **35**, pp. 102–14.

Sharp, A. and Green, R. (1975) *Educational and Social Control*, London: Routledge and Kegan Paul.

Sutherland, P. (1992) *Cognitive Development Today, Piaget and his Critics*, London: Paul Chapman Publishing.

Webb, R. and Vulliamy, G. with Hakkinen, K., Hamalainen, S., Kimonen, E., Nevalainen, R. and Nikki, M.-L. (1997), *A comparative analysis of the management of curriculum change in England and Finland.* Paper delivered to the BERA (British Educational Research Association) Annual Conference, University of York (obtainable from the Department of Educational Studies, University of York).

Section 2: Views of Learning

The previous section concluded with a chapter by Silcock who linked progressivist child-centred ideologies with developmentalism and constructivist theories of learning. Here constructivism was seen as having its roots in pragmatist views with links to both philosophical and psychological traditions. At one level constructivism offers an explanation of the nature of knowledge. At another, it describes how cognitive processes might be acquired and developed. It is used to provide models of learning and knowledge which could be used to provide insights into teaching and the curriculum. Section 2 considers what it means to be a learner through an examination of a number of views or theoretical models of the process of learning. Here, as elsewhere in this book, social, psychological and political perspectives are all featured. However, each of the chapters in Section 2 has a theoretical underpinning which can be traced to one or other developments of constructivism. A recurring idea within this section is that of revisiting earlier models of learning and illustrating how increases in our knowledge about learners forces us to change, extend or at least reexamine our existing conceptualizations whether it concerns adults or children.

The issues introduced and developed in this section include:

- the theory of multiple intelligences
- situated cognition theory
- notions of situated and non-situated learning
- a social-constructivist view of learning.

In Chapter 4, Mark Krechevsky and Steve Seidel draw upon evidence from studies of 'out of school' learning to challenge the traditional and fixed view of intelligence. They provide a succinct overview of the emerging theory of Multiple Intelligences. The theory of Multiple Intelligences provides a structure which recognizes fully the differences between individuals and the very distinctive nature of the educational pathways which potentially lead to achievement. The main thrust of this chapter lies in the way in which Krechevsky and Seidel relate this way of conceptualizing learning to actual practices in teaching and assessment. A key question for educators here would be whether to teach to existing strengths or work on areas of weakness.

In Chapter 5, R. P. McDermott clearly outlines the way in which Situated Cognition theory requires a critical shift from a focus on the individual to that on the settings and the activities contained within them. This is in sharp contrast to the highly individual perspective about thinking, learning and problem-solving identified previously by Krechevsky and Seidel. McDermott brings to the forefront the importance of context, language and discourse, and reflects the view that learning should not be thought of in individualistic terms. It is argued that at the centre of this view of learning we find the particular relationships which are established between people engaged in shared endeavour. Drawing on a case study of a pupil called Adam, McDermott illustrates that what Adam learns depends on what is around to be learned. Moreover, learning happens in the interactions within Adam's group as information is made available. With the same people and in the same physical environment of the school we are shown a number of Adams: what differs constantly are the context and the learning conversations.

In Chapter 6, Carl Bereiter develops the issues raised in the previous chapter by focusing on the idea of both situated and non-situated learning. To examine situated cognition, he suggests, we need an example of non-situated cognition for comparability. He explores this paradoxical relationship through a comparison between artificial intelligence and human thinking in terms of abstraction. In the school context, Bereiter makes comparison between two learners in the same physical environment but in different situations with regard to their own learning. In explaining these different situations Bereiter distinguishes between three learning goals. In his view completion, instructional and knowledge-building goals differ in their level of abstractedness and, correspondingly, their degree of situatedness. Completion goals are highly situated, whilst knowledge-building goals are only weakly connected with the immediate situation and thus highly transferable.

In Chapter 7, Mary Jane Drummond also draws on a view of learning in which knowledge is seen in relation to individuals and the social and cultural setting in which they find themselves. In particular she examines more closely the ways in which views of childhood are changed over time, in relation to gender, race, ethnicity and cultural practices.

4

Minds at Work: Applying Multiple Intelligences in the Classroom

Mara Krechevsky and Steve Seidel

A Brief Introduction to the Theory of Multiple Intelligences

All teachers have had at least one student who surprised them with the way the student solved a particular problem or demonstrated that he or she understood something. It may have been a child who solved a maths problem correctly but differently from the way it was taught. It could have been an adolescent who played Romeo's first scene with the Friar with surprising insight into Romeo's character. Or perhaps it was a shy seventh grader who shocked her classmates by becoming the most articulate voice in leading the group through a web of moral and social dilemmas and resolving a crisis over a case of cheating in the classroom. Why were these students surprising?

Perhaps there are two reasons. First, there were things about these children their teachers did not know, things about the ways their minds worked. (The students may not have known these things about themselves, either.) So their teachers did not anticipate that the students would solve a problem or express their ideas in a particular way. But a second reason may be that the teachers themselves may not have ever thought about the problem in that way.

Our sensitivity to the diverse ways in which children think, solve problems, and express themselves is often limited both by our notions of intelligence (for example, that it is something finite one is born with) and our own intellectual preferences. Intentionally or not, teachers design their classrooms (curriculum, instruction and assessment) to reflect their ideas about intelligence and how learning happens as well as their own ways of making sense of the world. Almost all of us can fall into believing that if we can only make clear the way we have come to understand something, others will understand, too.

Based on long and careful observation, especially of children who do not seem to understand easily what may seem obvious to others, many teachers recognize that there are, indeed, many different ways of perceiving the world and multiple ways of making sense of one's experiences. Certainly, in any group, each person notices and attends to different aspects of an experience. It often seems there are as many ways of knowing as there are

44

people. But a closer look at theories of intelligence can provide a middle ground between the idea that there is a single way in which minds work and the notion that every mind is unique. Theories, of course, are only theories; but in attempting to understand the mind and, particularly, the minds in a teacher's classroom, a good theory can help educators make sense of the surprising moves and strategies that students reveal.

Virtually every aspect of classroom life is, in some way, constructed around what teachers want children to learn, and how they think they are most likely to learn it. In some classrooms, desks are in rows and children sit quietly much of the day. In other rooms, there are stations or work areas, each designated for distinct kinds of activity. From the physical design of the room, to the structure of assignments, to the resources provided, to the questions posed in class discussions, each choice a teacher makes reflects, to some degree, an idea about intelligence and learning.

In this chapter, we discuss the theory of multiple intelligences (MI) posed by Gardner in his book, *Frames of Mind* (1993). We describe the ways teachers have considered the implications of a notion of intelligence that takes for granted that students bring a broad range of capacities, each in a distinctive balance, to their work as learners. In particular, we discuss how teachers in various grade levels have applied MI theory to their teaching and assessment practices. Acknowledging and working with diversity of almost any kind in the classroom often seems overwhelming initially. In time, however, this diversity becomes an opening into the creation of much more vibrant learning environments in which all kinds of minds can be encouraged to do their best work. Multiple intelligences theory can provide support for creating such environments.

What is MI theory and where does it come from?

For most of this century, psychologists' ideas about intelligence were derived from statistical analyses of short-answer tests. Using these instruments and analyses, psychologists articulated arguments isolating between 1 and 150 factors of intelligence (Carroll, 1993; Guilford, 1967; Horn and Cattell, 1996; Spearman, 1961; Vernon, 1950). However, 'g' or general intelligence often emerged as a factor common to various kinds of problem solving (Carroll, 1993; Spearman, 1904/1961).

In *Frames of Mind*, Gardner argued that using these instruments and methods does not adequately capture human problem-solving capabilities. Instead of defining intelligence in terms of performances on mental tests, Gardner (1993) defines an *intelligence* as the ability to solve problems or fashion products that are valued in at least one culture. Gardner identified eight criteria to determine whether or not a capacity qualifies as an intelligence. For example, he looked at the potential isolation of an ability by brain damage; distinctive and recognizable developmental paths; the existence of special populations like savants and prodigies who exhibit unusually jagged intellectual profiles; and an identifiable set of core operations (see Figure 4.1).

1. Potential of isolation by brain damage.

2. A distinctive developmental history with a definable set of expert 'end-state' performances.

3. The existence of savants, prodigies, and other exceptional individuals.

4. An identifiable set of core operations or information-processing mechanisms.

5. Support from experimental psychological tasks.

6. Support from psychometric findings.

7. Evolutionary history and evolutionary plausibility.

8. Susceptibility to encoding in a symbol system.

Figure 4.1   *Criteria for considering the intelligences*

Based on his survey of these types of data, Gardner suggested that all human beings possess at least seven relatively independent faculties. In addition to thinking of intelligence as involving linguistic and logical- mathematical abilities, Gardner said that we should consider musical, spatial, bodily-kinesthetic, interpersonal, and intrapersonal abilities intelligences as well (see Figure 4.2.) All human beings possess all of the intelligences, but we differ in our relative strengths and weaknesses.

Linguistic intelligence allows individuals to communicate and make sense of the world through language. Typical professions include journalists, novelists and lawyers.

Logical-mathematical intelligence enables individuals to use and appreciate abstract relations. Typical professions include scientists, accountants and philosophers.

Musical intelligence allows people to create, communicate, and understand meanings made out of sound. Typical professions include composers, conductors and singers.

Spatial intelligence makes it possible for people to perceive visual or spatial information, to transform this information, and to recreate visual images from memory. Typical professions include architects, sculptors and mechanics.

Bodily-kinesthetic intelligence allows individuals to use all or part of the body to create products or solve problems. Typical professions include athletes, dancers and actors.

Intrapersonal intelligence helps individuals to distinguish among their own feelings, to build accurate mental models of themselves, and to draw on these models to make decisions about their lives. Typical professions include therapists and certain kinds of artists and religious leaders.

Interpersonal intelligence enables individuals to recognize and make distinctions about others' feelings and intentions. Typical professions include teachers, politicians and salespeople.

Naturalist intelligence allows people to distinguish among, classify, and use features of the environment. Typical professions include farmers, gardeners and geologists.

Figure 4.2   *The multiple intelligences*

What is the relation between MI theory and traditional ideas about intelligence?

Aside from its unorthodox origins, Gardner's theory diverges from some traditional conceptions in several ways. Gardner, like other past and current theorists (see, e.g., Ceci, 1990; Guilford, 1967; Sternberg, 1985; 1988; Thurstone, 1938), argued for a more pluralistic notion of intelligence. Rather than fixing intelligence at birth, as some traditional ideas of intelligence imply (Eysenck and Kamin, 1981; Herrnstein and Murray, 1994; Jensen, 1969; 1980), MI theory suggests that intelligences change and grow in response to a person's experiences. Like a number of other scholars (e.g., Bronfenbrenner, 1979; Ceci, 1990; Feuerstein, 1980; Perkins, 1995), Gardner viewed the intelligences as educable. They are the result of a constant interaction among biological and environmental factors.

Moreover, traditional conceptions of intelligence hold that intelligence remains the same in all situations (Herrnstein and Murray, 1994; Spearman, 1961; 1927). That is to say, one's intelligence does not change, whether one is solving a maths problem, learning how to ski, or finding one's way around a new city. Modern conceptions point out that the thinking and learning required outside of school are often situated and contextualized (Brown, Collins and Duguid, 1989; Ceci, 1990; Resnick, 1987; 1991). Most intellectual work does not occur in isolation: when people work in different kinds of settings, their abilities to problem solve differ (Resnick, Levine and Teasley, 1991; Rogoff and Lave, 1984). Apart from traditional test settings, problem-solving is usually tied to certain tasks or goals and often aided by other people and an assortment of tools and resources (Brown, Collins and Duguid, 1989; Lave, 1988; Pea, 1990; Perkins, 1993; Salomon, 1993; Vygotsky, 1978).

In keeping with the theories of the thinkers just mentioned, Gardner's definition of *intelligence* is likewise highly contextualized. Further, an intelligence never exists in isolation from other intelligences: all tasks, roles and products in our society call on a combination of intelligences, even if one or more may be highlighted. For instance, concert pianists do not draw solely on musical intelligence to become accomplished in their field. They also must rely on interpersonal skills to connect to an audience or work with a manager, bodily-kinesthetic skills to develop manual dexterity and intrapersonal ability to understand and express the meaning and feeling of a piece of music.

Recent developments in MI theory

The theory of MI is constantly evolving. Recently, Gardner (1999) has suggested that another faculty should be added to the list – the naturalist intelligence. (The core ability of the naturalist intelligence is the ability to recognize and classify the species in one's environment.) Although some critics claim there is no empirical evidence to support MI, Gardner examined hundreds of empirical studies in identifying the original seven intelligences and he continues to review new data as they emerge. Indeed, Gardner added the naturalist intelligence to his list based on his examination of newly published studies. Several recent investigations provide evidence for the relative independence of interpersonal intelligence (e.g., Astington, 1993; Damasio, 1994) but refute the independence of musical and spatial intelligences (Rauscher, Shaw and Ky, 1993).

Even though to our knowledge, there have been no large-scale studies of schools using MI or the effectiveness of MI-based practices on student learning, some educators have reported educational benefits for their students (see, e.g., Campbell, 1992; Hecker, 1997; Mann, 1996). Clearly, more research on the impact of MI on schools needs to be conducted. Several researchers at Project Zero at Harvard are beginning to undertake such studies to look systematically at practices associated with effective use of the theory (Kornhaber and Hatch, 1996). They hope to convert these practices into practical resources and products that can support educators in their efforts to apply MI.

Some common misconceptions about MI theory

It may be helpful to clear up two common confusions with regard to MI. The first is the confusion between an intelligence and a domain of knowledge or discipline (Gardner, 1995). In Gardner's scheme, an intelligence is a biological and psychological potential – a capacity that resides in each person. A domain or discipline is the arena or body of knowledge that gives people the opportunity to use their intelligences in different ways and in which varying degrees of expertise can be developed (see Csikszentmihalyi, 1988; Kornhaber and Gardner, 1993). Examples of disciplines or domains in our culture are mathematics, medicine and gardening. Carrying out work in a domain or discipline requires that a person use several different intelligences, as we saw in the example of the concert pianist. Similarly, each intelligence can be used in a variety of domains – for example, bodily-kinesthetic ability contributes to proficiency in surgery, theatre and athletics.

Another source of confusion is the equation of multiple intelligences with learning styles. *Learning styles* refer to the different approaches that individuals take when trying to make sense of diverse kinds of content (see, e.g., Dunn and Dunn, 1978; 1992; Gregorc, 1985; McCarthy, 1982; Myers, 1980). Typically, a learning style is thought to cut across all content areas. So, if a person is a tactile learner, he or she will learn best when learning new material – whether history or cooking – by using his or her hands or sense of touch. In contrast, the intelligences represent potentials or capacities that are linked to neurological functions and structures and that respond to particular content in the world. We cannot assume that because one has demonstrated a good memory or ability to focus in music that he or she will behave similarly when presented with linguistic or spatial information.

Moreover, unlike learning styles, intelligences have distinct developmental paths that are tied to the achievement of valued roles in our society. If we want children to become skilled artists, mathematicians or solid citizens, then we need to nurture particular intelligences. Learning styles do not share this connection to meaningful societal roles. One can be a tactile or auditory learner and still become an accountant or a botanist. However, if one has not developed strong logical-mathematical or naturalist intelligences, success in those professions will be limited.

Implications of MI Theory for Instruction

MI theory raises many questions for classroom practice. Should teachers try to nurture all of the intelligences equally or should they focus on identifying and developing children's strengths? Should schools offer a wider selection of courses or should they maintain a traditional curriculum and provide more varied ways of engaging students in the standard subject matter? It is important to remember that MI is not an end in itself. If a colleague proclaims, 'I have an MI classroom', or 'I teach at an MI school', one's next question should be, 'What does that mean?' or 'What are your educational goals for your students and school and how does using MI theory help you get there?'

At first glance, MI appears to be compatible with many other educational philosophies and approaches, such as educating the 'whole child', 'project-based learning', an 'interdisciplinary curriculum', 'whole language', and so on. But this leads to the question of whether adopting the theory simply becomes a new label to describe existing practices and beliefs. Although MI may sometimes serve this purpose, it also can provide a theoretical foundation and validation for teachers' beliefs and practices, deepening and/or extending them to new domains (Kornhaber, 1994). The theory can become a framework for thinking about the students we teach and how to teach them, helping teachers become more reflective and explicit about the pedagogical choices they make. As with any theory, people may initially use MI in superficial ways, and some may continue to do so for years. But if educational goals and criteria for reaching those goals can be articulated, then MI can become an ally to rigorous learning.

There is never a single, direct route from scientific theory to daily practice and there are many different ways that MI can be applied in the classroom. As we noted above, applications vary depending on the educational goals and values for the class and the school (see also Gardner, 1993b). Although some people may believe it is important for students to be introduced to and develop competence in all areas, others think certain content (e.g. language or social skills) deserves more attention than others and spend a lot of time nurturing students' linguistic or interpersonal intelligences. Some teachers prefer to teach to children's strengths; others prefer to focus on deficits. Even though there is no one right way to apply the theory, we believe there are at least four important implications for classroom instruction.

Individualizing students' education

One implication of MI theory for instruction is that teachers need to get to know their students well enough to become familiar with each student's interests, strengths, and weaknesses, and shape their instructional practices accordingly. Of course, Gardner is not alone in suggesting that education needs to be individualized. Sizer (1984; 1992), the founder of the Coalition of Essential Schools at Brown University, also wrote about the critical importance of teachers' knowing their students well. At the elementary level, Comer (1988) talked about the value of understanding the six developmental pathways (physical, psycho-emotional, social-interactive, cognitive-intellectual, speech and language, and moral) along which all children progress. The theory of multiple intelligences adds a theory about intelligence and the way the mind works that supports such educational beliefs and practices.

MI provides a framework for individualizing education by helping us to understand the full range of students' intellectual strengths. Traditional schooling has focused on developing only math and language as cognitive abilities. Teachers who use a multiple intelligences framework recognize other abilities – musical, bodily-kinesthetic – as cognitive, too. But opening one's eyes to thinking about these other competencies in new ways is not enough. We must also be prepared to test and support hypotheses about a student's strengths. Several research and development projects have explored ways to do this in the classroom.

Project Spectrum, a collaboration between Harvard Project Zero and Tufts University, is an approach to curriculum and assessment in early childhood that gives teachers tools for identifying and providing evidence for children's strengths in different areas (Chen, 1993; Krechevsky, 1998). Spectrum researchers devised assessments ranging from structured activities to observational checklists in such domains as movement, music, science, art, and social understanding to help teachers recognize the various ways students can use their intelligences. For example, Spectrum divides the movement domain into athletic and creative movement. Athletic movement abilities include power, agility, speed and balance, and creative movement includes body control, sense of rhythm, expressiveness and generation of movement ideas. This delineation helps teachers make sense of key aspects of a domain with which they may not be familiar. Once a student's strengths and interests have been reliably identified, they either can be nurtured further or used to engage students in areas of difficulty.

At the middle-school level, students themselves can become recorders of their own strengths and can work with teachers to individualize their assignments. In the Practical Intelligence for School (PIFS) Project, a collaboration between Harvard Project Zero and Yale University, students are encouraged to learn about their own intelligence profiles and how to draw on their interests and strengths in carrying out their schoolwork (Gardner *et al.*, 1994; Williams *et al.*, 1996). PIFS is an effort to help students succeed in school in part by helping them understand the nature of school, why they attend, and how school activities can be useful in their current and future lives. One of the PIFS curriculum units introduces students to different notions of intelligence and encourages them to take more responsibility for their own learning. Students personalize their education by learning about how they learn best, reflecting on and sharing past experiences that reveal special talents and/or interests, and engaging in a set of problem-solving tasks and challenges that can be resolved in a variety of ways. These types of experiences and related discussion and reflection enable students to take more control of their education and build on their strengths by tailoring assignments to their own interests.

Decisions about whether to offer all students a broad education in many or all of the areas addressed by MI, or whether to tailor students' education to develop their strengths or remediate their weaknesses, may depend on the developmental level of the students. Many schools using MI choose to offer broad exposure early on, with increasing focus and specialization as students get older. One reason for adopting this approach is the belief that it is especially important in children's younger years to introduce them to many different forms of expression and meaning-making to provide them with experiences that are as rich as possible. But as students get older, going into depth in many different subject matters simply is not possible. Also, the pressures of college entrance exams and the job market demand that students be proficient in certain domains. Therefore schooling appears to become more focused. However, even with a more circumscribed curriculum, MI theory can be useful in helping students develop competence.

Teaching subject matter in more than one way

MI leads to teaching subject matter in multiple ways, providing students with different points of entry into learning a topic. Gardner talks about experts as individuals who are able to represent and explain thoughts and concepts in more than one way. The more ways a teacher can explain or teach a topic or concept, the more likely that both the teacher and the students will understand it deeply. Because most teachers do not feel comfortable or knowledgeable enough to teach by drawing on a variety of intelligences, applying MI in the classroom often leads to team-teaching or bringing in community experts to share their expertise. In one elementary school with three kindergartens, each teacher focused on developing her curriculum in two domains and then the children rotated among the three rooms. Classroom teachers often team up with the school's specialist to share knowledge and information about the children.

In his book, *The Unschooled Mind*, Gardner (1991) claimed that any substantive topic can be approached in at least five ways – through the use of narrative, logical analysis, hands-on experience, artistic exploration and philosophical examination (Gardner has since added participatory/ interpersonal experience). For example, students can learn about the theory of evolution by reading about Darwin and his trip on the *Beagle* (narrative); examining quantitative relationships in breeding dominant and recessive traits (logical); breeding fruit flies for certain characteristics (hands-on); looking for and drawing patterns of similarities and differences in fruit flies' wings (artistic); addressing fundamental questions such as whether evolution yields progress in all things (philosophical); or working together on a project where students assume different roles (interpersonal).

The experiences of two college-level English classes (one for students with learning disabilities) illustrate how students learn to articulate and craft arguments in writing using bodily kinesthetic and spatial techniques (Klein and Hecker, 1994). In these classrooms, teachers ask students to represent their arguments by walking across the room, changing directions to reflect shifts in logic. Students thought out loud as they stepped out their essays, asking themselves questions about where they wanted to go and how they could get there. New information was represented by a step forward, contradictory information by a step back, and additional examples by steps to the side. Having students step out their narratives seemed to trigger ideas, help word retrieval and aid in the sequencing of events.

Another set of strategies entails asking students to build models of the relationships between their ideas using coloured pipe cleaners, Lego or Tinkertoys. Rather than generating a written outline for an essay, students created models with differently sized, shaped or coloured pieces that represent different components of the essay like the introduction, main points and conclusion. Seeing concretely how different ideas are linked helped the students develop an overall sense for how the essay comes together. To bridge the spatial and linguistic domains, the teachers asked the students to describe and explain what they had built. Klein and Hecker reported that after several papers, students only had to imagine manipulating blocks or walking out an essay to write in a clear and organized fashion.

Project-based learning

Another natural partner of MI theory is project-based learning. As Katz and Chard (1989) pointed out, projects draw on a range of abilities, allow for multiple points of entry and often reflect meaningful, complex work over time (see also Steinberg, 1997). Projects offer students the opportunity to solve problems or create products – the definition of intelligence according to Gardner. In project work, the intelligences function as means, rather than goals, i.e., they are used in service of completing the work of the project, not as ends in themselves. Since projects also frequently involve collaborative work, they help students both to develop their own interpersonal intelligence and to value the intelligences of their peers (see, e.g., Greeley, 1996b).

An example from the earlier grades is a first grade classroom's project to study the school itself (Kornhaber, 1994). Children investigated the history of the school and wrote both fiction and non-fiction books about the school. They explored the school's physical structure and created scaled floor plans out of blocks. They graphed the number of doors and windows in the school and drew pictures of the pipes they discovered in the basement. Two other classrooms in the school undertook projects studying the community. These projects included such activities as transforming the classroom into a model community complete with churches, banks and beach pavilions, visiting a local restaurant and making pasta, conducting surveys of parents' occupations and graphing and posting the results, and drawing a mural of a passenger train. Many of these activities continued for five months or more.

Arts-infused curriculum

As we have seen, MI theory suggests that learning in and through the arts involves cognitive, problem-solving abilities just like more traditional subject matter. In many schools and classrooms influenced by MI, people turn to the arts and arts-based activities as a way to implement the theory in significant learning experiences. Teachers, parents, and students in MI-based classrooms value achievement in the arts as more than just frills.

Because many classroom teachers have not been trained as artists, they often find it useful to meet or team up with the school's arts specialists or artists from the community. One second grade arts team used dance and movement activities to help children understand place value. They asked children to create movement patterns to represent the 1s, 10s, and 100s places and then to represent their solutions physically (Kornhaber and Krechevsky, 1995). Teachers learned both from their own direct experience with the art form and from looking at student work under the guidance of a trained eye, learning to identify characteristics of unusual ability. The students got to experience at first hand the passion and mastery of expert practitioners.

Schools often draw on local institutions and resources like museums and arts groups to provide experiences or apprenticeships that they are unable to offer themselves. Many schools and districts write grants to host artistic residencies or bring in mentors or experts from the community to work with teachers or students. One middle school teacher asked local experts to come into her class one hour per week to work with students and to look at and critique their work on a play about immigrant life in the textile mills of the nineteenth century. A parent who was a professional composer helped students compose original music for the play. A set designer brought in books about mills and took the students to the library to do historical research. Because the students' notions of research were based on linguistic rather than visual information, the students had not previously thought of set designers as needing to conduct historical research. The teacher also took the students to visit one of the local mills, where they recorded the sound of the machines in operation, again extending their ideas about the nature of research. Through writing music and designing sets, students deepened their understanding of the immigrant experience in industrial America (Greeley, 1996a).

Some misuses of MI theory

It might be useful to identify some of the questionable instructional practices that purportedly follow from MI. Although many of these practices are understandable as initial attempts to apply the theory, ideally, educators trying to apply MI will be able to learn from and deepen their efforts over time.

First, MI is not a mandate to teach every topic in seven or eight ways. Many of the lesson plans and grids that are created to help teachers apply MI in the classroom contain seven slots or boxes, implying that teachers need to fill in just as many learning activities for each unit or lesson. Yet, not all topics and concepts lend themselves to being taught in seven or eight ways, and trying to force-fit activities into each box often leads to well-intentioned but contrived lessons. Suppose, for example, that one of the learning objectives in a maths unit is for students to understand fractions and their relationships. Asking students to sing a song about the operations they have learned, or playing classical music in the background during the lesson, are not particularly meaningful uses of music to support learning maths. However, it may be that learning about different rhythmic structures will help those students who are more musically inclined, especially if the link back to the maths can be made explicit.

Second, many schools and classrooms that have adopted MI encourage teachers and students to identify and honour students' strengths. However, celebrating strengths is not enough; the strengths need to be connected to what students need to know and understand. In either a societal or an academic context, nurturing meaningful achievement in a domain or discipline matters much more than nurturing intelligences per se.

Third, many of us fall into the trap of applying MI by labelling children. Or we may think that children learning to label activities as involving one or another intelligence is the same as demonstrating understanding in the different intelligences. But students need to know that there are different standards of performance and products in different domains, so they can learn what is considered quality work. Depending on the learning goals of a project, standards from a range of disciplines may need to be identified and used to judge the students' work in various genres.

Finally, infusing domains like the arts into the regular curriculum avoids the potential artificiality of separating out MI-based activities from the classroom. Ideally, attention to multiple points of entry and authentic activities in different disciplines should occur throughout the school, not just in a specially designated MI 'activity', 'discovery' or 'flow' room. Although such a setup has understandable appeal, if only for ease of implementation, it runs the risk of making MI something one 'does', as opposed to a way of thinking about children, how they learn, and how best to teach them.

[. . .]

Concluding Note

The theory of multiple intelligences suggests that it may be more instructive to consider how people are intelligent rather than 'how much' intelligence they have. Certainly, in classrooms, the prognosis for every child having a successful learning experience is greatly enhanced when the dominant paradigm is one in which all children are seen as having substantial ways of making sense of the world – including the worlds of academic disciplines – although those ways may not be immediately obvious to the teacher or the child. In part, the work of teaching, learning, and assessing is coming to understand such ways of knowing.

We have identified a number of approaches to curriculum and assessment, none of them entirely new, that reflect a perspective on intelligence that is consistent with the theory of multiple intelligences. Although their use is still far from widespread, most of these approaches have received considerable attention during the last decade of school reform. Some, like portfolios and project-based learning, have long histories of use in schools, especially in arts education. Yet these practices remain largely marginal in most schools in part because they reflect a view of intelligence that is still marginal. The paradigm of intelligence as a fixed, measurable quantity with limited forms of legitimate expression is convenient for certain models (e.g., transmission of knowledge through lecture) and functions (e.g., tracking and sorting by social class) of schooling. But it does not reflect what observation and empirical research indicate about the complexity of the human mind and the process of learning.

Those with alternative perspectives must take seriously the difficulty of implementing new practices in the classroom. In many schools, little time is devoted to explicit thinking through of how practice reflects theories and beliefs and how theory might inform practice. Whatever the practice

– old, new, borrowed or experimental – it is the responsibility of all practitioners and institutions to consider the beliefs and theories that justify what goes on in the classroom. Time must be allocated for the adults in a school to have reflective conversations, engage in such study and share this thinking with parents and the community. (Theorists, of course, also have a responsibility to consider practical implications of their perspectives.)

Short of this kind of restructuring of the school schedule and redefining of a school's culture, individual teachers can pursue these links between theory and practice in the classroom. Simply looking carefully at one's own or the classrooms down the hall and asking how students are encouraged to think, solve problems and express themselves is a good start. Some questions that are helpful to ask of curriculum, instruction and assessment are the following:

- Are students given the opportunity to make choices that reveal their intellectual proclivities and ways of thinking?
- Are there opportunities for assignments and projects that allow students to pace themselves and make decisions that suit their individual profiles?
- Do the approaches to assessment help both teacher and student to learn about and recognize the full spectrum of the student's intellectual strengths or weaknesses? Do these assessments help teachers teach and learn more effectively in subsequent classes?
- What options and resources are available in the classroom so students can exercise a variety of intelligences?
- What are the teachers' own strengths as learners? Are provisions made for understanding and supporting students whose strengths differ from theirs?

Intelligence is only one aspect of theory and beliefs about teaching and learning that needs to be examined. But it is a crucial aspect and one that is, arguably, at the heart of the educational enterprise. From the first day of school, students bring working minds to class. The educator's job is to create the best possible working environment for those minds.

Acknowledgements

Project Zero's work on applying MI in the classroom has been supported by generous grants from the William T. Grant Foundation, the Lilly Endowment, the James S. McDonnell Foundation, the Pew Charitable Trusts, Rockefeller Brothers Fund, the Rockefeller Foundation and the Spencer Foundation. We are grateful to Tina Blythe, Howard Gardner, Sara Hendren and Mindy Kornhaber, who gave many helpful comments on earlier drafts of this chapter.

References

Astington, J. (1993) *The Child's Discovery of the Mind*. Cambridge, MA: Harvard University Press.

Bronfenbrenner, U. (1979) *The Ecology of Human Development: Experiments by Nature and Design*. Cambridge, MA: Harvard University Press.

Brown, A. L., Collins, A. and Duguid, P. (1989) Situated cognition and the culture of learning, *Educational Leadership*, **18**(1), pp. 32–42.

Campbell, B. (1992) Multiple intelligences in action, *Childhood Education*, Summer, **68**(4), pp. 197–201.

Carroll, J. (1993) *Human Cognitive Abilities: A Survey of Factor Analytic Studies*, New York: Cambridge University Press.

Ceci, S. J. (1990) *On Intelligence . . . More or Less: A Bio-ecological Treatise on Intellectual Development*. Englewood Cliffs, NJ: Prentice Hall.

Chen, J. (1993) Building on children's strengths: examination of a project spectrum intervention program for students at risk for school failure, paper presented at the biennial meeting of the Society for Research in Child Development, New Orleans, April.

Comer, J. (1988) Educating poor minority children, *Scientific American*, **256**(11), pp. 42–8.

Csikszentmihalyi, M. (1988) Society, culture, and person: a systems view of creativity, in R. J. Sternberg (ed.), *The nature of creativity*, New York: Cambridge University Press.

Damasio, A. (1994) *Descartes' Error: Emotion, Reason, and the Human Brain*, New York: Putnam.

Dunn, K. and Dunn, R. (1978) *Teaching Students through their Individual Learning Styles: A Practical Approach*. Reston, VA: Reston Publishers.

Dunn, K. and Dunn, R. (1992) *Teaching Elementary Students through their Individual Learning Styles: Practical Approaches for Grades 3–6*. Boston: Allyn and Bacon.

Eysenck, H. and Kamin, L. (1981) *The Intelligence Controversy: H. J. Eysenck versus Leon Kamin*, New York: Wiley.

Feuerstein, R. (1980) *Instrumental Enrichment: An Intervention Program for Cognitive Modifiability*, Baltimore, MD: University Park Press.

Gardner, H. (1991) *The Unschooled Mind*, New York: Basic Books.

Gardner, H. (1993) *Frames of Mind*, New York: Basic Books. (Original work published 1983.)

Gardner, H. (1993a) Assessment in context: the alternative to standardized testing, in H. Gardner, *Multiple Intelligences: The Theory in Practice*, New York: Basic Books.

Gardner, H. (1993b) 'Choice points' as multiple intelligences enter the school, *Intelligence Connections*, **3**(1), pp. 1, 3, 7, 8.

Gardner, H. (1995) Reflections on multiple intelligences: myths and messages, *Phi Delta Kappan*, November, **77**(3), pp. 200–9.

Gardner, H. (1999) Are there additional intelligences? The case for naturalist, spiritual, and existential intelligences, in J. Kane (ed.), *Education, Information and Transformation*. Englewood Cliffs, NJ: Prentice-Hall.

Gardner, H., Krechevsky, M. Sternberg, R. J. and Okagaki, L. (1994) Intelligence in context: enhancing students' practical intelligence for school, in K. McGilly (ed.), *Classroom Lessons: Integrating Cognitive Theory and Classroom Practice*, Cambridge, MA: MIT Press.

Greeley, K. (1996a) Making theater, making sense, making change, in D. Udall and A. Mednick (eds). *Journey through our Classrooms*, Dubuque, IA: Kendall/Hunt.

Greeley, K. (1996b) Windows into students' thinking: interweaving curriculum and assessment, in D. Udall and A. Mednick (eds), *Journey through our classrooms*, Dubuque, IA: Kendall/Hunt.

Gregorc, T. (1985) *Inside Styles: Beyond the Basics*. Maynard, MA: Gabriel Systems.

Guilford, J. P. (1967) *The nature of human intelligence*, New York: McGraw-Hill.

Hecker, L. (1997) Walking, Tinkertoys, and Lego: using movement and manipulatives to help students write, *English Journal*, **86**(6), pp. 46–52.

Herrnstein, R. J. and Murray, C. (1994) *The Bell Curve: Intelligence and Class Structure in American Life*. New York: Free Press.

Horn, J. and Cattell, R. B. (1996) Refinement and test of the theory of fluid and crystallized general intelligences, *Journal of Educational Psychology*, **57**(5), pp. 253–70.

Jensen, A. (1969) How much can we boost IQ and scholastic achievement? *Harvard Educational Review*, **39**(1), 1–123.

Jensen, A. (1980) *Bias in mental testing*, New York: Free Press.

Katz, L. and Chard, S. (1989) *Engaging Children's Minds: The Project Approach*, Norwood, NJ: Ablex.

Klein, K. and Hecker, L. (1994) The 'write' moves: cultivating kinesthetic and spatial intelligences in the writing process, in A. Brand and R. Graves (eds), *Presence of Mind: Writing and the Domain beyond the Cognitive*, Portsmouth, NH: Heinnemann-Boynton-Cook.

Kornhaber, M. (1994) The theory of multiple intelligences: why and how schools use it, qualifying paper, Graduate School of Education, Harvard University, Cambridge, MA.

Kornhaber, M. and Gardner, H. (1993) *Varieties of Excellence and Conditions for their Achievement*, NCREST: Teachers College, Columbria University.

Kornhaber, M. and Hatch, T. (1996) Advancing intelligent models for schools using the theory of multiple intelligences, Proposal submitted to the Geraldine R. Dodge Foundation, Morristown, NJ.

Kornhaber, M. and Krechevsky, M. (1995) Expanding definitions of learning and teaching: notes from the MI underground, in P. Cookson and B. Schneider (eds), *Transforming Schools*, New York: Garland.

Krechevsky, M. (1998), *Project Spectrum: Preschool Assessment Handbook*, New York: Teachers College Press.

Lave, J. (1988) *Cognitive in Practice: Mind, Mathematics, and Culture in Everyday Life*, New York: Cambridge University Press.

Mann, C. (1996) Integrating the multiple intelligences theory into classrooms, unpublished doctoral dissertation, Nova Southeastern University, Richmond, British Columbia.

McCarthy, B. (1982) the 4mat system. Arlington Heights, IL: Excell.

Myers, I. B. (1980) *Gifts Differing*, Palo Alto, CA: Consulting Psychologists Press.

Pea, R. (1990) Distributed intelligence and education, paper presented at the annual meeting of the American Educational Research Association, Boston, April.

Perkins, D. N. (1993) Person plus, in G. Salomon (ed.), *Distributed Cognitions: Psychological and Educational Consideration*, Cambridge: Cambridge University Press.

Perkins, D. (1995) *Outsmarting IQ: The Emerging Science of Learnable Intelligence*, New York: Free Press.

Rauscher, F., Shaw, G. L. and Ky, X. N. (1993) Music and spatial task performance, *Nature*, **365**, pp. 611.

Resnick, L. (1987) Learning in school and out, *Educational Researcher*, **16**(9), pp. 13–20.

Resnick, L. (1991) Shared cognition: thinking as social practice, in L. Resnick, J. M. Levine and D. Teasley (eds), *Perspectives on Socially Shared Cognition*, Washington, DC: American Psychological Association.

Resnick, L. B., Levine, J. M. and Teasley, S. D. (eds). (1991) *Perspectives on Socially Shared Cognition*, Washington, DC: American Psychological Association.

Rogoff, B. and Lave, J. (eds) (1984) *Everyday Cognition: Its Development in Social Context*, Cambridge, MA: Harvard University Press.

Salomon, G. (ed.) (1993) *Distributed Cognitions: Psychological and Educational Considerations*, Cambridge: Cambridge University Press.

Sizer, T. (1984) *Horace's Compromise: The Dilemma of the American High School*, Boston: Houghton Mifflin.

Sizer, T. (1992) *Horace's School: Redesigning the American High School*, Boston: Houghton Mifflin.

Spearman, C. (1961) The proof and measurement of association between two things, in J. J. Jenkins and D. G. Patterson (eds). *Studies in Individual Differences: The Search for Intelligence*, New York: Appleton-Century-Crofts. (Original work published 1904.)

Spearman, C. (1927) *The Nature of Intelligence and Principles of Cognition*, London: Macmillan.

Steinberg, A. (1997) *Real Learning, Real Work: School-to-Work as High School Reform*, New York: Routledge.

Sternberg, R. J. (1985) *Beyond IQ: A Triarchic Theory of Human Intelligence*, New York: Cambridge University Press.

Sternberg, R. J. (1988) *The Triarchic Mind: A New Theory of Human Intelligence*, New York: Viking.

Thurstone, L. L. (1938) *Primary Mental Abilities*, Chicago: University of Chicago Press.

Vernon, P. E. (1950) *The Structure of Human Abilities*, London: Methuen.

Vygotsky, L. S. (1978) *Mind in Society: The Development of Higher Psychological Processes*, Cambridge, MA: Harvard University Press.

Williams, W., Blythe, T., White, N., Li, J., Sternberg, R. J. and Gardner, H. (1996) *Practical Intelligence for School*, New York: Harper Collins.

5

The Acquisition of a Child by a Learning Disability

R. P. McDermott

Sometimes if you try harder and harder, it just gets worser and worser.
(Adam, 1977, third grade)

From 1976 to 1978, Michael Cole, Lois Hood, and I gathered a series of videotapes from one classroom of 8- and 9-year-old children in various settings. Our effort at the time was to locate the children 'thinking' aloud in the hope that we could identify naturally occurring examples of some mental activities that seemed so well defined in experimental settings. Our concern was that activities like attending, remembering, problem-solving and the like, although often invoked in formal institutional descriptions of our children, in fact had few referents in their daily lives. It was not just that no one had ever seen a memory, for various unseen things (electrons, gods, missing stars that fill out a navigator's imagination) have had a useful theoretical career without being seen; it was rather that we had no way to gauge the usefulness of the theories we had available about memory, attention or problem-solving. [. . .]

As an offshoot of our main concern, we became fascinated by how we might describe the learning biographies of different children. There was Nadine, who seemed to know most things and to learn quickly whatever she did not already know; there was Reggie, who seemed to know a great deal about everything but how to get along with his peers; there was Matt, who hid out for the year and seemingly never engaged in any official, school-learning task; and there was Adam, who suffered as an officially described learning disabled (LD) child, but who seemed always eager to try. It was this last child who most captured our focus. [. . .] The present chapter revives Adam's story in order to raise some questions about various approaches to the explanation of learning failures and to provide a focus for an account of notions of context and learning.

The Argument

[. . .]
We might just as well say there is no such thing as LD, only a social practice of displaying, noticing, documenting, remediating, and explaining it. This

theoretical shift makes LD no less real to the participants of life in schools where occasions for displaying LD are so frequent, but it should at least make us wonder what we all do that makes LD so commonly sensible and ubiquitous in our experiences with institutionalized learning. [. . .]

After following Adam for 18 months, we gave up on specifying his traits as the explanation of his behaviour and began talking instead about what happened around him daily that seemed to organize his moments as an LD person. Even at this most local level, we could find that many people were involved in Adam's problem. On any occasion of his looking inattentive, for example, it took Adam to look away at just the right time, but it took many others to construct the right time for Adam to look away; it took others to look away from his looking away, and still more to discover his looking away, to make something of it, to diagnose it, to document it and to remediate it. Whatever was Adam's problem inside his head, we had forced on us the recognition that Adam had plenty of problems all around him, in every person on the scene, in most every scene called educative. It is in this vein that we claimed that Adam's disability was not just visible in the sense that the world was a neutral medium for what he could not do, but that the world was precisely organized for making his disability apparent, that he was the negative achievement of a school system that insisted that every-one do better than everyone else (Hood, McDermott and Cole, 1980).

In order to describe Adam, or better, in order to figure out what we had described after we spent a year trying to describe Adam, we needed a theory of learning that could take into account that learning is not an individual possession. The term *learning* simply glosses that some persons have achieved a particular relationship with each other, and it is in terms of these relations that information necessary to everyone's participation gets made available in ways that give people enough time on task to become good at what they do. If that happens enough, it can be said that learning happens. It probably makes more sense to talk about how learning acquires people more than it makes sense to talk about how people acquire learn-ing. Individually we may spend our time trying to learn things, but this phenomenon pales before the fact that, however hard we try, we can only learn what is around to be learned. If a particular kind of learning is not made socially available to us, there will be no learning to do. This is a primary fact that we have made little use of theoretically. If we can stop focusing on who learns more or less of particular, culturally well-defined fragments of knowledge, and ask questions instead about what is around to be learned, in what circumstances and to what end, learning achievements would become statements about the points of contact available to persons in various social settings (Lave, 1988a; 1988b). What could LD be in such a world?

Before extending the arguments about context and learning in a discus-sion of various approaches we have available for the description of children like Adam, it is necessary to introduce Adam in the various settings in which we came to know him.

Adam, Adam, Adam and Adam

We videotaped all the children in their classrooms, in some one-to-one
testing settings and, most extensively, in afternoon activity clubs that we set
up for them two days a week. We were often struck with how much some
children varied across the different settings. Adam stood out as the child
who varied the most.

There were four settings in which we knew Adam fairly well: Everyday
Life, Cooking Club, Classroom Lessons and Testing Sessions. We can
roughly gloss them along a continuum displaying either Adam's visibility as
a problem (from invisible to a source of constant embarrassment), or
school-like demands (from fairly loose to very constrained). Adam was
least visible as a problem in Everyday Life situations. He appeared in every
way competent and, more than most of the children, he could be wonder-
fully charming, particularly if there was a good story to tell. In the Cooking
Club, Adam was only a little more visible as a problem. When he worked
with his friend Peter, he got his cake made without any trouble. When he
had to work with someone else, there were often some arguments, some
tears, and some taunting from others before he could get his work done.
Classroom Lessons presented the same story, although troubles were more
frequent, and the adults seemed to be drawn more obviously into his
problem in the sense that they would try to reframe the task he was facing
or they would chastise him for his misbehaviour. Finally in the Testing
Sessions, Adam stood out from his peers not just by his dismal performance but by the wild guesswork he tried to do.

As the settings differed in the degree to which Adam stood out as a
problem, so they differed along a continuum to the extent that they were
school-like in their constraints and their demands. Our effort in this chapter is to identify some of the approaches one could take to the description
of the continuum, to point to some of the pre-theoretical assumptions each
makes about the nature of context and learning, and to extract what might
be the most useful notions for our own purposes. The first approach
focuses on the inadequacy in Adam's head, the second on the arbitrariness
of the tasks Adam is asked to work on, and the third on the interactional
dilemmas thrown in Adam's way as he moves through school.

The Continuum of Difficulty and Deficit

[. . .]

By our most popular line of folk reasoning, Adam becomes more visible
as we move across the continuum because he is performing less well in the
face of increasing demands. Under the loose constraints of Everyday Life,
Adam can blend into the crowd and do what he has to do without anyone

worrying about the quality of his mind. In the Cooking Club, this is equally true when he can work with Peter, who can read the recipe and oversee the step-by-step planning of the cake. When he cannot work with Peter, he has to work hard to arrange for someone else's co-operation, and, if that is not forthcoming, he begins to stand out. In Classroom Lessons, the tasks can be even more demanding, and Adam appears even less adequate to meeting the challenge. A close inspection of the classroom tapes showed Adam acting out on those occasions when he could be called on to perform. For example, while the teacher was asking the class questions and calling on children for answers, Adam could be found crawling under his work table, giving the finger to a friend, and so on; when the teacher switched to the next part of the lesson and called the children forward to see a demonstration, Adam would join the crowd. When the going gets cognitively demanding, Adam stands out; otherwise, he is part of the crowd.

Adam had not been spared professional labels. His LD was well documented not just by the school, but by a university reading clinic that he attended for tutoring. As much as he seemed fine in Everyday Life, school work seemed terribly hard for him. Although Adam's case was extreme, this is an experience that we all recognize. That Everyday Life seems easier than Testing Sessions is a basic fact of life for us all, and tying it to cognitive difficulties makes great intuitive sense. In addition, once questions about children are framed in these terms, once our inquiry is narrowed down to the question of what is wrong with this or that child, support for a deficit theory can be found wherever one looks. [. . .]

The deficit approach rests on a number of assumptions of questionable validity, however. Although it is true that Everyday Life *seems* easier than life in school, there is no reason to assume that the difference has only to do with increased cognitive demands. The tasks do not have to be cognitively more complex for us to experience them as harder. The trouble could lie along other dimensions; for example, school tasks could be harder simply because they are more arbitrarily constructed, or because an inadequate performance on school tasks could lead to a degradation ceremony.

If we examine the notions of context and learning inherent in the deficit approach, we can gain a little more insight into what we are getting ourselves into when we describe someone as LD. In the deficit theory, as in all common-sense uses of the term, context refers to an empty slot, a container, into which other things are placed. It is the 'con' that contains the 'text', the bowl that contains the soup. As such, it shapes the contours of its contents; it has its effects only at the borders of the phenomenon under analysis. [. . .]

Accompanying this sense of context is a static theory of learning. By this account, knowledge and skill enter heads, where they wait passively for situations in which they might prove useful. School-derived knowledge and skill are supposed to generalize and to make children ready for a wide range of adaptive behaviours. The learner is a passive container, filled up by his or her efforts in school, slowly gathering up the skills purportedly essential to some jobs that will eventually have to be tackled. The problem with LD children is that they enter school without some rudimentary skills for paying attention and processing information. They are hard to fill. Some school situations are easier on them than some others, but in the long run their inability to keep pace with their peers forces them to stand out and fall even further behind. They are what they are; learner and environment are seperable, and they do not greatly alter each other.

These static assumptions about context and learning are supported by static notions of both language and culture. The deficit theory assumes that language and culture are storehouses from which children acquire their competence. Some children get more and some get less. These are assertions about which we should be most uncomfortable. [. . .]

The social policy that flows from these static notions of context, learning, language and culture are easily recognizable to us. Those who do not get enough knowledge from home or school need to be encouraged to get some more. They need to acquire more language and culture in order to be ready for more situations. They cannot afford to learn on the job; they cannot afford to assume that they will be shaped by new contexts, or that the language and culture that they need will be available to them *in situ*. They need to get more things in their heads to cut down their deficits in the face of difficult demands.

[. . .]

The Continuum of Arbitrary Demands and Left-out Participants

The second way of looking at the range in Adam's performances has us focusing less on Adam and more on the tasks he is asked to perform. In Everyday Life, Adam can use any resources to get a job done. If he has to remember a telephone number, he can memorize it, write it down, call information or ask a friend. School tasks are different from this in that a person is often restricted in what he or she can make use of; procedure is of the essence. On tests, this trend is exaggerated. What else is a test but an occasion on which you cannot use any of the resources normally available for solving some problem; memory notes or helping friends are now called cheating. Is it possible that Adam is better understood as a child who is faced not by increasingly more difficult tasks, but increasingly more arbitrary tasks?

In Everyday Life, Adam found the resources at his disposal more than adequate. In the Cooking Club, he had an equivalent freedom if he was working with a friend. If, however, he was working with someone who was not willing to help, or if the people around him were trying to outdo him, then the task of cooking suddenly became more difficult. It is not just the case that Cooking Club can be made easy by someone helping Adam to do what he cannot; it is rather that, under the gentle circumstances of working with the friend to make a cake together, he can do what he cannot do if the task is both to make a cake and not to get caught not knowing how to read a recipe. In the Cooking Club, we quite by accident organized some confusing circumstances for children of this age: for example, a two-cup cup, teaspoon and tablespoon, baking soda and baking powder, ingredients on one side of the page and instructions on the other side. Adam's friend Peter is one of the children who could sort out these problems; when working with Peter, Adam not only follows the directions Peter reads to him, he sometimes reads the recipe himself. When working under less gentle circumstances, he will rarely look at the page. The task is obscured by the social work he must do to arrange not looking incompetent. In this way, reading 'teaspoon' for 'tablespoon' becomes more likely, not because Adam's head does not work, but because he barely looks at the page and ordinary resources for the solution to the problem are disallowed. In the Testing Session, Adam is so preoccupied with getting the answer that it is not clear he even hears many of the questions. He might be handling more mental steps avoiding the questions than he would have to handle if he addressed the questions. Arbitrary demands make him stand out. There may be more to LD than disability.

Understanding Adam by way of the arbitrariness of the demands placed on him represents an advance over the blind ascription of the deficit approach. It encourages, for example, a more careful look at the child and his or her circumstances and insists that we be more sensitive to what might be going on in the child's surround.

Upon careful examination, the continuum of arbitrariness leaves us with the same sense of context, learning, language, and culture as the deficit account. The conceptual assumptions remain the same. Contexts and their demands are still static, although there are more of them than allowed by the deficit approach. Adam is still Adam, and tests are tests. Context and their members are still separable. Learning still sits inside the student waiting to be called forth, although now in the form of specific sets of skills that must be used in situationally specific ways. Language and culture are still the sorts of things one can have more or less of, as if those who had less were not a systematic version of the culture everyone else had.

A Continuum of Degradation and Labelled Children

A third approach to Adam's behaviour focuses on how much and on what grounds a person is liable to degradation in the different settings. What is at stake here is an appreciation of how much each setting organizes the search for and location of differential performances and how much that search further organizes the degradation of those found at the bottom of the pile. Garfinkel (1956; Pollner, 1978; see also Pollner and McDonald-Wikler, 1985, for a stunning reverse case) has shown how degradation is always a ceremony in which public agreement on what one can be degraded for is displayed and directed against the total identity of others. This means that it takes much work across persons to make an individual liable for some part of their behaviour; a person must not only do the wrong thing, but exactly the wrong thing that everyone is looking for someone to do and then at just the right time.

By this line of reasoning, Adam is a problem in Everyday Life, primarily because everyday life is well organized for the systematic location of problems (Scott, 1985). Cooking Club is mostly about cooking, and only occasionally a source for a learning-related degradation ceremony. On one occasion, Adam and a friend made a green cranberry bread (a physical possibility, we are told, in an aluminium bowl with ingredients inserted in just the wrong order). When the others gathered around to see and laugh, he simply said, 'So I made a goddamn mistake, so what'. The issue passed. Other occasions for degradation do not move along so easily, no matter what Adam's response. Classroom Lessons, for example, can be so well organized for putting the spotlight on those who are doing less well than the others that hiding becomes a sensible strategy for all of the children some of the time and for some of the children all the time. Adam seemed to suffer in the classroom, and this is in part how he became visible to us. During one small-group reading lesson, Adam was having a difficult time matching words with accompanying pictures. Reading 'fake' for 'face', he became tangled in a complex conversation with the teacher as she walked in and out of his group with occasional tips for the kids. It took us days of looking even to guess at the ways they seemed to be not understanding each other. What kept us curious was the attention paid to Adam's disability by the other children in his group. Adam's LD generally played to a packed house. Everyone knew how to look for, recognize, stimulate, make visible and, depending upon the circumstances, keep quiet about or expose Adam's problem.

There may be more to LD than disability. There may be many other people involved: certainly everyone in Adam's classroom, in various ways everyone in the school, everyone in the schooling business, all of us. [. . .]

Could Adam be disabled on his own? Only if he could work on a task that was not culturally defined and had no consequences for his life with others; that not being a possibility, he can only be disabled through his interactions with others. Culture is a sine qua non of disability. There are basic questions asked in all scenes called educative in America: Who can do it? Who can't? Who is smart? Who is dumb? These are not the dominant questions that are asked in all scenes in America; they can leak by way of school into homes and on to some jobs, much less in school playgrounds, and not at all in singles bars, but they are ubiquitous in schools. How is it, Goffman (1979) once asked, that a young man cannot know a word in school and feel dumb and not know a word in a car garage and have not his intelligence but his masculinity put on the line? An identical cognitive absence can be interpreted different ways depending on the scene. These questions acquire their answers, and in the process, with the help of tests, diagnoses, specialists and government-sponsored budgets, LD acquires its share of the children.

The degradation account of Adam's behaviour along the continuum of scenes relies on a different sense of context, learning, language and culture than the previous approaches. If the assumptions of this approach are a little better tuned with our experiences, and possibly a little less lethal to our children, then we may have grounds to prefer a degradation approach to the others.

Context

Context is not a fixed entity to Adam, for it shifts with the interactional winds. Each new second produces new possibilities along with severe constraints on what is possible. In this sense, context is not so much something into which someone is put, but an order of behaviour of which one is a part. Adam was a contributing member of various organizations that made his behaviour relevant to the life of LD; this happened more often in Testing Sessions and Classroom Lessons than it did in Cooking Club or Everyday Life, and this was made possible by people, including Adam, organizing these scenes in ways that made LD diferentially available in the different scenes.

Adam's LD is made available for all to see, because everyone was looking for it. In the Cooking Club, it is not so much the difficulty of the material as that Adam cannot address the material without worrying about whether he can get it straight or whether anyone will notice if he does not. This is not paranoia; everyone is often ready to notice and, depending on the situation, ready also to look away or to make Adam's problem even more public. Looking for Adam's LD has become something of a sport in Adam's class, a subset of the wider sport of finding each other not knowing things. Adam spends his day arranging not to get caught not having information that he could get from print. His every move is designed not to have LD again ascribed to him and, as such, his every move confirms and re-creates the possibility that the label of LD will be available in the classroom for anyone to ascribe to Adam. 'Where is the LD?' Behaviourally, the answer is clear. It is all over the classroom as an interactional possibility. Everyone stands in some relation to it. Everyone is part of the choreography that produces moments for its public appearance. LD is distributed across persons, across the moment, as part of the contextual work members do in the different scenes. Neither Adam, nor his disability, can be separated from the contexts in which they emerge.

Learning

Learning traditionally gets measured on the assumption that it is a possession of individuals that can be found inside their heads. By the degradation approach, learning is not in heads, but in the relations between people. Learning is in the conditions that bring people together and organize a point of contact that allows for particular pieces of information to take on relevance; without the points of contact, without the system of relevancies, there is no learning and there is little memory. Learning does not belong to individual persons, but to the various conversations of which they are a part.

When Adam works in the Cooking Club he gets no time to read, but he gets constant instruction on how to look LD. The instructions stored in the system are not simply about how to read. Reading to get the cake made is not Adam's only point of contact with the other members of the class. The instructions stored in the system are also about who is to finish first, with the best cake, with the recognition that they are the most competent. Given this more inclusive agenda, information about how to read can get lost easily, and Adam can get acquired by LD. It is the business of degradation and not education that seems to organize selected moments in the Cooking Club, even more moments in Classroom Lessons and more still in the Testing Sessions.

Language and culture

The language and culture that Adam encounters in his daily round may not be what most of us assume them to be. Language is easily understood as a neutral tool of expression that helps us to say and write what we like and to interpret what others have said and written for us. On these grounds, Adam needs more language. Like most children called LD, he loses his words at various important times, and reading and writing are pure torture for him. More language for sure. By the degradation stand, however, Adam's language may be quite complete. Language is not a neutral medium; it comes to us loaded with social structure. It comes to us loaded with sensitivities to the circumstances under which it was born and maintained in previous encounters. It comes to us biased with the social agendas of a school system that pits all children against all children in a battle for success. Indeed, all American culture seems well poised to have Adam and millions of others failing in school. By this standard, Adam has exactly the language required of his position. Culturally, he is taking one of two perfectly normal pathways through school: he is failing. There is a language waiting in every classroom in America for anyone who might take that road, and Adam has done his job well. He acquired and was acquired by a culturally recognized and mandated absence. He had achieved school failure. Adam had been acquired by the language of LD that was in place before he was born.

Languages help us to build the scales along which we calculate our pluses and minuses. So it is with culture. Cultures and languages fill the world before any given child's arrival, and they define what must be present and what must be noticed as absent. Culture and language define what each of us needs, force us to attend to those of us who are left short, and ideally equip us to help them over their disabilities. Unfortunately, cultures are never so magnanimous, nor can they be. As a series of ideal types, *cultures are defined most essentially by the inability of all to live up to their directives*. Cultures offer only 'collective illusions', prescriptions that give us a way to talk about how we should live together in exchange for an inarticulateness about how we actually do live together (Murphy, 1971; 1987). Cultures cannot supply the resources members need in order to live in them without exposing the arbitrariness of their particular way of life. They exist by their promises, and they feed off each of us to the extent that we try to follow them and fail.

Languages acquire their speakers. So disabilities acquire their learners. Who is there first? Long before Adam was born, we had LD – or an equivalent. It is an absence we know how to look for. American culture makes the absence of learning real as presence. Before any teachers of children enter the schools every September, failure is in every room in America. There is never a question of whether everyone is going to suc-ceed or fail, only of who is going to fail. Because everyone cannot do better than everyone else, failure is an absence real as presence, and it acquires its share of the children. Failure and success define each other into separate corners, and the children are evenly divided as if by a normal curve, into successful and failing. Among those who fail are those who fail in ways that the system knows how to identify with tests, and these children are called special names. LD acquires its share of the children.

Context and learning no longer have individual subjects as variables, but refer instead to the organizing devices people have available for dealing with each other. Similarly, language and culture are no longer scripts to be acquired, as much as they are conversations in which people can particip-ate. The question of who is learning what and how much is essentially a question of what conversations they are a part of, and this question is a subset of the more powerful question of what conversations are around to be had in a given culture (Goodwin, 1991). To answer these questions, we must give up our preoccupation with individual performance and examine instead the structure of resources and disappointments made available to people in various institutions. To do this job, we may not need a theory of individual learning and, given its use in our current educational system, we may not be able to afford one.

Acknowledgements

Richard Blot, Eric Bredo, Robbie Case, David Charnow, Michael Cole and Jean Lave offered helpful comments on a previous draft. Mimi Cotter helped greatly with the occasional Gestalt flavour. This chapter is dedi-cated to the late Robert F. Murphy who understood well how a culture can disable. I owe him a letter.

References

Garfinkel, H. (1956) Conditions for a successful degradation ceremony. *American Journal of Sociology*, **61**, pp. 420–4.

Goffman, H. (1979) *Gender Advertisements*, London: Macmillan.

Goodwin, M. (1991) *He-Said-She-Said*, Bloomington, IN: Indiana University Press.

Hood, L., McDermott, R. P. and Cole, M. (1980) 'Let's try to make it a good day' – some not so simple ways, *Discourse Processes*, **3**, pp. 155–68.

Lave, J. (1988a) *Cognition in Practice*, Cambridge: Cambridge University Press.

Murphy, R. F. (1971) *Dialectics of Social Life*, New York: Basic Books.

Murphy, R. F. (1987) *The Body Silent*, New York: Holt.

Pollner, M. (1978) Constitutive and mundane versions of labeling theory, *Human Studies*, **1**, pp. 269–88.

Pollner, M. and McDonald-Wikler, L. (1985) The social construction of unreality. *Family Process*, **24**, pp. 241–57.

Scott, J. (1985) *Weapons of the Weak*, New Haven, CT: Yale University Press.

6

Situated Cognition and How to Overcome It

Carl Bereiter

The first half-century of American psychology is often represented nowadays as a dark age of rat-running and rote verbal-learning experiments, which ended only when it was overwhelmed by the rise of the new cognitive psychology that started in the 1950s (cf. Gardner, 1985). But throughout that early period, there was a strain of mainstream experimental psychology that dealt with what we would now call situated learning. It was rat psychology, to be sure, but it was a psychology of situated rat behaviour. The central tenet was that animals do not simply learn responses, they learn their environments. Run rats in a maze under typical tightly controlled conditions, and they learn a fixed route to the goal. Change things a little and they are lost. But let them run around on their own and they quickly learn the whole maze, so that they can get from wherever you drop them to wherever they want to go by an efficient route. [. . .]

Contemporary ideas about situated cognition, having come to us from anthropology, are heavily loaded with human cultural concerns. They are connected with Vygotsky and his belief in the social origins of cognitive structures. We tend to forget that animal cognition is situated, as well.
[. . .]

Outgrowing Animal Cognition

We do not come by situated cognition through a cultural or learning process. Our brains evolved to deal with situations in which we find ourselves. We have, however, managed to transcend our animal heritage in certain ways, and in this chapter I argue for the value of viewing these as ways of overcoming the situatedness of cognition. Like other adventures in overcoming nature, overcoming the situatedness of cognition has risks as well as benefits and is, in a fundamental sense, illusory. But identifying the risks and benefits and separating illusion from reality is part of the programme I am advocating here.

The most obvious way in which we humans transcend our animal heritage is through transforming physical environments and creating new social structures and practices along with them. The second way is through acquiring expertise, which enables us to function in a novel environment much as if we had evolved within it (Bereiter and Scardamalia, 1993).

Environmental transformation and expertise are to be found in every society, but there is a third way of transcending biological givens that is much less common and that represents a far more radical departure from the kinds of cognitive adaptations we share with other species. This is the kind of departure most dramatically exemplified by science. It amounts to creating a world of immaterial knowledge objects and acquiring expertise in working with them. Although these knowledge objects may refer to spatially and temporally located situations, they are not bound to those situations. Thus, this third way represents a stronger sense in which humans may be said to overcome the situatedness of cognition. The third way, furthermore, greatly extends the other two. A modern city is a physical environment within which human beings have developed many new forms of practice and expertise, but this environment could not exist were it not for centuries of development of abstract knowledge now put to use in the construction of tall buildings, electrical power grids, heating and air-conditioning systems, and the countless other technological underpinnings of a modern city.

These three kinds of advances beyond animal cognition map nicely on to Popper's (1972) metaphoric schema of three worlds – World 1 being the material world of inanimate and animate things (including human beings), World 2 the subjective world of individual mental life and World 3 the world of immaterial knowledge objects. Lacking other handy labels, I use Popper's terms without implying a necessary commitment to other aspects of Popper's epistemology.

Situated cognition researchers have contributed substantially to our understanding of the relations between Worlds 1 and 2, arguing that these are much more directly and intimately connected than previous cognitive theories had supposed. But they have not done the same for World 3. Instead of according knowledge existential status in its own right, as epistemologists have traditionally done, they have tried to account for it in terms of the practices of particular groups, such as scientists or mathematicians; concrete embodiments of knowledge, such as books and instruments; and, occasionally, as content in individual minds – as mental models, for instance (Greeno, 1994).

Although these are important aspects of knowledge, they seem to me to miss the core. That core is represented in the metaphor of World 3 – a world, wholly created by the human intellect, that enables us, for better or worse, to escape the situational embeddedness of cognition. Without that core, formal education becomes meaningless (as, indeed, some advocates of situated cognition seem to believe it is). Again, for better or worse, formal education is our individual escape route from the confines of situated cognition.

Can There Be Non-situated Cognition?

Greeno, a leading exponent of situated cognition, expressed dissatisfaction with the term. It seems to refer to a type of cognition and, thus, to imply that there also exists a type of cognition that is not situated (Greeno, 1994). Situativity theorists (to use Greeno's suggested replacement term) deny this: all cognition is situated and could not be any other way. If we accept this premise, then the title of this chapter, 'Situated cognition and how to overcome it', is an oxymoron.

But, in fact, there is non-situated cognition, and situativity theorists have devoted a lot of effort to criticizing it. The catch is that non-situated cognition is not found in nature (at least not in nature as it is known to earthlings); it is found only in machines. Most of artificial intelligence has been constructed according to a model radically at variance with the kind suggested by situativity theory. In situated cognition, people (or other agents) carry on activity in the world, adapted to the constraints and affordances of the environment. Cognition is the individual or collective process by which people negotiate these constraints and affordances, according to their individual or collective purposes. Machine intelligence of the classic AI variety is not like that. Cognition is an entirely internal process of symbol manipulation (Vera and Simon, 1993). Interaction with the outside world is done by means of transducers that translate inputs from sensors into symbols that the machine can manipulate or that translate symbols into actions. Thus, a robot controlled by AI of this kind will contain a plan – for getting from Point A to Point B, let us say – that controls how data from its visual sensors are translated into symbols that its program can then convert into instructions to its servomechanisms so that the plan is executed through physical movement. The robot may also contain a program for revising the plan in case of mishap. One very important line of argument in favour of situated cognition comes from roboticists, who find that this kind of robot cognition does not work very well (Beer, 1991). It is too slow and crude and prone to catastrophic failure. But these kinds of criticisms acknowledge that there is such a thing as non-situated cognition, making the case that it is not a very good kind of cognition for getting around in the world.

The existence of non-situated cognition, albeit artificially created, is, I believe, profoundly important for understanding human cognition and its situatedness. For one thing, it allows us to talk about advantages and disadvantages of situated cognition, which would make no sense if there were nothing to compare situated cognition with. It also affords the possibility of identifying degrees of situatedness. With such possibilities in view, it is no longer absurd to talk about overcoming situated cognition. The questions are: why would anyone want to, and how could it be done?

Advantages and Disadvantages of Situated Cognition

If we take rule-based AI as exemplified non-situated cognition, then looking at what it does well and poorly (compared to human beings) may offer us insights into the advantages and disadvantages of situated cognition. Using rule-based programs, computers are much better than we are at carrying out long chains of reasoning and at exhaustively searching memory (Anderson, 1985). Thus, they excel at chess. The best programs, which can beat all but a few human experts, succeed by reasoning farther ahead and along more paths than their human opponents (Charness, 1991). We are abysmally bad at searching memory in a listwise fashion. Try naming the 50 United States – or some other familiar set of about that size, if the states are not familiar enough. Almost everyone misses one or two and has a terrible time finding the missing ones, whereas computers have no trouble with this sort of task.

What we do remarkably well in comparison to rule-based AI is recognize patterns – for instance, recognizing a face from the past, even though it has aged 20 years since last we saw it. Computers, by contrast, have trouble identifying letters of the alphabet under the normal variations of handwriting and typography, a task many preschool children can handle easily. Another relative strength of human cognition is associative retrieval – for instance, reading a research report and being reminded of a related finding from a decade past, on a slightly different topic. This is a chancy business for us, but rule-based AI cannot do it at all unless the stored items have been appropriately indexed beforehand (Schank, Collins and Hunter, 1986). Pattern recognition and associative retrieval seem to be the means by which we grasp analogies and metaphors, and this gives us a great imaginative edge over the literal-minded machine (Margolis, 1987).

The relative strengths of computer and human cognition directly reflect differences between non-situated and situated cognition. Rule-based AI works very well when all the necessary information can be explicitly represented and indexed, as is the case with a game of chess or a gazeteer. The rule-based system can then go to work on its stored information and produce a result appropriate to the part of the real situation of which it contains a representation; for example, it can compute a move appropriate to a real chess game. When all the necessary information is coded into rules or propositions, formal logic comes to the fore as a powerful tool for arriving at decisions, and logical operations are what computers excel at. The trouble is that the great bulk of real-world situations cannot be represented in this way. Chess games can, but as simple a game as tag cannot. This is because chess has a set of rules that allow all the possible moves to be computed, whereas the possibilities inherent in a dozen kids running around on a playground are, for practical purposes, limitless. Representations are necessarily abstractions. Abstractions based on Newton's laws work for physical situations involving a small number of inanimate objects, but when objects have minds of their own and can twist and dodge the way agile children can, such abstract representations become relatively useless. It is not that Newton's laws cease to hold, of course; it is just that the variables are too numerous and are impractical to measure and compute.

A tag-playing robot would need a different kind of mind from the one that rule-based AI would give it. Instead of a mind that works on internal representations of the playground and the participants, it would need a mind more directly attuned to the physical and social environment, responding quickly to opportunities for tagging, switching from one pursuit to another the instant that a more promising target presented itself. In short, it would need situated cognition.

At this point, my account sounds like much of what appears in the situated cognition literature. The situated actions of just plain folks come off as flexible, adaptive and elegant – in a word, intelligent – whereas action based on formal procedures and principles comes off as brittle, plodding, insensitive to nuance – in a word, stupid. It is time, therefore, to look at the other side. Although non-situated cognition may not be very good for guiding a robot in a game of tag, it has proved capable of guiding a space vehicle to Mars. Surely there is a lesson for us in that.

The Problem of Transfer

The main weakness of situated cognition is, it seems, precisely its situatedness. In traditional language, the limitations of situatedness are referred to as problems of transfer. What we learn in one situation, we often fail to apply in another. Situativity theory helps us to understand why this is so. The progress of situated learning consists of increasingly fine attunement to the constraints and affordances of the particular situation. Thus, as learning proceeds, it tends to become less and less generalizable to other situations. In your first job as a store clerk, you will begin by learning many things that are applicable to store clerking in general – how to address customers, ring up sales, bag purchases, watch for shoplifters, and so on. But as the weeks go on, your skills will become more and more specific to the particular store and its merchandise, clientele, management, physical layout, staff, and so on.

Advanced stages of situated learning may, in fact, begin to yield negative transfer, as habits are acquired that will need to be overcome in a new situation. There is a deeper problem of transfer, however. Elsewhere, I have tried to show that what mainly fails to transfer is learned intelligent behaviour (Bereiter, 1995). The course of situated learning typically has the aspect of a progression from being inept and prone to stupid mistakes to being competent and smart. Although important parts of what is learned in one situation may transfer to a new one, the part that does not transfer is likely to include the being smart. Again, this makes sense in light of situativity theory, for being smart just means becoming so nicely attuned to specific constraints and affordances of a situation that you can effortlessly cope with whatever problems arise. In a new situation, you are liable to have to start over being stupid.

If, categorically, learned intelligent behaviour is not transferrable from old situations to new, this has grave implications for education, of not for humankind in general, what with the accelerating pace of change. But there we have an irony worth pondering. The accelerating pace of change is increasingly driven by technological innovations, virtually every one of which is an instance of transfer of intelligent behaviour from one situation to another. I do not want to make space travel out to be the highest achievement of human intelligence, but it is surely our most colossal example of transfer of learning. No amount of situated cognition or legitimate peripheral participation would get people to the moon and back. It took something more to produce that kind of transfer, and we must try to pin down what that is. Failing in that, we may face a future in which a small number of people have caught on to some secret of transferrable learning, and thus are able to keep creating and adapting to new situations, while the rest of us find it increasingly difficult to cope.

[. . .]

Learning Beyond What the Situation Calls For

Flora and Dora are both A students in Algebra I. The next year, they take Algebra II. Flora again aces the course, whereas Dora finds herself at a loss and just manages to scrape by with the C minus awarded to students who try hard but do not get it. Here we have an apparent case of the same learning transferring for one person but not for another. Few mathematics educators would buy that interpretation, however. They would conjecture that Flora and Dora learned quite different things in Algebra I. What Flora learned evidently provided a good basis for Algebra II, whereas what Dora learned did not. So it is not that something failed to transfer for Dora, it is that she failed to learn what was transferrable. How are we to account for these different learnings, and how do they relate to situated cognition?

In the last 20 years, there has been quite a bit of research on the Floras and Doras of the world. Even without the research, it is easy to divine that Flora probably understood the mathematics presented in Algebra I and that Dora did not, getting by instead on rote procedures. What the research has done is give us an idea of what Flora did differently from Dora in order to produce this result. Stepping down from algebra to arithmetic, a nice example of this research comes from Resnick and Neches (1984). They examined a practice common in elementary arithmetic, in which children carry out operations with concrete objects that mirror such symbolic operations as borrowing and carrying (or regrouping, as it is now called). Most children, although they were able to carry out both the concrete and the symbolic operations, failed to make a connection between them. Some children did make the connection, however. On interviewing the children, it was found that the children who made the connection reported that they were trying to make a connection.

That may not sound very surprising, but consider it from the standpoint of situated cognition. Clearly, the situation was designed to afford experimenting with the relationships between concrete and symbolic quantitative operations. But any situation affords innumerable opportunities for inquiry. Why we would exploit one and not another – or any at all, for that matter – depends partly on our own goals and partly on, to put it broadly, what the situation calls for. Generically, the situation in which the children in Resnick and Neches' study found themselves was that of schoolwork (Doyle, 1983). A schoolwork situation is rather like that in a garment factory. Although a number of workers may be present in the same room, each one is independently engaged in carrying out a task specified by the supervisor or teacher. What the situation calls for is defined by the task constraints. The tasks are usually defined in such a way as not to put undue strain on the capacities of those performing them. There usually are time constraints, however, and so there is motivation to find ways of satisfying task requirements that economize on time. Another characteristic shared by schoolwork and garment work is a very limited time horizon. Although the teacher or supervisor may have long-range objectives, the students or workers are not expected to look beyond the immediate day's task. (School projects are an exception, as their name implies.)

Given these characteristics of schoolwork, it then becomes remarkable that some children would take it on themselves to try to discover a logical connection between the concrete and symbolic components of the task they were assigned to carry out. The task assignment did not require it. The task components were easily enough executed that it was unlikely that an impasse would drive them to deeper analysis. And the time horizon, suggesting that it would all be over soon, offered no reason to think ahead to the possible relevance of the current task to future situations.

Returning to Flora and Dora, their first-year algebra class probably provided opportunities – through textbook explanations and worked examples, class discussions and problems – to develop a basic understanding of algebraic functions. But what the situation actually called for was just solving lots of linear equations. By learning a few procedures and applying them carefully, an assiduous student could solve the equations without any need for conceptual understanding. That, we may surmise, is what Dora did. It worked well through Algebra I. But then she got to Algebra II and encountered an explosion of different types of equations and complications in procedures for solving them. Try as she might, she made frequent errors. Having no sense of how algebra related to arithmetic, she never checked her answers with trial values. (Perhaps arithmetic did not make much sense to her, either, and therefore provided no basis on which to build an understanding of algebra.) Consequently, her errors went uncorrected and the marks on her schoolwork plummeted.

Flora, we surmise, did acquire an understanding of algebra in the course of her first year. But on the basis of related research, we may further surmise that this did not just happen. Despite the fact that the situation did not actually call for it, Flora must have expended effort in trying to understand what algebra was about and how it connected with what she already knew. This is what Scardamalia and I have elsewhere defined as intentional learning (Bereiter and Scardamalia, 1989). Intentional learning is primarily a matter of goals rather than strategies. Examining the goal-related statements of people studying computer programming, Ng and Bereiter (1991) were able to identify three levels of goals. The first and most common are task completion goals. In the Flora and Dora case, these would be goals associated with correctly completing assigned algebra problems. At the next level are instructional goals. These are goals related to what the teacher or textbook is trying to teach. They can vary greatly in how explicitly and saliently they are put before the student. In a typical algebra textbook, they would be discernible from section headings and the like, but they could easily be ignored in the pursuit of task completion goals. Finally, and rather rare, are knowledge-building goals, which pertain to the learner's personal agenda for constructing knowledge. Among other things, the three kinds of goals differ greatly in their time horizons. In a conventional algebra class, the time horizon for task completion goals is usually the next day. The time horizon for instructional goals is likely to be the next examination or, at most, the end of the course. The time horizon for knowledge-building goals, by contrast, may extend indefinitely far into the future, and may also extend into the past, encompassing a history of past learning that is consciously built on in the present.

[. . .]

These three levels of goals differ in their level of abstractness. Correspondingly, we may say that they differ in their degree of situatedness. Action in pursuit of task completion goals is highly situated, being directly linked to manifest constraints of the situation. The pursuit of instructional goals is less so. And when we get to pursuing knowledge-building goals, we are talking about action that is only weakly connected with the immediate situation, that consists largely of mental work on symbolic objects, some of which are abstracted from the current situation but others of which originate quite outside it.

Situativity theorists might concede that something like this continuum of abstraction exists, but they would argue that the more abstract kind of mathematical activity is just as situated as the more concrete. This is where the relational character of situativity becomes important. Although Flora and Dora may be in the same physical environment, they are in different situations. The affordances and constraints are different, reflecting their differing motives and capacities. But even though one may be plodding through a workbook assignment while the other is reflecting on the nature of mathematical functions, each is engaged in a cultural practice that is adapted to situational constraints and affordances.

[. . .]

Schooling and Knowledge Work

Although situated cognition researchers have taken a lively interest in learning, both in and out of school, they have not come up with anything that could be called a new educational vision. Instead, situativity theorists have tended to endorse various innovations of a social constructivist cast, interpreting them within their own frameworks. As has been pointed out (Wineburg, 1989) and acknowledged (Brown, Collins and Duguid, 1989), however, the educational ideas coming from situativity theorists have not advanced notably beyond those of Dewey. The main difficulty, I would suggest, is that situativity theory has not been able to provide a cogent idea of the point of schooling. This difficulty, in turn, derives from a serious confusion between product and process.

[. . .]

The source of the confusion is that knowledge production, like any kind of human activity, takes place in some physical and social situation, and accordingly situated knowledge also develops. This is knowledge constituted in the practice of the community and intimately involved with the affordances and constraints of the situation. But this is not the same as the knowledge that is the product of the situated activity, any more than the situated knowledge of the workers in the paint factory is the same as the paint they produce.

Some knowledge-production situations are less confusing than others, however, so let us consider one of those first. A forensic chemistry laboratory produces knowledge of a particular kind. Through analysis of materials obtained at a crime scene, knowledge is produced that contributes to creating an account of what went on at the scene. In this case, it is not difficult to distinguish between the knowledge embedded in the practice of the chemists and the knowledge that they deliver to the detectives. The two kinds of knowledge relate to entirely different situations. The distinction becomes trickier if the chemists are doing basic research. In this case, the knowledge they produce relates to their own practice as well as to others'. But with a little effort, the distinction can be maintained. If, however, chemical research is being carried out by students in a school laboratory, then the distinction becomes even less obvious. This is because the students are likely to be the only users of the knowledge they produce. Nevertheless, I believe that the school situation, like the other situations in which knowledge is created, can best be understood by striving to distinguish knowledge implicit in the process from knowledge that is the product of the process.

No such distinction is normally made in education, even with the popularization of constructivist ideas. The results of knowledge construction are thought of as entirely internal – internal to the minds of individual students under most construals, or internal to the distributed cognition of the classroom community under construals influenced by sociocultural theories (Cobb, 1994). Accordingly, constructivism becomes more or less synonymous with learning by discovery, and it competes – not always successfully – with direct instruction (Harris and Graham, 1994).

The observable goings-on in this activity that we call collaborative knowledge-building fall easily within the spectrum of what others might call constructivist learning, cognitive apprenticeship, inquiry learning or talking science. The distinctiveness is conceptual; it is a matter of how teachers and students conceive of what they are doing and the effect this has on efforts to do it better. One thing that must be recognized about the many exciting experiments in educational uplift that are going on (it is true of all the ones I have knowledge of, and so I confidently generalize to the rest) is that reality falls well short both of the ideal and of the exemplary episodes reported in the literature. Hence, in pedagogy as in science, improvability is of the essence. The following are ways in which a knowledge-building conceptualization of schooling offers advantages over other approaches that regard both knowledge construction and the knowledge produced as situated:

1. The focus of classroom activity shifts from improving students' minds to improving their theories or other knowledge objects. This is a clearer objective and one that students and teachers alike can more readily track.
2. A developmental continuum may be recognized that runs from unconscious learning in early childhood (Montessori, 1967) to self-aware, intentional learning (Bereiter and Scardamalia, 1989) and then to inquiry that is focused on the external world and finally to inquiry that is focused on World 3 objects as they relate both to the external world and to one's own purposes (Scardamalia, Bereiter and Lamon, 1994). Helping students advance along this continuum then becomes a meaningful educational objective.
3. Production of knowledge objects inevitably involves building on or otherwise dealing with existing knowledge objects (hence Newton's avowal that he stood upon the shoulders of giants). Consequently, familiarity with culturally significant World 3 objects – the goal of cultural literacy (Hirsch, 1987) – comes about naturally rather than through a didactic regimen.
4. Progressive education sought to avoid inert knowledge by having learning come about naturally through the social life of the community. But the social life of school communities does not naturally give rise to much learning of an abstract or theoretical nature. Students experience the power of concepts in science and other disciplines by using them to help solve problems in their own knowledge-building efforts.

5. Knowledge-building is not in competition with instruction. In schools, there is no reason why time cannot be taken out from knowledge building, to whatever extent is judged necessary, and devoted to explicit learning activities.
6. Knowledge-building provides a natural basis for involving people outside the school who are engaged in related activities – scientists, curators and librarians, experts in various trades and professions, and so on. This involvement of talents beyond the classroom is almost obligatory if students are free to follow a knowledge-building project wherever it leads them (Scardamalia and Bereiter, 1994).
7. The knowledge objects students produce in school will tend naturally to be ones of very basic and general applicability. This is because there is no particular job that the knowledge must serve (as there is, for instance, in the forensic chemistry laboratory); and students' questions, when freely generated, tend to be *why* questions that lead toward deep principles (Scardamalia and Bereiter, 1992). Consequently, the knowledge that students produce is the kind that serves broadly to overcome the limits of situated cognition.
8. The situated learning that does occur is learning how to function in a community of practice whose work is work with knowledge. The transferrability of this learning to knowledge work in out-of-school situations is, of course, chancy; but it seems reasonable to assume that students who have had years of experience in explicitly working with knowledge will have an advantage over ones whose experience has been limited to the traditional kinds of scholastic learning and doing in which knowledge, as such, is seldom the object of attention.

[. . .]

A major social issue for our time is whether the world will be run by an expert elite on one side of the divide while the bulk of humanity remains on the other. It seems to me that today's schools are on the wrong side of the divide. That bodes ill for prospects of moving much of the population to the post-industrial side.

One of the most disturbing indicators that I encounter comes from my experiences in speaking publicly about the ideas discussed in this section. People in modern businesses understand what I am talking about immediately. Educators usually do not. They think I am just talking about active learning. Educators are immersed in World 3, but they are like the proverbial fish immersed in water. They cannot see it. They do not conceive of knowledge as something that can be manufactured, modified, worked with and, in some cases, even packaged and sold. Unfortunately, the rise of situated cognition theory does not help in this regard. It has contributed greatly to our understanding of the kind of knowledge that is implicit in practice, but by treating all knowledge as situated, it renders the world of knowledge objects invisible.

In a famous statement, Sir Isaac Newton likened himself to a child finding pretty stones on the shore 'whilst the great ocean of truth lay all undiscovered before me'. Those pretty stones, however, were the foundation of the modern world. We need schools in which students learn to work with pretty stones. As for the great ocean of truth, all we can say with confidence is that, if it ever is discovered, it will not be by fishes.

References

Anderson, J. R. (1985) *Cognitive Psychology and its Implications* (2nd edn), San Francisco: Freeman.

Beer, R. D. (1991) *Intelligence as Adaptive Behavior*, Cambridge, MA: MIT Press.

Bereiter, C. (1995) A dispositional view of transfer, in A. McKeough, J. L. Lupart and A. Marini (eds), *Teaching for Transfer: Fostering Generalization in Learning*, Hillsdale, NJ: Lawrence Erlbaum Associates.

Bereiter, C. and Scardamalia, M. (1989) Intentional learning as a goal of instruction, in L. B. Resnick (ed.), *Knowing, Learning, and Instruction: Essays in Honor of Robert Glaser*, Hillsdale, NJ: Lawrence Erlbaum Associates.

Bereiter, C. and Scardamalia, M. (1993) *Surpassing Ourselves: An Inquiry into the Nature and Implications of Expertise*, La Salle, IL: Open Court.

Brown, J. S., Collins, A. and Duguid, P. (1989) Debating the situation: a rejoinder to Palincsar and Wineburg, *Educational Researcher*, **18**(10–12), p. 62.

Charness, N. (1991) Expertise in chess: the balance between knowledge and search, in K. A. Ericsson and J. Smith (eds), *Toward a General Theory of Expertise: Prospects and Limits*, Cambridge: Cambridge University Press.

Cobb, P. (1994) Where is the mind? Constructivist and sociocultural perspectives on mathematical development, *Educational Researcher*, **23**(7), pp. 13–20.

Doyle, W. (1983) Academic work, *Review of Educational Research*, **53**, pp. 159–99.

Gardner, H. (1985) *The Mind's New Science: A History of the Cognitive Revolution*, New York: Basic Books.

Greeno, J. G. (1994) Understanding concepts in activity, in C. Weaver, C. R. Fletcher and S. Mannes (eds), *Discourse Comprehension: Essays in Honor of Walter Kintsch*, Hillsdale, NJ: Lawrence Erlbaum Associates.

Harris, K. R. and Graham, S. (eds). (1994) Special issue on implications of constructivism for students with disabilities and students at risk: issues and directions, *Journal of Special Education*, **28**(3), pp. 233–378.

Hirsch, E. D., Jr. (1987) *Cultural Literacy: What Every American Needs to Know*, Boston: Houghton Mifflin.

Margolis, H. (1987) *Patterns, Thinking, and Cognition*, Chicago: University of Chicago Press.

Montessori, M. (1967) *The Absorbent Mind*, New York: Holt, Rinehart and Winston.

Ng, E. and Bereiter, C. (1991) Three levels of goal orientation in learning, *Journal of the Learning Sciences*, **1**(3–4), pp. 243–71.

Popper, K. R. (1972) *Objective Knowledge: An Evolutionary Approach*, Oxford: Clarendon.

Resnick, L. B. and Neches, R. (1984) Factors affecting individual differences in learning ability, in R. J. Sternberg (ed.), *Advances in the Psychology of Human Intelligence*, Hillsdale, NJ: Lawrence Erlbaum Associates.

Scardamalia, M. and Bereiter, C. (1992) Text-based and knowledge-based questioning by children, *Cognition and Instruction*, **9**(3), pp. 177–99.

Scardamalia, M. and Bereiter, C. (1994) Computer support for knowledge-building communities, *Journal of the Learning Sciences*, **3**(3), pp. 265–83.

Scardamalia, M., Bereiter, C. and Lamon, M. (1994) CSILE: Trying to bring students into world 3, in K. McGilley (ed.), *Classroom Lessons: Integrating Cognitive Theory and Classroom Practice*, Cambridge, MA: MIT Press.

Schank, R. C., Collins, G. C. and Hunter, L. E. (1986) Transcending inductive category formation in learning, *Behavioral and Brain Sciences*, **9**, 639–86.

Vera, A. H. and Simon, H. A. (1993) Situated action: a symbolic interpretation, *Cognitive Science*, **17**, pp. 7–48.

Wineburg, S. S. (1989) Remembrance of theories past, *Educational Researcher*, **18**, pp. 7–10.

7

Children Yesterday, Today and Tomorrow

Mary Jane Drummond

In this chapter I will explore the proposition that the most important considerations in the debate about how primary education should be reformed for the twenty-first century are not questions of power politics, nor of whose definitions of curriculum should prevail. The core of the debate must focus on the children who will be living and learning in this century; we need to consider the characteristics of these children, before we can shape a curriculum that is fit for them. As a starting point, here are the first few lines from a book I sometimes use on in-service courses, in my work with teachers and other educators.

> Once upon a time there was a little girl.
>
> She had a Father, and a Mother, and a Grandpa, and a Grandma, and an Uncle, and an Aunty; and they all lived together in a nice white cottage with a thatched roof.
>
> This little girl had short hair, and short legs, and short frocks (pink-and-white striped cotton in summer, and red serge in winter). But her name wasn't short at all. It was Millicent Margaret Amanda. But Father and Mother and Grandpa and Grandma and Uncle and Aunty couldn't very well call out 'Millicent Margaret!' every time they wanted her, so they shortened it to 'Milly-Molly-Mandy,' which is quite easy to say.
>
> Now everybody in the nice white cottage with the thatched roof had some particular job to do – even Milly-Molly-Mandy . . .
>
> And what did she do? Well, Milly-Molly-Mandy's legs were short, as I've told you, but they were very lively, just right for running errands. So Milly-Molly-Mandy was quite busy, fetching and carrying things, and taking messages. (from *Milly Molly Mandy Stories*, Joyce Lankester Brisley)

First published in 1928, the Milly-Molly-Mandy stories were reprinted in paperback right through the 1970s, 1980s and 1990s. They are still in print, still being asked for in bookshops, still being read by children today.

When I ask early years educators on in-service courses to read a chapter or two of Milly-Molly-Mandy's adventures, many of them admit to having loved her dearly during their own childhoods. Those educators who meet Milly-Molly-Mandy for the first time are divided: some cannot get excited by this relic of a bygone age, but others are disgusted by her vacant expression and little beady eyes. With encouragement, the educators list her other characteristics: her obedience, her immature speech, her dependence (it takes six mature adults to protect and provide for her) her politeness, her sweet tooth, her thrift, her innocence of pain and grief (and mud). We go on to note how quiet, clean, safe and snug is her thatched cottage, how enclosed and self-contained her well-kept village, how the adults in her life rarely talk to one another and never, ever, say anything the slightest bit disagreeable.

What's the point of this discussion? To trigger an investigation into the taken-for-granted concepts *childhood* and *children*; to stimulate questions about the nature of children, especially 'child-like children'. This is a concept that the Japanese have a word for (see Tobin, Wu and Davidson, 1989). I have found it useful in the process of examining my own values and beliefs about children and childhood. What about this child, for example?

We lit fires. We were always lighting fires.

I preferred magnifying glasses to matches. We spent afternoons burning little piles of cut grass. I loved watching the grass change colour. I loved it when the flame began to race through the grass. You had more control with a magnifying glass. It was easier but it took more skill . . . We'd have a race; burn, blow it out, burn, blow it out. Last to burn the paper completely in half had to let the other fella burn his hand. We'd draw a man on the paper and burn holes in him; in his hands and his feet, like Jesus. We drew long hair on him. We left his mickey till last.

We cut roads through the nettles. My ma wanted to know what I was doing going out wearing my duffle coat and mittens on a lovely nice day.

– We're doing the nettles, I told her.

The nettles were huge; giant ones. The hives from their stings were colossal, and they itched for ages after they'd stopped stinging. They took up a big corner of the field behind the shops. Nothing else grew there, just the nettles. After we hacked them over with a sideways swing of our sticks and hurleys we had to mash them down.

(Doyle, 1993)

I use this extract like the first, to raise questions that may not get asked very often among those who live and work with children, questions that are however, still worth thinking about. Is Paddy Clarke a child-like child? If Milly-Molly-Mandy misses out on noise and danger and rough words, what's absent in Paddy Clarke's life? Is he more or less of a child than she is? If an intelligent Martian, with a working command of English but no conception of children or of childhood, were to be confronted with these two extracts, what sense could he, she or it make of them?

Where these questions lead is towards other, and more serious ones: whose definitions of children and childhood do we, parents and educators, subscribe to, probably without even knowing it? Whose images of the child-like child do we carry, deep in our mind's eye, as we care for and educate children? Do we know enough about the effect these images, definitions, expectations might have on the children in our families and our primary schools? It is not difficult to accept the proposition that the way we (you, I, society at large) see children in general affects the ways in which we treat them as a whole; it is harder to disentangle cause and effect in particular adult interactions with children, in individual adult–child relationships. And yet I believe this is an area well worth exploring, since our practices in educating children must be inextricably tangled up with our aspirations about what kind of people we think they are, and what kind of people we want them to become.

As such an exploration gets under way, as it now is, in numerous research studies and seminars, in books and journals – (e.g. Pilcher and Wragg, 1996; Walkerdine, 1997), it is necessary to be aware that it can only proceed on the basis of our rejection of a different way of understanding children, a mindset that James and Prout (1990) diagnose as the 'old paradigm' of childhood. In this version, children are seen in stark contrast to the adults whom they will one day become. James and Prout list the characteristics of adults and children, in this 'old paradigm', as if they were two different instances of the same human species.

Children	**Adults**
immature	mature
irrational	rational
incompetent	competent
asocial	social
acultural	cultural

(adapted from James and Prout, 1990, p. 13)

The passage from one state of being to another is achieved, according to socialization theory, by the natural process of development (from the simple to the complex, from the irrational to the rational) and by the equally natural process of parenting. The adults direct, the children respond; the adults trigger learning and co-operation by operating reward and punishment systems; the social order is perpetuated, as the irrational, passive infant becomes the competent, active adult. In this model, the universal child, natural and culturally naked, as it were, is transformed into the adult at home and at ease in a particular, ordered, taken-for-granted, social world.

James and Prout reject this way of seeing, forcefully arguing that although the physical, biological facts of infancy and childhood are fixed, their cultural manifestations can and do vary dramatically. The facts get taken over by the ways in which society (which includes parents and teachers) apprehend, interpret and give shape to the facts. In the 'new paradigm', James and Prout claim, it is recognized, first, that childhood is always socially constructed and, second, that children are also social constructivists, that they make meanings for themselves, as they contribute to the shaping of the world of childhood they inhabit.

Tobin, Wu and Davidson (1989) provide vivid, chapter-long illustrations of the social construction of childhood in three very different worlds, in China, Japan and the USA. English early years educators with whom I have used this challenging book are often especially excited by the description of Hiroki, a 4-year-old boy in a Buddhist preschool in Kyoto:

> On the day we videotaped at Komatsudani, Hiroki started things off with a flourish by pulling his penis out from under the leg of his shorts and waving it at the class during the morning welcome song. During the workbook session that followed, Hiroki called out answers to every question the teacher asked and to many she did not ask. When not volunteering answers, Hiroki gave a loud running commentary on his workbook progress ('now I'm coloring the badger, now the pig . . .') as he worked rapidly and deftly on his assignment. He alternated his play-by-play announcing with occasional songs, entertaining the class with loud, accurate renditions of their favourite cartoon themes, complete with accompanying dancing, gestures, and occasional instrumental flourishes. Despite the demands of his singing and announcing schedule, Hiroki managed to complete his workbook pages before most of the older children (of course, those sitting near him might have finished their work faster had they a less distracting tablemate) . . .
>
> Lunch over and the room cleaned up, Fukui-sensei (the teacher) returned to the balcony where, faced with the sight of Hiroki and another boy involved in a fight (which consisted mostly of the other boy's being pushed down and climbed on by Hiroki), she said neutrally, 'Are you still fighting?' Then she added, a minute later, in the same neutral tone, 'Why are you fighting anyway?' and told everyone still on the balcony, 'Hurry up and clean up (the flash cards). Lunchtime is over. Hurry, hurry.' Hiroki was by now disrupting the card clean-up by rolling on the cards and putting them in his mouth, but when he tried to enter the classroom Fukui-sensei put her hand firmly on his back and ushered him outside again. Fukui-sensei, who by now was doing the greatest share of the card picking-up, several times blocked Hiroki from leaving the scene of his crime, and she playfully spanked him on the behind when he continued to roll on the cards.

There is plenty more to read about Hiroki's exciting day, and typically the discussion becomes quite heated, especially when we turn to comments made by other participants in Tobin's study – the educators representing the 'three cultures' being investigated.

Comments Arising from the Observation of Hiroki

- Staff team at Hiroki's school:
  'We think Fukui-sensei (Hiroki's teacher) dealt with Hiroki in a satisfactory way. We think it is right to ignore the most provocative, aggressive and exhibitionist actions. This is a strategy we have agreed on.'
- Higashino: Assistant Principal of Hiroki's school:
  'We should not punish Hiroki. He has pride and he will be hurt if we yell at him or make him sit alone. We must avoid confronting or censuring Hiroki'.
- American early years specialist:
  'Hiroki is bored, he finishes his work quickly, his behaviour is an attempt to make things more exciting, better matched to the pace and level of stimulation he needs. He is gifted, talented, intelligent.'

- Fukui-sensei – Hiroki's teacher:
  'Hiroki is not especially intelligent; if he is so clever, why doesn't he understand better? If he understood better, he would behave better.'
- Yoshizawa: Principal of Hiroki's school:
  'Misbehaving, including fighting, is a lost art for today's sheltered nuclear-family raised children.'
- Fukui-sensei – Hiroki's teacher:
  'I let the boys fight because it is natural for boys of that age to fight, and it is good for them to have the experience while they are young of what it feels like to fight.'

When the heat of the discusssion has died down, it is time to think about what Hiroki can teach us about our own observations and perceptions of children. What internal categories, invisible to ourselves but glaringly obvious, we must assume, to Hiroki's educators, govern our understanding and our practices? And are these categories compatible with our most cherished aspirations for our children?

As the discussion continues, the participants begin to disentangle the strands that make up *our* version of *Tobin's* account of *Hiroki's* story. It becomes easier to see which bits of children, and of a particular child, are necessarily part of being a child; these can then be set apart from those parts that are the outcomes of firm expectations, however unselfconsciously enforced, those parts that are a projection of our most optimistic aspirations, and those parts that children construct for themselves. For if Hiroki teaches us nothing else, he certainly reminds us that children have voices and important things to say, just as much as their educators.

We need not, of course, travel to Japan to find differences in the ways we construct children and childhood. Here in England, in January 1996, the School Curriculum and Assessment Authority (SCAA) published a slim document called *Desirable Outcomes for Children's Learning on Entering Compulsory Education*. Reactions from the early years professional community were, on the whole, hostile. But in one quarter, the early years educators were more than hostile: they were implacably opposed, on principle, to the desirability of some of the 'desirable outcomes' set out in the document. These educators were speaking on behalf of the Steiner-Waldorf kindergarten movement, an international group who draw their inspiration from the philosophical writings of Rudolf Steiner (1861–1925), and whose kindergartens number more than 1000 worldwide. Their work is dedicated to a particular view of childhood, and the ways in which children under 7 (or, in their own terms, before the second dentition) grow, develop and learn. Their account of the essential features of early childhood parts company with SCAA's desirable outcomes approach in several important particulars. The chief of these is the way in which the SCAA document sets out key expectations for early achievement in literacy.

Children enjoy books and handle them carefully, understanding how they are organized. They know that words and pictures carry meaning, and that, in

English, print is read from left to right and from top to bottom. They begin to associate sounds with patterns in rhymes, with syllables, and with words and letters. They recognize their own names and some familiar words. They recognize letters of the alphabet by shape and sound. In their writing, they use pictures, symbols, familiar words and letters, to communicate meaning, showing awareness of some of the different purposes of writing. They write their names with appropriate use of upper and lower case letters.

(*Ibid.*)

These capacities – outcomes or achievements – whatever we might choose to call them, have no place in the Steiner kindergarten. There the educators use no picturebooks or printed material of any kind. They do not require their children to learn either the names or the sounds of the letters of the alphabet.

The rationale for their approach is to be found in Steiner's teaching about certain key stages in the development of children. Drawing on a threefold model of adult humanity, comprising the powers of the head, the heart and the will (thinking, feeling and doing), Steiner educators maintain that young children are essentially in 'doing' mode, exercising their whole bodies, under the control of their will, in sustained, creative, imaginative exploration of their world. In the Steiner kindergarten, there is no place for the abstraction of the printed page or the letters of the alphabet. But their 3- to 7-year-olds are not deprived of stories, folk tales, myths, poetry and song. Their lives are daily enriched by the most entrancing stories and songs, as I know from my own observations in the Rosebridge Kindergarten in Cambridge.

The programme for these young children is built on very different foundations from the 'areas of experience' familiar to mainstream nursery educators. The Steiner programme is based on rhythm, routine, reverence, ritual, creativity, stories and song. At the centre of this programme are the children, who, like children anywhere, are by turns boisterous, dreamy, fretful, absorbed, noisy, joyful, wondering, inventive and energetic. During the morning session they move from a period of spontaneous imaginative play to gather round the big table for painting, baking or craft activities. There is a time for ring-games and songs, and for outdoor play in a wonderful garden. There are times to come together to eat the bread they have baked, to celebrate festivals, to listen to their teacher tell them stories. These stories are selected not just for their rich language and literacy worth, but for their moral meanings; they are stories that will act as a grounding for the children's moral life. All knowledge, claims one Steiner educator, starts with a state of wonder; the kindergarten seeks to support and foster this sense of wonder. The adults in the kindergarten are the guides who protect the children absorbed in exploring their world, and who feed their energies with nourishing activities.

Several times now, I have invited Steiner educators to contribute to my in-service courses for early years practitioners. They are listened to in a profound silence, which is half born of incredulity (that a system so different could exist on one's very doorstep), and half born of respect for the reverence and intensity with which these people speak of their work with children. Once, however, I remember, a nursery teacher from a huge inner-city primary school, serving an economically disadvantaged estate, with all its associated problems, was moved to object to what she was hearing. The essence of her strenuous objection was that the Steiner kindergarten and its trappings – muslin, candles, wooden blocks, flowers, shells, logs, brown bread and freshly made jam – could not be said to constitute a preparation for the *real* world, where the children she knew best were living and learning. The Steiner educator paused for a moment and gently replied: 'Surrounded by the beautiful, being shown what is good . . . I don't think that makes you *un*prepared for the world.' Needless to say, the discussion did not end there.

But the point the speaker was making has a wider relevance than a discussion about the advantages – or disadvantages – of the Steiner approach. At the heart of her proposition is the simple principle that the prime responsibility of educators, of whatever philosophical or political conviction, is to give their children the intellectual and emotional nourishment that will match their growing and developing powers. Difficulties and differences only arise when educators disagree about what these powers are, and which are the most important. Where Steiner educators prioritize the good and the beautiful, the authors of SCAA's *Desirable Outcomes* prioritize (among other things) capital letters, word recognition and numbers up to ten. At stake here are different constructions of childhood, different conceptualizations of what it is that young children should do and feel, know and understand, represent and express.

Where do we go from here? Recognizing differences, and accepting the inevitability of such differences is only a first step. But it is an important step, because it reminds us that we – parents, teachers, society at large – do have real choices to make. In early years provisions in nurseries, infant, first and primary schools, it is possible for people, parents and educators, to come together to do some thinking work around these issues, returning perhaps, as a starting point, to the Japanese concept of the child-like child. What *do* we understand by 'child-like children', of 3, of 5, of 7 or 11?

Any attempt to come to terms with these difficult questions will be immeasurably enriched by close attention to the work of the early years educators in the region of Emilia Romagna in Italy. Here the services to young children, from birth to 3, and from 3 to 6, are justly world famous. Their work has been celebrated in a staggeringly impressive travelling exhibition *The Hundred Languages of Children*, which was seen in England for the first time in the summer of 1997, in two venues, under the auspices of the British Association for Early Childhood Education. The title of the exhibit refers to the principle at the heart of the Reggio-Emilia approach, (as it has come to be known) – the principle that children have at their disposal 100 languages, of which the school steals 99. In Italy children start elementary school at the age of 6; in the full day childcare available from birth to 6 in the preschools, nurseries and toddler centres of Reggio-Emilia, the educators are committed to restoring the full 'one hundred languages of children'.

Their approach

> fosters children's intellectual development through a systematic focus on symbolic representation. Young children are encouraged to explore their environment and express themselves through all of their natural 'languages' or modes of expression, including words, movement, drawing, painting, building, sculpture, shadow play, collage, dramatic play and music.
>
> (Edwards, Gandini and Forman, 1994)

These are not empty words, or wishful thinking; this description of the educators' aspirations is followed through into practice.

In every provision for young children there is a richly equipped workshop-cum-studio – the *atelier* – staffed by a professionally trained artist/educator, the *atelierista*. In the *atelier*, children's powers to represent their experiences, their questions, their problems, and their dreams, are given the richest opportunities for growth. Using the multitude of materials available, children are daily engaged in complex representations of their pressing emotional and cognitive concerns. Child-like children, in Reggio-Emilia, are honoured for characteristics that make 'the appropriate use of upper and lower case letters' look like very small beer. Carla Rinaldi, a pedagogical co-ordinator who works to support curriculum development and in-service work in a group of preschools, sums up their principled position:

> The cornerstone of our experience, based on practice, theory and research, is the image of children as rich, strong and powerful . . . They have the desire to grow, curiosity, the ability to be amazed and the desire to relate to other people . . . (They) are open to exchanges and reciprocity as deeds and acts of love, which they not only want to receive but also want to offer.

In describing the Reggio-Emilia approach so enthusiastically I am not trying to suggest that it could simply be transplanted, root, branches and flowers, into primary education in this country. But I do believe that British teachers and other educators would do well to assimilate the understanding that Rinaldi refers to as their 'cornerstone', their confident belief in children's powers.

In the years since 1988, and the passing of the Education Reform Act, untold time and energy (and forests of paper) have been expended in the project of devising and revising curriculum structures (programmes of study, attainment targets, end of keystage descriptions, desirable outcomes), through which a whole generation of primary and preschool children have passed. These structures have been elaborated in terms of knowledge, concepts and skills; their reference points are to the external world, as we apprehend it through the subject studies of the National Curriculum, themselves derived from the academic disciplines of the grammar schools of earlier centuries. The curriculum review now under way, which will take us into the twenty-first century, is an opportunity to start again with a different set of conceptions in mind, the conceptions that are the theme of this chapter. If we decided to design a primary curriculum for the future by *starting with children*, we would be well on the way to constructing a curriculum fit for children. This would be a more truly educational enterprise than perseverating in our attempts to fit children into a curriculum imposed from without.

Starting with children would entail, as the Italian educators do, recognizing their powers. It would mean abandoning our tendency to focus on children's weaknesses and incapacities, as evidenced in hundreds of items in baseline assessment schedules that record what children cannot do, or do not seem to know. It would mean recognizing that all children learn, that learning is what they do best and that they have been doing it from birth. It would mean that child-like children, right through the primary school, would have their powers acknowledged, exercised and strengthened. Their power to speak at least two languages, for example, grossly neglected in many present-day schools, could be recognized. Their powers to imagine, 'to see into the life of things', in Mary Warnock's expressive phase (Warnock, 1978), could be more effectively nourished if we accepted that the absolutely logical consistency required of the flight controller or income tax inspector is not a characteristic of children's thinking. As the celebrated American kindergarten teacher, Vivian Gussin Paley (1981), puts it:

> (The 5 or 6-year-old child) is at a singular period. He is not a captive of his illusions and fantasies, but can choose them for support or stimulation without self-consciousness. He has become aware of the thinking required by the adult world, but is not committed to its burden of rigid consistency.
>
> (pp. 29–30)

Magical and imaginative thinking, in Paley's version of the child-like child, is not a weakness, but young children's way of deploying their power to see things as they might be, not simply as they are. And this power brings insight and understanding.

> The child is the ultimate magician. He credits God and lesser powers, but it is the child who confirms the probability of events. If he can imagine something, it exists . . . As soon as he learns a language well enough, and *before* he is told he cannot invent the world, he will explain everything.
>
> (*Ibid.*, p. 81)

Warnock (1978) pushes home the point in terms of what educators must do if these powers are to survive in school:

> I have come very strongly to believe that is is the cultivation of imagination which should be the chief aim of education, and in which our present systems of education most conspicuously fail, where they do fail . . . in education we have a duty to educate the imagination above all else.

When Diderot and his associates, a group of radical French philosophers, drew up the syllabus for the great Encyclopaedia, published in 35 volumes between 1751 and 1776, they used the simplest of frameworks. All of humanity's great achievements, all of society's accumulated knowledge and wisdom, all was subsumed under just three heads: Memory, Reason and

Imagination (see Furbank, 1992). Such bold simplicity, with its emphasis on the powers of the human intellect, encourages me to argue that acknowledging what we know about young children's intellectual and emotional powers is a promising starting point for their education. The Italian educators in Reggio-Emilia choose to start here, and they have convincingly documented the exceptional quality of children's lives in their nurseries and preschools.

But not every society chooses to start from the same premise. In the USA, the *Quality 2000 Project* has announced that the first national educational goal for the twenty-first century is to be: 'All children will start school ready to learn.' This is an absurd inversion of the priority for the future as I see it; the first step must be to ensure that all schools are ready for children who have been learning since birth, who are already, when they cross the threshold of formal education, dedicated learners, adventurous explorers, committed scientists, expressive artists and compassionate friends. It is up to schools to make sure they stay that way, while they lead them on to greater things.

Not all educationalists are convinced that schools are capable of meeting this responsibility. Mary Willes's challenging study of what happens to young children when they become pupils stands as an awful warning of what does happen in some schools, where she carried out her observations, and what could happen in many more, if teachers and other educators ignore or neglect the essential characteristics of the children in their classrooms.

> The minimal inescapable requirement that a child must meet if he is to function as a participating pupil is not very extensive. It is necessary to accept adult direction, to know that you say nothing at all unless the teacher indicates that you may, to know that when your turn is indicated you must use whatever clues you can find, and make the best guess you can.
>
> (Willes, 1983, p. 83)

The pupils evoked in this chilling passage have had their powers stripped from them. Even more pessimistic is Willes's scathing summary of what it is to be a pupil: 'Finding out what the teacher wants, and doing it constitutes the primary duty of a pupil' (*ibid.*, p. 138).

Even allowing for exaggeration, which can be attributed to the author's passionate desire for a better deal for children, there is an uncomfortable grain of truth in Willes's observation. Everyone who has ever worked with young children in large numbers knows that, for at least part of the time, harmony in the classroom depends on compliance. Many aspects of life in the primary school routine are predicated on obedience. What would happen, I sometimes wonder, if one day, when the teachers of England rang the bell for the end of morning playtime, the children simply refused to respond?

This fantasy of country-wide school refusal has been strengthened by reading Iona Opie's painstaking observations of *The People in the Playground* (Opie, 1993). Opie made weekly visits to observe in a junior school

playground from January 1970 until November 1983. Her prime purpose
was a continuation of her and her husband's earlier researches into school-
child lore, games, songs, riddles and jokes; she found in the playground an
astonishingly rich vein to mine. The main interest for the primary educator
is in what Opie saw that the teachers on playground duty rarely see (because they are busy looking for trouble): the energy and enthusiasm that
the children (or *people* as they always refer to themselves) invest in their
imaginative and physical play. One image sticks in my mind: two girls
plunging down the steps into the playground; one calls to the other 'going
on with witches and fairies, right?' The fractions and the apostrophes on
the blackboard are left far away as the children fly back to their shared
imaginative worlds. In schools of the future, my fantasy continues, this
energy, and this power to live through the imagination, will be characteristic of classrooms as well as of playgrounds.

It is interesting to note that for Kieran Egan (1988), this possibility is no
fantasy, but an educational necessity. Egan's work starts by considering the
traditional opposition between the powers of logical reason and those of
fantasy. Education as we know it, so far, has been constructed around the
primacy of rationality; fantasy, 'which ignores the boundaries of reality, is seen
as the enemy' (p. 11). He goes on to call for a redistribution of emphasis;
drawing attention to young children's mental lives, of which a prominent part
is fantasy, he argues that the education of young children must take account of
this way of thinking, which is, he claims, energetic, wholesome and important
for intellectual growth. In *Primary Understanding* he sets about the project of
devising a whole primary curriculum, and a range of teaching methods, that
would enable teachers to get in tune with children's robust imaginative
powers.

Kieran Egan's version of the child-like child is a person who may, on the
one hand, 'be unable to conserve liquid quantity, (but who) may, on the other,
lead a vivid intellectual life, brimming with knights, dragons, witches and star
warriors' (*ibid.*, p. 23). The children of today – and tomorrow – argues Egan,
deserve a curriculum 'made up of *important* content, rich in meaning . . . our
curriculum concern will be to get at what is of human importance to our social
and cultural lives' (*ibid.*, p. 199). And so, once again, we see there are choices
to be made; the choices we make in constructing our own versions of child-like
children will in turn affect the decisions we make in selecting important educational content, which makes human sense to them.

Conclusion

In this chapter, I have argued that the children of tomorrow, who will live
and learn in the primary schools of the twenty-first century, deserve an
education that fosters and strengthens their powers to do, to feel and to
think: an education for the domains of the will, the heart and the head, as

the Steiner educators would put it. To be able to provide such an education, parents and educators, the whole community of those concerned for children's lives, will need to recognize that there is work to be done, together, in thinking through what these words entail. The quality of this thinking is crucial. The task is a challenging one: to debate what sorts of children we want to become the citizens of the future, to consider what sort of lives we want them to lead, in childhood and in adulthood, to investigate the conception of the 'good life' for children, and for the society in which they learn. The rigour and creativity of the thinking we engage in, the openness with which we explore difference and dissent, the energy with which we collaborate in the task – all these will affect the quality of the primary education of the future.

Acknowledgement

I am deeply grateful to Janni Nicol and Stephanie Grögelein for allowing me to observe from a corner of their kindergarten, and for giving so much time to help me understand what I saw.

References

Doyle, R. (1993) *Paddy Clarke Ha Ha Ha*, London: Secker and Warburg.
Edwards, C., Gandini, L. and Forman, G. (1994) *The Hundred Languages of Children*, NJ, Norwood: Ablex.
Egan, K. (1988) *Primary Understanding*, London: Routledge.
Furbank, P. N. (1992) *Diderot: A Critical Biography*, London: Minerva.
James, A. and Prout, A. (eds) (1990) *Constructing and Reconstructing Childhood: Contemporary Issues in the Sociological Study of Childhood*, London: Falmer Press.
Opie, I. (1993) *The People in the Playground*, Oxford: Oxford University Press.
Paley, V. G. (1981) *Wally's Stories*, Cambridge, MA: Harvard University Press.
Pilcher, J. and Wragg, S. (eds) (1996) *Thatcher's Children? Politics, Childhood and Society in the 1980s and 1990s*, London: Falmer Press.
Tobin, J. J., Wu, D. and Davidson, D. (1989) *Pre-school in Three Cultures*, Princeton, NJ: Yale University Press.
Walkerdine, V. (1997) *Daddy's Girl Young Girls and Popular Culture*, London: Macmillan.
Warnock, M. (1978) *Imagination*, London: Faber.
Willes, M. (1983) *Children into Pupils*, London: Routledge and Kegan Paul.

Section 3: Outcomes of Assessment

As identified in the introduction to this book, considerations of the traditions of assessment bring to the foreground the debate about the purpose of education, the dilemmas inherent in the ideas of democratic education and the tension between inclusivity and elitism. A constructivist view of learning assumes that everyone has the potential to learn and that there exists also the possibility of incremental improvement. However, it also accepts that learning will be different when social, cultural and contextual variations occur. In an individualistic and elitist system not everyone can have prizes, but in a democratic one everyone is of equal worth. Given the intensity of the debate surrounding the purposes, practices and procedural aspects of assessment it is no longer possible to believe that making judgements about children's ability is a straightforward thing. Deciding that one construction of learning is more appropriate at a certain point or in a certain place is not about controlling the learning process or imposing one specific view. The teacher's role is to achieve a sense of balance by identifying, analysing and challenging misunderstandings in order that learners can refine their knowledge constructions. The difficulty in classrooms is that pupils quickly learn what the teacher has in mind as a preferred outcome by the way in which praise or marks are allocated. Respecting autonomy and making assessments are not easily accommodated.

Taken together the chapters in this section:

- consider the importance of achievement within the learning process
- explore how attainment might be measured
- examine where current ideas about assessment and testing have their roots
- show that psychological, political and cultural beliefs and values have important and significant effects on children's construction of themselves as learners
- consider some possible outcomes of assessment in terms of ability grouping.

In Chapter 8, Patricia Broadfoot outlines the development of a number of key issues and identifies links between them and models of learning. She argues that assessment should be located in learning and not in measurement. The challenge here is to the nineteenth-century ideology of objective, scientific classification achieved through reliable and valid techniques. Although this is a long-standing criticism, there are many echoes today of these assumptions to be found in the comments of advocates of tests, value-added measures and unjust and unjustifiable league tables. Much of the debate in this area arises from our unexamined beliefs. Understanding where we stand in relation to the traditions of assessment and the different views and practices linked to its various purposes can only be helpful to those involved in making fair and representative judgements about standards of achievement.

In Chapter 9, Patricia Murphy develops the themes of the book by examining the relationship between assessment outcomes and sources of gendered learning within and outside school. She identifies the way in which assessment practice is implicated in the creation of gender gaps in children's performance. In her exploration of recent developments in thinking about learners and learning she distinguishes between 'processing' and 'constructing' views of learning. She also explores the way in which a cultural view of learning and assessment has to take into account the different cultural beliefs and experiences of boys and girls. Of particular importance here are the ways in which gendered roles create different learning opportunities. Gender differences in achievement are discussed in relation to a number of curriculum areas, specifically, mathematics, English and science. The chapter concludes by considering the implications for curriculum and assessment.

In Chapter 10, Judith Ireson and Susan Hallam remind us that the debate about the selection and grouping of pupils has been rekindled in response to the perceived need to raise academic standards. As a contribution to the debate their chapter reviews the literature on ability grouping and its effects on academic and non-academic outcomes for pupils, including self-esteem, attitudes towards school and alienation. In addition, they consider aspects of the school environment that may mediate the influence of organizational grouping on pupil outcomes. Drawing on their reading of this research evidence, Ireson and Hallam argue that a return to a system of selection and structured grouping is unlikely to raise standards. They conclude by suggesting some alternatives to ability groupings.

In Chapter 11, Cathy Nutbrown considers how educators might demonstrate their respect for learners through careful observation and assessments. Drawing on case study observations of young children in a variety of settings within and outside school Nutbrown discusses practical aspects of observation and shows just how important the careful collection and analysis of evidence can be. She then focuses on assessment, what that might mean and, in particular, issues leading to the notion of respectful assessment. She concludes the chapter with some ideas that educators may wish to consider if they wish to respect children's achievements.

8

Liberating the Learner through Assessment

Patricia Broadfoot

Since the earliest days of mass educational provision, terminal assessment procedures have largely governed the content of the curriculum, the way in which schools are organized, the approach to teaching and the learning priorities of students. Assessment has become both the vehicle and the engine that drive the delivery of education as we currently know it in schools and colleges. Because of this, it is arguably assessment that has been, for most students, the single most significant influence on the quality and shape of their educational experience, on their motivation and hence on their learning. The central role played by assessment in shaping the way in which education is delivered has come into increasingly sharp focus in recent years as governments have shown a growing awareness of the capacity of assessment policies to effect desired changes in the education system. Thus unless there is some fundamental breakdown in the long-standing link between education and employment, or governments are persuaded that accountability does not need formally to be provided for, the results of educational assessment are likely to continue to constitute the language by which the achievements of individuals, institutions and even whole education systems are judged.

But what model of learning do these powerful assessment traditions assume? How far are the assumptions that underpin their use appropriate for today's 'learning society'? Do traditional forms of assessment 'liberate the learner', or do they rather inhibit the pursuit of more and better learning? These are the questions which this chapter will address. In seeking an answer to them the chapter will first of all consider briefly the reasons why we have inherited the particular assessment traditions which are currently so pervasive. Second it will argue for an approach to assessment which is rooted in what we know about *learning* – especially the kind of learning needed for today's society – rather than what we know about *measurement*. Third it will consider the extraordinary resilience of the measurement paradigm. In offering this analysis, the chapter concludes with some suggestions for possible ways forward in assessment that do offer the potential for liberating, rather than locking up, the learner.

The Social and Historical Context

The assumptions on which most educational activity is based are rooted in notions of 'measurement' that date back to the changes that started to take place in Europe during the seventeenth century: to the growing beliefs in the power of science and of rational forms of organization which are the cornerstones of the 'Enlightenment' (Broadfoot, 1996). New types of test were invented to provide a 'scientific' – and hence apparently rational – basis of determining individual levels of competence, which could thus provide a fair basis for selection. The long-standing emphasis on the demonstration of practical competence in a trade or craft, which had been until this time virtually the only formal assessment practised, gave way to tests and examinations which were designed as much for selection as they were for attesting competence, and so had to provide for the ranking of candidates *against each other* rather than against some set and explicit standard. To this end the content of the test, its conduct and its subsequent grading all had to be standardized, if the tests were to be a truly equitable, and hence rational, basis for selection. Thus entered the formal syllabus with its emphasis on content to be covered; the written test that lent iteslf to controlled conditions of administration; and the language of marks and grades that provided some common basis for interpreting the results so produced.

Associated with this change, as Claxton (1996) points out, was a transformation in theories of learning. Claxton contrasts the 'psychomythology' of the pre-Enlightenment, pre-Cartesian era, in which learning was seen as involving many different types of activity and outcome, to the current situation in which learning is closely associated with the deliberate application of the concept of 'intelligence' and in which assessment, consequently, is based on 'the ability to describe and explain what one knows, rather than to reveal it spontaneously under appropriate real-life conditions'. Thus new types of test were invented that reflected the new emphasis on candidates' *relative* achievement, rather than the previous emphasis on standards.

Particularly significant in this respect was the advent of intelligence testing. This represented a move away from the assessment of some kind of achievement towards the assessment of *innate ability*. The assumption that individual potential could be measured in an objective, scientific way underpinned the growth of a pervasive and powerful belief that, among other things, educational assessment could somehow be detached from its context of operation and like, a ruler, be used in an absolute way to produce measurements of both achievement *and potential*. At the time, there was little substantial critique of this notion either in terms of principle or in terms of the techniques which were developed to operationalize it. Perhaps more surprising still is the fact that, although many such critiques have subsequently emerged concerning both the accuracy of the measures used and their impact on the processes of teaching and learning, they have yet seriously to dent the assumptions which underpin the measurement paradigm in general and notions of intelligence in particular.

Yet the model of learning that informs this chapter – integrated learning theory – makes such a view of assessment untenable. This theory argues that learning takes many forms, some of which are more measurable than others. It maintains that whether, and to what extent, learning occurs is a function of individuals' strategic judgement, their cost-benefit analysis concerning the risk-reward ratio of their investing effort aimed at achieving a given goal. Social constructivism, of which integrated learning theory is a variant, suggests that learning is a messy business which is influenced in idiosyncratic ways for any given individual by the complex mixture of understanding, beliefs and attitudes which is the product of past learning experience. Such a view is simply not compatible with any of the unidimensional or even fixed notions of ability which have for so long informed educational thinking and practice.

Nor are such conceptions of assessment compatible with the knowledge and skills that will be needed by tomorrow's citizens. Just as a shift in employment patterns provoked the emphasis on measurement for the purposes of selection with which we have become familiar over the last hundred years, so advances in technology and management practices are now prompting employers to call for educational systems in developed countries which equip the workers of tomorrow with transferable skills, a high level of adaptibility and, above all, the commitment to go on learning. Thus Resnick (1994) is typical of many in emphasizing the need for a more 'pragmatic epistemology' which conceives learning as rooted in interactive cognition.

Describing the influential 'New Standards Project' in the USA, Resnick stresses the need to challenge several centuries of tradition in which the conception of knowledge has been theoretical rather than interactionist, and has therefore not, of itself, led to the capacity actually to perform. By contrast, the New Standards Project, with its emphasis on projects and portfolios, large-scale investigations and idiosyncratic learning goals, emphasizes a variety of ways of interpreting quality and defining achievement. It recognizes that learning can involve many different 'genres' of both activity and outcome. The power of new priorities, and hence practices, to challenge the domination of the measurement paradigm and its associated epistemology of learning is evidenced by the rapid growth of the movement in the USA. Nineteen states are now involved in the initiative which in consequence has begun to achieve the status of a quasi-governmental body (Resnick, 1994). Similar testimony to such changing priorities is evident at the present time in many other countries which are seeking to introduce assessment practices that support the full range of learning goals.

Yet these initiatives, which include the move to introduce records of achievement and student self-assessment in the UK during the 1980s, have still seriously to challenge the prevailing orthodoxy in the minds of politicians and public. It is still a reliable vote-catcher for politicians to talk of increasing the level of testing as part of a bid to raise standards (Airasian, 1988). In England, the government's retreat since 1993 from continuous assessment in favour of traditional unseen exams, despite a chorus of protest from many of the communities involved – teachers, employers and even parents – provides a telling example.

Thus while it may be true to say that there is a growing acceptance of more learning-centred theories of assessment among educational professionals around the world, such novel perspectives have done little, as yet, to challenge the power of traditional forms of assessment, and the way in which they in turn influence conceptions of learning and teaching. In countries where the selection imperative is still overwhelmingly important – where, in effect, education has to be rationed – this is hardly surprising. In such contexts, examinations and especially multiple-choice tests provide the 'least worst' means of rationing educational opportunity: that is, both cheap and accepted as broadly fair, in that they are based on demonstrated merit and therefore seen as legitimate (Heynemann, 1993). But the assessment problems facing *developing* countries are more akin to those which originally gave rise in the West to the current assessment orthodoxy during the nineteenth century than they are to the assessment problems which post-industrial countries now face.

The measurement paradigm in assessment developed, as we have seen, as a specific response to the pressing need for a trustworthy and widely acceptable means of rationing educational opportunity according to some idea of 'merit'. Despite the inevitable technical limitations of any such device, the advent of a measure of professionalism and technical expertise to assist in the important business of deciding life chances was, on the whole, a step forward. And it is no doubt for this reason that the examination and testing industry is one of the most lasting legacies of colonial influence. Indeed it has now developed into one of the most successful international industries, which, like Coca-Cola, touches the life of almost everyone on the planet. Activity on this scale implies many entrenched interests, as well as a good deal of inertia and the sheer impossibility of even conceiving of forms of educational provision which have not been shaped by the discourse of measurement.

Nevertheless such new conceptions must be not only realized but implemented if we are to 'liberate the learner' in the way that is now required. Whilst it may have been reasonable to turn a blind eye to some of the well-documented shortcomings of traditional forms of assessment when, on the whole, they were doing their job well, it makes very little sense to allow such practices to continue when the limitations lie not only in their technical characteristics but much more fundamentally in their capacity to inhibit urgently needed change in education, and to obscure the real imperative facing education for the twenty-first century, which is the creation of committed and effective learners. The following sections elaborate this argument.

Testing Testing

It is argued in this chapter that learning, and hence, by implication, performance, is the result of feelings, values and other learned attitudinal responses, as well as of cognitive processes. If this is so it should not be seen as surprising that so much research exists demonstrating the inaccuracies of conventional assessment techniques (see, for example, reviews by Satterly, 1994, and Ingenkamp, 1977). Apart from the possible sources of error in the measurement itself – for example, the teacher may not have taught what is tested in the examination; students may guess, if the format is a multiple-choice one; the test may be incorrectly normed for a given population of students; and so on (Lee Smith, 1991, provides a comprehensive list of these flaws) – performance itself has been shown to be neither constant nor a necessarily true reflection of learning.

At the most obvious level, the test may measure performance on a given day which has no connection with long-term retention by the student. Students may be bored or disaffected and not engage to the best of their ability with the test or examination. They may find the questions confusing or ambiguous. They may not be able to apply their knowledge because of the limitations of handwriting or other mechanical abilities. Many achievement tests merely measure endurance or persistence rather than learning. Some students who are divergent thinkers may read too much into the question. Some students become frightened and 'freeze up' in the testing situation, especially those who have little self-confidence or some kind of emotional or family disturbance. Furthermore, research in the psychology of assessment has consistently demonstrated that small changes in task-presentation, in response mode, in the conditions under which assessment takes place, in the relations between assessor and assessed, and within students on different occasions – all can affect performance (Black, 1993; Wolf and Silver, 1993).

Thus the measurement paradigm offers us what is, at best, only a rough and ready tool for identifying achievement. It offers us even less as a basis for predicting potential – which now is widely recognized as being neither innate nor fixed (Vernon, 1957; Karier, 1972). The increasingly extensive research literature on assessment in operation shows quite clearly that assessment is an essentially social process. That is to say, it is to a greater or lesser extent an interactive operation, in which a whole range of circumstances will affect the outcome: who the assessor is (even in an apparently objective multiple-choice test) or where the assessment takes place (Gipps and Murphy, 1994). Clearly this does not mean there is no place for measurement techniques in the tool-cupboard of educational activity. Indeed there are many situations in which it is important to try to generate an accurate picture of individual or indeed group achievement – for diagnosis of a learner's strengths and weaknesses; to gauge the success of a particular course in achieving its objectives; to provide information on the overall performance of an education system; and, not least, the certification of achievement. Rather what it does mean is that it is time to challenge the 'sacred cows' of assessment, the concepts and preoccupations that have for too long inhibited the educational community from engaging with the quite different, but potentially much more important, assessment agenda which concerns its role in promoting learning.

The work of the French philosopher Michel Foucault traces the power to control the way reality is defined which is embodied in the evaluation of particular discourses. One such discourse, he suggests, legitimates the 'hierarchical authority' and 'normalizing judgement' which are the defining characteristics of the traditional examination. Students can be located, according to their demonstrated success, in an evaluative framework in which the whole territory of the development of learning has already been mapped out. External assessment represents the imposition of these standardized norms of progression according to the criteria of worth already laid down by the hierarchical authority (Broadfoot, 1996). Whether or not one is disposed to accept the finer points of Foucault's structuralist analysis, it is difficult not to accept its central tenet, namely that the language we use to articulate a particular subject has built into it particular concepts and assumptions that tend to delimit the arena of debate, and hence to preclude other ways of theorizing experience, for which an equivalent language, and hence conceptual base, is lacking. Thus what we think assessment is, what it can do and how it might be improved, have all been questions that, until recently, could only be raised in terms of the dominant assessment paradigm.

To a great extent this remains the case. Despite a growing international obsession with assessing quality, this does not seem to have prompted an equivalent measure of development in assessment thinking. Indeed the opposite is the case, as the obsession with league tables, performance indicators and standards reinforces the preoccupation with measurement, while questions which focus on how such performance can most effectively be encouraged go not only unheard but even *unthought*. One explanation for the persistence of an assessment status quo which is increasingly out of step with the priority of raising and broadening learning thresholds is doubtless the inertia of habit, and the tendency to fall back on the tried and tested. Among politicians – who play a key role in perpetuating such thinking – traditional approaches to assessment have acquired a legitimacy which makes them invaluable, both as a rhetorical device and as a means of managing the aspirations of individuals. For the last hundred years or so, traditional forms of assessment have proved themselves to be vital tools in the hands of those responsible for managing the priorities and procedures of the education system.

But, if historically, educational assessment has been driven by a perceived need to measure individual capacity, it now needs to be driven by the need to develop that capacity – and to create new kinds of capacity in people of all ages, in short, to 'liberate the learner'. Problem-solving capacity, personal effectiveness, thinking skills and a willingness to accept change are typical of the general competencies straddling both cognitive and affective domains that are now being sought by employers. It is becoming increasingly apparent, however, that until we develop new kinds of assessment procedures that can relate to this wide range of skills and attitudes, not only will it be impossible to produce valid judgements about the success of the educational enterprise as a whole in terms of its goals; it will also help to ensure that certain desired learning outcomes will be neglected in practice. Not surprisingly perhaps, this is a lesson which is rapidly being learned in those areas of education which are most closely connected with the world of employment. In many countries, including the UK, Australia, New Zealand, Canada and the USA, efforts are under way to introduce more flexible and meaningful systems of vocational qualifications based on demonstrated, rather than inferred, competence (Curtain and Hayton, 1995). Characteristic of such frameworks is the inclusion of competencies which break down the inevitably artificial division between the *capacity* to perform a task at a given level and the *attitudes* that predispose an individual so to do. But if the English National Vocational Qualifications (NVQs) and those of other countries with similar characteristics represent a significant attempt to break out of the straitjacket of marks and grades, formal examinations, set syllabuses and built-in failure levels – in short of the whole paraphernalia of traditional assessment thinking and practice – they nevertheless stop well short of fulfilling the criterion of an approach to assessment that has the capacity to 'liberate the learner'.

[. . .]

Claxton (1996) argues for the critically important role of motivation – and of non-cognitive factors generally – in promoting or inhibiting learning. Assessment is perhaps the most powerful influence on such drives and feelings. Although some students are motivated by the spur of competition and the glitter of potential reward, many more learn not to try for fear of failing. Claxton cites Dweck's work concerning students whose self-esteem is progressively eroded by negative assessment results and who frequently, in consequence, become what Dweck terms 'helpless prone'. Indeed research by Bandura (1977) and others shows that the amount of persistence exhibited by students is a function of how successful they expect to be. In short, students who have an image of themselves as successful learners are likely to be more motivated than those who have formed a more negative view of themselves in this respect.

A moment's thought confirms that it is assessment that is the purveyor of such messages. For students, the daily diet of evaluative language which is an inescapable, and probably essential, part of teaching is regularly reinforced by more formal evaluative communications in the form of marks and grades, and still further reinforced by the weighty messages of reports and parents' evenings, a process that ultimately culminates in the 'summing up' (Harlen, 1994) of the formal examination. Given that in this latter respect at least, failure is built into the system by definition, in that a given proportion of candidates is expected (and often required) to fail, it is unlikely that many learners will be liberated by such assessment.

Ironically perhaps, it was in an attempt to address directly the demotivating effects of such built-in failure that the educational community began to stumble on far more significant insights concerning how assessment might be used to transform the process of teaching and learning itself. In the UK, the Records of Achievement movement started with the idea that by broadening the range of achievements that could be formally acknowledged in a school-leaving document, this would improve the motivation of students who could not hope to succeed in public examinations. Gradually, however, the teachers committed to these initiatives came to realize that what was really making a difference in students' motivation and in the quality of their learning were the changes they were introducing actually in the classroom. These changes included sharing and discussing curriculum goals with students; encouraging students to set their own learning targets and to draw up more general 'action plans'; involving students in assessing their own work so that they were both more willing and more able to monitor their own learning; and teacher and student reviewing progress together. The opportunity for one-to-one discussion in particular made an enormous impact on many students who had never before had the chance of an individual conversation with a teacher about their learning on a regular basis.

Elsewhere I have argued that the educational community in general, and students in particular, have paid a heavy price for the failure to locate this ferment of activity in a scientific rationale that was capable of being every bit as convincing as that on which the previous assessment orthodoxy had been based (Broadfoot, 1993). In Crooks's (1988) comprehensive review of the psychological literature concerning the impact of assessment on learning is all the ammunition required to construct such a case. Caught up in their enthusiasm for the exciting things that were happening in their classrooms, however, teachers were content to trust their own experience, and to seek for no further explanation for the changes in motivation and capacity to learn that they were witnessing in their students (Broadfoot *et al.*, 1988). In other countries the pattern has been essentially similar. Thus, in each case, when the politicians have begun to huff and puff they have apparently succeeded, with relatively little difficulty, in blowing down a house that lacks solid theoretical foundations. As the 'standards' agenda has become increasingly dominant internationally; as many governments have sought to create a market in education using a currency of test results and league tables; as 'performance indicators', quality assessment and inspection have come to define the *Zeitgeist* of the 1990s, so schools have had to revert to a very different set of enthusiasms and imposed priorities.

It is one of the odd ironies of educational research, however that, as Nisbet and Broadfoot (1981) argue, its impact is rarely direct. Rather ideas gather momentum – sometimes quite indirectly – until the time comes when conditions are right for them to make a specific impact. So it has been with new assessment thinking. Ideas that were forged out of the more obvious shortcomings of traditional assessment practices, as these impacted on schools, have been taken up and developed in circumstances where the combination of needs and constraints has been more auspicious for their growth. It is in the arena of professional learning in particular that there has been a recognized need to engage learners with developing the full range of professional skills, and a rapid realisation of the value of the new approaches to assessment, involving student learning, diaries, target setting, self-assessment, regular reviews of progress on an individual basis, the collection of portfolios of evidence, and so on – approaches which were often developed in rather different learning contexts (Gonczi, 1994). It emphasizes the mixture of knowledge, skills, attitudes and values involved in such learning and the necessarily central role that reflection and self-evaluation play in promoting it.

It is not hard to find other, similarly inspired examples of this trend. While schools have been drawing back from implementing the more radical aspects of the new assessment thinking as far as pupils are concerned, the implementation of its rationale has become commonplace in the context of teacher appraisal. Here again the emphasis is typically on using assessment – in the shape of personal review, discussion and target setting – to promote professional learning. In initial teacher education too, as Figure 8.1 illustrates, the new concern with identifying competencies is frequently integrated into a more formative assessment design, aimed at encouraging the learner teacher to develop skills of self-reflection and review.

Such approaches are rapidly approaching the status of a received orthodoxy in this kind of learning context, where there is an obvious necessity for professionals to be broadly equipped with a mixture of both cognitive and affective skills. The rapid spread of such practices in the arena of professional and vocational training has also helped to establish notions such as self-assessment and action planning as mainstream educational concepts, despite their relatively recent origins. Thus although the battle to 'liberate the learner' through assessment may temporarily have been lost in schools, the war continues. The beginnings of a new assessment discourse, of concepts which reflect a preoccupation with learning, rather than with dependable measurement, suggest that we are witnessing a genuine paradigm shift; that the tyranny of testing is at last being challenged. To measure or to learn: that is the question.

References

Airasian, P. (1988) Symbolic validation: the case of state-mandated High Stakes Testing, *Educational Evaluation and Policy Analysis*, **10**(4), Winter, pp. 301–15.
Bandura, A. (1977) *Social Learning Theory*, Englewood Cliffs, NJ: Prentice Hall.

Comments by PGCE student				Staff assessment of the student's level of achievement. Please incorporate future development comments.
	SUBJECT KNOWLEDGE • Understand the knowledge concepts and skills of the main teaching subject. • Know and understand the NCATs and PoS for the main subject if applicable.			
	SUBJECT APPLICATION **1. *Lesson Planning*** • Plan both individual, and a series of, lessons setting appropriate aims and allowing for differing abilities in your students. • Foster a range of learning styles and use a variety of teaching strategies appropriate to the age, ability and attainment level of pupils.			
	SUBJECT APPLICATION **2. *Communications*** • Communicate clearly and suitably with students, both orally and in writing.			
	SUBJECT APPLICATION **3. *Information Technology*** • Select and make appropriate use of a range of equipment and resources.			

Figure 8.1   *Part of the University of Bristol PGCE Professional Practice Student Profile Record.*

Black, P. (1993) Conference Paper – Association of Assessment Inspectors and Advisers, reported in *Times Educational Supplement*, 1 October.

Broadfoot, P. (1993) Exploring the forgotten continent: a traveller's tale, *Scottish Educational Review*, **26**(2), pp. 88–96.

Broadfoot, P. (1996) *Education, Assessment and Society*, Milton Keynes: Open University Press.

Broadfoot, P. James, M., McMeeking, S., Nuttall, D. and Stierer, B. (1988) *Records of Achievement. Report of the National Evaluation of Pilot Scheme*, London: HMSO.

Claxton, G. (1996) Implicit theories of learning, in G. Claxton *et al.*, *Liberating the Learner*, London: Routledge.

Crooks, T. J. (1988) The impact of classroom evaluation practices on students, *Review of Educational Research*, **58**(4), pp. 438–81.

Curtain, R. and Hayton, G. (1995) The use and abuse of a competency standards framework in Australia: a comparative perspective, *Assessment in Education*, **2**(2), pp. 205–25.

Gipps, C. and Murphy, P. (1994) *Fair Test? Assessment, Achievement and Equity*, Milton Keynes: Open University Press.

Gonczi, A. (1994) Competency based assessment in the professions in Australia, *Assessment in Education*, **1**(1), pp. 27–44.

Harlen, W. (ed.) (1994) *Enhancing Quality in Assessment*, London: Paul Chapman Publishing.

Heynemann, S. (1993) Keynote lecture to the World Congress of Comparative Education Societies, Prague.

Ingenkamp, K. (1977) *Educational Assessment*, Slough: NFER.

Karier, C. (1972) Testing for order and control in the corporate liberal state, *Educational Theory*, **22**(2).

Lee Smith, M. (1991) The meanings of test preparation, *American Educational Research Journal*, **28**(3), pp. 521–42.

Nisbet, J. and Broadfoot, P. (1981) *The Impact of Research on Policy and Practice in Education*, Aberdeen: Aberdeen University Press.

Resnick, L. (1994) The New Standards Project, Seminar given at University of London Institute of Education, June.

Satterly, D. (1994) Quality in external assessment, in W. Harlen (ed.) *Enhancing Quality in Assessment*, London: Paul Chapman Publishing.

Vernon, P. (1957) *Secondary School Selection*, London: Methuen.

Wolf, A. and Silver, R. (1993) The reliability of test candidates and the implications for one-shot testing, *Educational Review*, **45**(3), pp. 263—78.

9

Gendered Learning and Achievement

Patricia Murphy

Introduction

Concern about gender and achievement has emerged in recent years in relation to boys' achievement in, and attitudes to, schooling. Policy recommendations suggest that these gender differences can be addressed by changes in the curriculum and its teaching (QCA/DfEE, 1999). This raises the question of what in the current curriculum, its teaching and assessment is implicated in creating differences between girls and boys. Policy recommendations have also raised assessment as an issue but in relation to teacher assessment rather than national tests. However, no assessment is socially neutral, rather assessment practices need to be viewed as social techniques that have social consequences (Connell, Johnston and White, 1992). From this perspective it is essential that children's understanding in relation to assessments are not assumed but are made problematic both in the development of assessments and in the interpretations of their outcomes.

The chapter examines the relationship between assessment outcomes and sources of gender differences in children's learning both within and without school. The evidence discussed indicates how, if not taken into account, the consequence of children's learning *out of school* impacts on their achievement throughout schooling. The chapter looks at the way assessment practice is implicated in the *creation* of gender gaps in children's performance. The chapter is organized in sections. The first section introduces issues arising from recent developments in thinking about learners and learning, and the implications of these for assessment and how we understand gender. The second section explores these implications by looking at gendered learning. The main section examines gender differences in achievement in a number of curriculum areas and highlights research about the sources of these differences. The chapter concludes by considering the implications for curriculum and assessment.

Background

How we understand the influence of gender on children's learning and how this in turn affects the way they understand and respond to assessments depends on our perceptions of the ways children make sense of their worlds. There are various theoretical traditions that influence our perceptions of learning in schools. One tradition of long standing sees learning as 'mental' processing. In this view thinking is a stage separated from sensory input and precedes activity, which is seen as an outcome of thinking. The human mind 'sees', 'thinks' then 'acts'. In this approach to learning the learner is separate from the environment and *acts on it*. This has been described as a mind and body separation. An emerging tradition, culturalism, challenges this way of thinking about learners. In a cultural approach to learning thinking is not separate from or interposed between perception and action. Viewed in this way 'There is no separation of mind and body, because the physical interaction involved in inquiry is simply a part of the process of acting mindfully' (Bredo, 1994, p. 1).

In a 'processing' view of the human mind the learner plays a passive, receptive role in the learning process. The teacher dispenses knowledge, learners process it and thus acquire it. Increasingly the emphasis on learning as an individual's internal mental processing has been challenged. One key challenge sees learning not as processing but, rather, as *constructing*. In other words, reality is made not found. Bruner describes this view of the learner as 'proactive, problem-orientated, attentionally focused, selective, constructional, directed to ends' (Bruner, 1996, p. 93).

Whilst these challenges to learning are currently being debated in the context of teaching little attention is paid to them in assessment. Current views of assessment reflect a 'processing' model of mind. The task of assessment being 'how to read out the stored knowledge [of the learner] in the most accurate and reliable way' (Roth, 1997, p. 9). If the challenges are taken seriously they require us to think critically about the tasks we set in assessment. In a processing view of learning it is assumed that information is given and that tasks are therefore stable across learners, i.e., children perceive and interpret them in the same way. In a cultural view of learning the *whole task* for children includes *the task of figuring out what the task is*. The tasks we give to children either in formal or informal assessments are therefore *strategic fictions*, i.e., their meaning is determined by the learners and changes during activity (Newman, Griffin and Cole 1989). Consequently communicating tasks and their goals becomes much more complex, and establishing children's perceptions becomes an essential part of the learning and assessment process. A cultural approach to learning is so labelled because it views mind as shaped by culture. As Bruner puts it 'Although meanings are "in the mind" they have their origins and their significance in the culture in which they are created' (Bruner, 1996, p. 3). That is not to say that learners are mirrors of their cultures rather that the meanings they make reflect both their unique history and sense of self and the culture's ways of constructing reality. One of these ways includes cultural beliefs about what it is to be a girl and a boy. Culturally defined stereotypes and expectations of girls and boys are in evidence at all levels of socialization. Duveen (1999) argues 'a new born infant is not a neutral object but one which is invested with the characteristics of a social identity'. Duveen emphasizes the transition from 'external identities as children are incorporated into the social world through the actions of others to inter-nalised identities as children become independent actors in the field of gen-der' (Duveen, 1999). From birth, girls and boys experience different socialization processes. Parents' expectations differ for boys and girls. These different expectations are reflected in the activities and toys parents provide and in their reactions to their children. Consequently boys and girls engage in different hobbies and pastimes from an early age, and their interests continue to diverge with age. An outcome of different socialization patterns is that children develop different ways of responding to the world and making sense of it, ways which influence how they learn and what they learn. In this way children learn to value those activities, traits and behaviours associated with their gender and, consequently, gender becomes a self-regulating system. The more children engage in gendered activities, the more they develop the skills and understandings associated with them, understand-ings which emerge as gender-related ways of being in the world.

It is important to remember that gender is only one cultural representation that influences children and its influence will vary across children within a group. The data discussed are about group not individual performance, however.

Gendered Learning

Studies of preschool children have helped to characterize some of the gender differences in interests that emerge as a consequence of children's socialization. Murphy (1997) reported the role play differences between boys and girls:

> You see the maternal instinct in girls from a very early age and this does tend to motivate their play. Boys bring their own agendas – they get into some very active, very physically involved games.
>
> Boys like to be people in authority, policemen, fire fighters or super-heroes.
>
> (p. 120)

In these roles children become involved in the activities associated with them. These create different learning opportunities. From an early age children are paying attention to different details in the environment and developing different views of what is salient. In the same study play care staff described girls' and boys' interests:

> Girls are much more interested in drawing and as a result quite often are more forward than boys when it comes to using pencils and scissors. Girls seem to enjoy the colours and the process of drawing. Boys just aren't interested.
>
> As soon as you have a sort of machinery gears or something the boys are inter-ested straight away. I think it inclines them more to the sort of mathematical side of things.
>
> (Murphy, 1997, pp. 121 and 122)

Browne and Ross's (1991) results were similar in their large-scale study of preschool children. They described children's first choice of activity on entering day care in the following way:

> Many girls chose to play in the home corner to do a drawing to become involved in a creative activity read a book or to talk to an adult. It was extremely rare to observe a girl choose to play with a construction toy . . . whereas it was very common to observe boys doing so.

(p. 42)

Perhaps, unsurprisingly, baseline assessments of children entering school show girls ahead of boys in social skills, letter identification, writing and drawing (Arnot, David and Weiner, 1996). Studies in the USA of children's toys have also suggested that typical girls' toys and boys' toys provide different opportunities for learning mathematical skills. Damarin (1990) observes that girls' toys tend to be single objects or sets of objects whose relations to each other are one-to-one correspondence. Boys more than girls have access to toys with interrelated parts (blocks, Lego, Meccano, K'Nex, etc.). She argues that extensionality, i.e., length and thickness as well as other geometric features, are key features of such toys. Play with such toys allows children to build understanding of part–whole relations, a concept central to fractional arithmetic; and the relations between and among objects based on their extensionality. In contrast, play with typical girls' toys provides understanding of ideas of correspondence. Damarin describes girls' play as a continuing process never finished, whereas boys' toys tend to focus their attention on projects or products in which the order of operations is crucial. One can imagine this contrast if one compares the social play of girls with dolls versus the production of a Lego model of a moving vehicle. Girls may be disadvantaged in their learning in two ways: by not having the relevant prior experience that boys have; and having their alternative approaches judged inappropriate.

A further feature of gendered learning of particular significance for children's achievements in school are their approaches to reading and writing. The earlier observations suggest that girls are more likely than boys to come to school with initial writing skills. It is also the case that preschool boys are seen to have less interest than girls in reading: 'Getting them to settle down to a story was really quite a task. What I resort to is any book that has a tractor, a dumper in it, any sort of machinery. I don't have a problem settling the girls' (Murphy, 1997, p. 121).

Two potential effects arise from such a response. It can orientate boys further towards particular experiences and to paying attention to specific aspects of their environment. It also introduces boys from an early age to texts of a particular style. Thus boys' future choices of reading materials and learning about appropriate styles of expression may be influenced. Evidence of this self-regulating characteristic of gender is available. For example Browne and Ross (1991) observed that children in infant classes continued to follow their gendered interest even when apparently engaged in the same activity. When observed playing with Lego, girls made houses and simple structures as part of their social play, boys made vehicles or guns incorporating movable parts and focused on movement, structure and balance.

Gendered Achievement: Mathematics

Evidence from international surveys in mathematics show girls and boys differ in the way they achieve their scores in tests. Girls' superior performance is associated with computation, whole number and estimation and approximation as well as algebra. Boys' superior performance is associated with geometry, particularly three-dimensional diagrams, measurement and proportional thinking. These findings bear close relationship to the gendered learning referred to earlier. National surveys in the USA and in England and Wales also found boys outperformed girls on the use of measuring instruments but only where boys had more experience of using them outside school. These achievement differences can therefore be understood in terms of children's *opportunity to learn* rather than their *ability to learn*.

In national assessments of mathematics in England and Wales overall similarities in girls' and boys' performances are reported and very little attention paid to performance at question level (QCA, 2000a; 2000b). This is despite findings that more boys than girls achieve the highest level 5 and, more girls than boys the intermediate and lower levels. Damarin (1990) linked the emergence of boys' superior performance in mathematics at grade 4 to the appearance in the curriculum of fractional arithmetic. In the report of national assessment it is noted that only level-5 pupils (where there are significantly more boys than girls) answer these questions well. It is also noted that children in levels 3 and 4 (where girls are more highly represented than boys) do significantly less well on 'shape, space and measures'.

Teachers' expectations differ for boys and girls and this is reflected in their decisions about tier entry in maths assessment (Stobart *et al.*, 1992). Boys more than girls are entered for higher tiers to motivate them and are more likely to be excluded from entry because teachers see disaffection as a problem for boys. Girls are seen to be less confident than boys and tend to be entered for lower or middle tiers as a consequence. Affective factors, such as children's confidence, easily become translated in practice into cognitive ones, i.e., high confidence equates with ability, low confidence with its lack. Teachers' beliefs about pupils do influence pupils' self-concepts in relation to subjects. Head (1996) describes the way boys tend to attribute success to their own efforts and failure to external factors while girls do the converse. A review of research studies concluded that boys dominated class interactions. Teachers selected boys more often than girls, in part because they attracted more attention (Howe, 1999). Boys also received more feedback from teachers both positive and negative. Although girls received less negative feedback what they received was more often focused on their work and influenced their expectations of themselves and their abilities negatively (Dweck *et al.*, 1978). Davies and Brember (1995) in their longitudinal study of children in primary schools found that by the end of primary schooling all pupils were less positive about school but boys were even less concerned about discipline and conforming to the rules, whereas girls were even more concerned to do what the teacher required of them. Assessment plays an important role in providing feedback to children and therefore in influencing their developing sense of self. The increased role of assessment in the primary curriculum suggests that care in how we treat each child is particularly critical. As Pollard (1997) noted in a study of national assessment in the primary years, 'assessment structures may unwittingly be undermining positive disposition to learning'. Another finding from research into assessment in mathematics concerns children's perceptions of questions and solutions.

We have argued from a cultural view of learning that it is learners who construct sense in assessments. That is assessment questions are not given, rather they are reformulated. Research by Cooper and Dunne (2000) has highlighted the different ways that groups of children respond to questions set in what they refer to as 'realistic' settings. An example of a realistic setting would be using pie charts to represent the different types of socks worn by boys and girls in a school day, and asking children to interpret them. They studied 10–11-year-old children's understandings of national test questions in mathematics and their views of what are appropriate solutions. They found that working- and intermediate-class children performed less well than those from higher socio-economic backgrounds on these questions because they drew on their everyday knowledge rather than their mathematical knowledge. For example, one boy disputed the 'reality' represented which showed no boys wearing white sports socks and 20 per cent wearing patterned ones. This was described as an inappropriate use of everyday knowledge. However, the charge seems more appropriately levelled at the assessor and not the pupil. The research also found that this effect resulted in the mathematical achievements of those children being misrepresented. The biggest performance gap was between boys in the highest social class grouping and girls in the lowest social class grouping. The authors argue that much more thought needs to be given to what these national test questions assess: 'Is it primarily children's "mathematical" knowledge and understanding . . . or is it primarily their capacity to negotiate the boundary between the "mathematical" and the "real" as part of the process of discovering the test designers' intentions . . . ?' (*ibid.*, p. 200). An examination of such questions, the 'sock' one being a good example, often reveals that the real setting is irrelevant to the question and acts as an unnecessary barrier to some pupils. If however, the intention is to assess children's understanding of the application of mathematics then the setting must be central to the question and the solution and the mark scheme should give appropriate credit. If not then the interpretation of scores for different children will not be the same. The way in which the setting of a task can influence children's responses is considered again in the discussion of science performance.

Gendered Achievement: English

International surveys show that girls outperform boys in reading and writing across the 5–16 range. In reporting national assessments of reading in England and Wales attention to gender differences occurs because a problem is identified when the assumption of equality of outcome for boys and girls is interrupted (QCA, 2000a). However, if opportunity to learn varies between children, such an assumption is not justified.

At age 6–7 years girls perform better than boys in reading but it mattered if the text was story or information based. The performance gap in favour of girls was reduced on questions drawing on information texts. Boys were found to outperform girls on some multiple-choice questions. Girls' performance was enhanced on questions to do with feelings and motivation, boys where reasons for actions were sought. What the task was about mattered, for example, if it was about a girl's viewpoint or a boy's viewpoint. Girls performed better on the former and boys better on the latter.

At the older ages (10–11) more girls achieved the expected level than boys (76 per cent compared with 65 per cent). Boys' superior performance was associated with questions drawing on information with short or multiple-choice responses. Girls' superior performance was associated with open-ended questions requiring extended responses involving interpretation and explanation. Girls tended to do better than boys when questions involved imagery and poetic language.

In writing tasks girls were ahead of boys at both ages but little detail about the sources of the gender gap were provided. Girls spell significantly better than do boys though the size of the difference declines with age. Girls also use punctuation more and structure and organize their work better than boys (QCA, 2000b). Boys do better when questions required short responses or right/wrong answers, as in multiple choice, and overall writing competence was not required.

These gender differences in English persist through school even when there is no evidence to suggest they reflect differences in innate linguistic ability (OFSTED, 1993). An argument to explain this is again related to gendered choices and learning. Girls' and boys' preferred writing styles reflect their choice of reading materials *outside* of school and there are marked differences in their choices. In the infant phase boys' choices are as described earlier. The tendency for teachers and others to promote boys' interest in reading by enlisting their interests develops by the age of 7 into a preference for hobbies and sports books. Girls read widely in a range of genres (Collins, Hunt and Nunn, 1997).

Girls' styles of writing have been described as extended, reflective composition, boys' as more often episodic, factual and focusing on commentative detail. The source of these differences can readily be linked to the style of writing that children meet in their choice of reading. The link between the content of questions and performance can be traced to the different subjects that children pursue through their reading and mirror children's play interests.

There appears to be a link between ways of responding more typically associated with girls and the widespread finding that multiple-choice items disadvantage girls irrespective of the subject being assessed (Gipps and Murphy, 1994). Research evidence shows that extracting is a 'masculine' approach to thinking whereas females are more likely to apply an embedded model (Head, 1996). Girls' responses to tasks across a range of subjects have been described as reflecting: 'multiple perspectives' (English); 'an ability to take on a wide range of issues' (Design and Technology); and 'a willingness to consider a range of views' (History). Multiple-choice items rely on extraction. Ambiguity in distractors is also more likely to be perceived if multiple perspectives are applied. Add to this, girls' preference for extended written responses, then the finding that girls more than boys do not respond to multiple choice items or tick more than one box comes as no surprise. Mode of response is another potential source of differential validity therefore in that a zero score may not be because of a lack of the achievement being assessed, merely an outcome of a thoughtful response to an ambiguous item.

Gendered Achievement: Science

In science as in mathematics performance overall shows little difference between boys and girls of primary age. There is again the tendency for boys to achieve in the higher levels and girls in the intermediary levels. How girls and boys achieve their scores also differs. A long-standing finding is that boys across the ages outperform girls on tests of physical sciences and this holds true still (Preece, Skinner and Riall, 1999). There are several links that can be made between this finding and gendered learning. Girls' and boys' interests in science related topics vary. In national surveys of science systematic content effects were observed across different types of achievement and these were found for primary and secondary pupils (DES, 1988; 1989). The content is what the task is about, for example, it could be reading a table about different fibres used in clothing or the different metals used in car production. Across the ages girls and boys as groups avoided certain contents irrespective of the question being asked. Questions that involved health, reproduction, nutrition and domestic and social situations showed girls performing at a higher level than boys. This gap arose as more boys failed to respond to such tasks and more girls approached them with confidence. The converse occurred with 'masculine' contents, e.g., traffic, building sites, submarines, space flight, etc. In physics assessments 'masculine' contents dominate and there is often use made of diagrams to represent phenomena. Girls more than boys will have less experience of these contents, consider them to be gender inappropriate and so lack confidence in their approach to them. This may lead some girls to not respond, and others to engage more tentatively with the question. Overall this will lead to a reduction in girls' score as a group.

There is an issue here in relation to how we interpret assessment outcomes as a content effect prevents children showing what they know. There is a further issue about the selection of content for assessment tasks in that the selection should not alter what is intended to be assessed, i.e., the construct, nor should it disadvantage some children over others.

Other gender differences in performance that overall results can mask relate to children's different views of salience. For example when given the choice girls and boys focus on different aspects of phenomena. Girls more than boys pay attention to colour, sound and smells. Boys on the other hand pay attention to structure and movement more than girls (Murphy and Elwood, 1998). In both cases these differences link closely to those noted in the play of preschool and infant pupils. However, these views of salience often go unobserved and emerge later in assessments as achievement differences (Kimbell *et al.*, 1991). Recent observations of year 6 children (age 10–11) in Design and Technology showed the self-regulating nature of gender development in operation but in ways unremarked and therefore unchallenged by teachers. The children had to design a vehicle of their choice. The issues for learning were to do with the design and make aspects of the task. What vehicle was made and, therefore, what aesthetic issues if any obtained were irrelevant. Typically boys made sports cars, army vehicles, rocket carriers and the occasional train. Girls' vehicles were to transport food, e.g. pizzas, circus animals, families and the occasional stretch limousine. The finish of the product therefore engaged the children in different details but it was the quality of the finish rather than the details that were noted by the teacher. This is another example of differences in *opportunity to learn* that needs to be taken into account to inform interpretations of assessment outcomes.

Another issue that has already emerged but is understood slightly differently in the context of science assessment is the effect of the question setting. If realistic settings are used in science they are intended to enhance the relevance of the work and therefore the motivation of the children. Girls, however, more than boys pay attention to features of a setting and incorporate them in their task and their solutions to them. For example, using the setting for a scientific investigation of the effect of temperature on the rate of dissolving, of a father not being able to get his sugar to dissolve in his tea, can have unintended effects that lead to the misrepresentation of children's achievement. In the example mentioned a mixed group of children were observed in a science lesson. These children aged

9–10 were competent investigators. However, in this situation they could not agree a strategy as the girl did not want to test cold water as one of the temperatures whereas the boy was adamant that it would be a 'rubbish' test without it. The girl, however, insisted on many occasions that 'nobody drinks cold tea'. For her the problem was to use her science to solve the father's dilemma of when to put sugar in his tea. For the teacher and the boys in the group that was irrelevant, the task was the scientific investigation (Murphy, 2000). Setting is therefore a critical issue in assessment both in informal and formal situations as it influences the task as it is understood by the individual. This understanding will reflect the views of salience that children have developed both within and without school.

Summary

If we consider overall test results, gender differences in achievement may appear to be only an issue in relation to boys' achievement in English. This is far from the case. The pattern of achievement in maths and science for example is not equally distributed for boys and girls. Boys typically are represented in greater numbers in the highest levels of achievement compared with girls. This pattern appears to hold across schooling and has been associated with the differential expectations of teachers and pupils. Feedback is critical in shaping pupils' perceptions of themselves in relation to subjects and schooling generally. Assessment plays a key role in this. One concern is the way that affective characteristics often acquired through schooling become understood as cognitive abilities. Thus girls' conformity can be understood as intellectual timidity and lack of flair, and some boys' disruptive behaviour as lack of ability and others' independence and risk-taking as brilliance. Patterns of achievement which see girls typically clustered in the middle levels and boys spread more and at the extremes begins to make sense seen in this light. Differences in the distribution of boys and girls across levels and grades in assessment may also arise when the selection of achievements in subject tests reflect those skills and understandings they acquire through their gendered choices and ways of interacting in the world. There is evidence of this across the core subjects.

Another problem is the assumption that there should be equality of outcome between girls and boys which presumes equality of opportunity to learn. The chapter has drawn attention to the way that gendered learning can constrain the opportunities available to children. The chapter has provided examples of the way assessment practice can compound gender differences by the use of particular contents, settings and modes of response and, therefore, serve to create the gender gaps they purport to measure. Gender differences arise from an interaction of subeffects in questions.

The recent controversy over the 1999 reading test provides a useful example of this. It highlighted the way we need to look at assessments in order to understand the potential for creating barriers or indeed reducing them for pupils. The Spinners poem about spiders was judged to be more boy-friendly than poems used in previous tests. Of course whether or not you agree with the criticism depends on how you understand gender differences in performance emerge statistically. The evidence presented in the chapter would support the criticism. The question combined a multiple or short response format with a content that interests boys more than girls, and used cartoon illustrations that boys like. These combined effects will mean that some boys' confidence in their ability to tackle the question, and therefore their engagement with it, is enhanced and some girls' confidence in their ability in relation to the task is reduced. Some girls' beliefs that they know nothing about spiders will mean they fail to respond at all. Hence gender actively mediates the possibilities available for individuals to demonstrate their achievements on this question. These effects may or may not result in an overall difference in girls' and boys' scores, this data is not available in the public domain. We have argued that if we adopt a cultural approach to learning assessment cannot be viewed as objective. It can, however, aim to be just. To achieve this children need to be given opportunities to show what they know and interpretations of scores need to recognize and distinguish between a *lack of achievement* and a *lack of opportunity*. Interpretations of outcomes also need to take account of assessment artefacts such as mode of response that can create barriers for some children and lead to a misrepresentation of their achievements.

In the short term it would help children if assessments were examined critically as *part* of a subject's curriculum. This is not teaching to the test, rather looking at tests as representation of subjects. In this way children can consider the types of response and views of salience valued and at the same time consider those accorded less value. This allows them to develop a critical stance to the curriculum and their own learning. The use of particular contents in subject assessments can also be examined to help children see through the content to the task. In looking at question settings children can examine the extent to which these have any thing to do with what is being assessed. They can also reflect on their own and other children's responses to different settings. Using assessments in these ways has long-term consequences as well.

Gender differences increase with schooling as we unwittingly build on children s strengths and fail to recognize the limitations that gendered learning can create. Children's responses to both teaching and assessment situations can be used to make explicit alternative views of salience. Examining typical boys' responses and girls' responses reveals how they are equally valid and partial views of the world. If the examination includes a consideration of the possibilities for learning in different perspectives, children can come to understand how gender mediates their learning. This examination will also provide insights for teachers about missed opportunities for learning that will inform future planning.

Gendered styles of response put children at an advantage or disadvantage depending on the subject being assessed. If styles are taught explicitly as part of a subject's curriculum and justified in terms of the different goals of that subject, then this constraint upon pupils can be addressed to the benefit of all.

Assessment has the ability to inform and misinform, to liberate and to control. Attention to children's ways of knowing is essential if its benefits for learning are to be realized.

References

Arnot, M., David, M. and Weiner, G. (1996) *Educational Reforms and Gender Equality in Schools*, London: Equal Opportunities Commission.

Bredo, E. (1994) Reconstructing educational psychology, *Educational Psychologist*, **29**, p. 1.

Browne, N. and Ross, C. (1991) Girls' stuff, boys' stuff: young children talking and playing, in N. Browne (ed.), *Science and Technology in the Early Years*, Milton Keynes: Open University Press.

Bruner, J. (1996) *The Culture of Education*, Cambridge, MA: Harvard University Press.

Collins, F., Hunt, P. and Nunn, J. (1997) *Reading Voices*, Plymouth: Northcote House.

Connell, R. W., Johnston, K. and White, V. (1992) *Measuring Up*, Canberra: Australian Curriculum Studies Association.

Cooper, B. and Dunne, M. (2000) *Assessing Children's Mathematical Knowledge Social Class, Sex and Problem-Solving*, Buckingham: Open University Press.

Damarin, S. (1990) Gender and the learning of fractions, paper presented to the American Educational Research Association, Boston, MA, April.

Davies, J. and Brember, I. (1995) Attitudes to school and the curriculum in Year 2, Year 4 and Year 6: changes over four years, paper presented at the European Conference on Educational Research, Bath, England, 14–17 September.

Department of Education and Science (DES) (1988) *Science at Age 11 – A Review of APU Survey Findings*, London: HMSO.

Department of Education and Science (DES) (1989) *Science at Age 13 – A Review of APU Survey Findings*, London: HMSO.

Duveen, G. (1999) Representations, identities, resistance, in K. Deaux and G. Philogene (eds), *Social Representations: Introductions and Explorations*, Oxford: Blackwell.

Dweck, C. S., Davidson, W., Nelson, S. and Enna, B. (1978) Sex differences in learned helplessness: the contingencies of evaluative feedback in the classroom, *Development Psychology*, **14**, pp. 268–76.

Gipps, C. and Murphy, P. (1994) *A Fair Test? Assessment, Achievement and Equity*, Buckingham: Open University Press.

Head, J. (1996) Gender identity and cognitive style, in P. Murphy and C. Gipps (eds), *Equity in the Classroom: Towards Effective Pedagogy for Girls and Boys*, London: Falmer Press/UNESCO.

Howe, C. (1999) *Gender and Classroom Interactions*, Edinburgh: Scottish Council for Educational Research.

Kimbell, R., Stables, K., Wheeler, T., Wosniak, A. and Kelly, V. (1991) *The Assessment of Performance in Design and Technology*, London: Schools' Examination and Assessment Council.

Murphy, P. (1997) Gender differences – messages for science education, in K. Harnqvist and A. Burgen (eds), *Growing up with Science: Developing Early Understanding of Science*, London: Jessica Kingsley.

Murphy, P. (2000) Science education a gender perspective, in S. Capel, J. Dawson, J. Arthur and J. Moss (eds), *Issues in the Teaching of Science*, London: Routledge.

Murphy, P. F. and Elwood, J. (1998) Gendered experiences, choices and achievement – exploring the links, *International Journal of Inclusive Education*, 2(2), 85–118.

Newman, D., Griffin, P., and Cole, M. (1989) *The Construction Zone: Working for cognitive change in school*, Cambridge: Cambridge University Press.

Office for Standards in Education (OFSTED) (1993) *Boys and English*, London: DFE.

Pollard, A. (1997) *The Basics and an Eagerness to Learn: A New Curriculum for Primary Schooling*, SCAA: International Conference London, June.

Preece, F. W. P., Skinner, C. N. and Riall, A. H. R. (1999) The gender gap and discriminating power in the National Curriculum Key Stage 3 Science Assessments in England and Wales, *International Journal of Science Education*, 21(9), pp. 979–87.

QCA/DfEE (1999) *The Review of the National Curriculum in England*, London: QCA.

Qualifications and Curriculum Authority (QCA) (2000a) *Standards at Key Stage 1, English and Mathematics*, London: QCA.

Qualifications and Curriculum Authority (QCA) (2000b) *Standard at Key Stage 2, English, Mathematics and Science*, London: QCA.

Roth, W.-M. (1997) Situated cognition and the assessment of competence in Science. Paper presented at the 7th Conference of the European Association for Research in Learning and Instruction, Athens, Greece, August 26–30, 1997.

Stobart, G., White, J., Elwood, J., Hayden, M. and Mason, K. (1992) *Differential Performance in Examinations at 16+: English and Mathematics*, London: Schools Examination and Assessment Council.

10

Raising Standards: Is Ability Grouping the Answer?

Judith Ireson and Susan Hallam

Introduction

During the 1990s debate about the selection and grouping of pupils has been rekindled, initially in relation to the issue of selective schooling and more recently in relation to ability grouping within schools. The concern about pupil grouping is in response to the perceived need to raise academic standards nationally and to the difficulties some schools have been experiencing in relation to the behaviour and attendance of some pupils.

In this chapter we will present an overview of the research on ability grouping and its effects on pupils' academic achievement. We will also review the research on other important outcomes associated with ability grouping, such as pupils' attitudes towards school, their self-esteem and attendance at school. Finally, we will consider aspects of the school environment that may mediate the influence of organisational grouping on pupil outcomes. The review will refer extensively to British research but will draw on international research where appropriate. It must be recognized, however, that differences in cultural attitudes and education systems limit the relevance of research in other countries.

Overall, the research suggests that there are both advantages and disadvantages in formalizing the grouping of pupils through selective schooling, streaming, banding or setting. Perhaps because of this it is an area which fuels intense debate. Those favouring structured grouping tend to stress its effectiveness in terms of pupil achievement, whereas those against stress the inequity of the system and its social consequences.

Types of Grouping

Historically, grouping in the UK has been based on measures of general ability or intelligence, such as verbal reasoning or cognitive abilities. During the 1960s and 1970s such tests were used by many secondary schools to allocate pupils to streams on entry. Pupils were then taught in their streamed classes for all lessons. Since then, many schools have introduced less rigid forms of grouping such as banding and setting. Banding introduces flexibility by restricting the number of streams to two or three, so that each band contains a moderate range of ability and pupils may be placed either into mixed ability classes or regrouped into sets within a band for different subjects. Setting is used to group pupils into classes on the basis of their attainment in a particular subject. This means that a pupil may be in a high set for one subject and a lower set for another. Practical constraints such as timetabling and availability of staff sometimes reduce the amount of flexibility in setted systems. Where pupils are in sets for all subjects, setting may approximate streaming, as certain pupils end up in all the bottom sets while others are in all the top sets. Sometimes different forms of grouping may be operating simultaneously at different levels within the same school (Rutter *et al.*, 1979; Laarhoven and de Vries, 1987; Slavin, 1987) with schools typically increasing the amount of ability grouping in the later years (Benn and Chitty, 1996). In addition, the grouping practices may differ from one year to the next, in response to pressure from school inspections or changing views of staff. Even where a school has a policy of mixed ability grouping, individual teachers may group pupils by ability in their classes. Because schools have such a variety of groupings, it has been difficult for researchers to establish with any clarity just what grouping particular pupils have experienced during their time in school.

Effects on Academic Achievement

A number of large-scale studies in the UK have investigated the impact of selective and non-selective school systems on pupil achievement. Some have demonstrated minimal differences in terms of learning outcomes on standardized reading and mathematical tests and examination performance (Gray, McPherson and Raffe, 1983; Marks and Pomian-Srednicki, 1983; Steedman, 1980) when prior ability is controlled for, while others have found that pupils' performance becomes increasingly differentiated depending on the kind of school they are in (Lughart *et al.*, 1989). Pupils of average ability seem to perform better in high-ability schools than comparable students in schools where the majority are pupils of lower ability.

At primary level in the UK, streaming was introduced after the 1931 Primary School Report. By the early 1950s, articles criticizing the practice had begun to appear and it was largely phased out with the demise of the 11-plus examination. During this time several studies were undertaken, the most comprehensive by Barker Lunn (1970) which compared the achievement gains of students in 36 streamed and 36 unstreamed junior schools, matched on social class. There were no meaningful differences in achievement between the pupils in streamed and unstreamed schools. The size and quality of this study provides particularly strong evidence that ability grouping is not by itself a major factor affecting achievement at primary level.

Among the American elementary school studies, a study by Goldberg, Passow and Justman (1966) stands out as providing particularly strong evidence. This study involved 86 Grade 5 classes in New York elementary schools. Pupils were assigned to classes on the basis of IQ scores according to 15 different grouping patterns that varied in terms of homogeneity. They remained in those classes for two years. Most achievement comparisons were not significant, and those that were supported heterogeneous rather than homogeneous grouping. This evidence is consistent with that of the Barker Lunn study, referred to above.

Kulik and Kulik (1992) concluded that the clearest effects on achievement are obtained in enrichment programmes and accelerated classes, which involve the greatest curriculum adjustment. Generally the higher-ability groups benefit, but there do not appear to be negative effects on the achievement levels of middle and low groups. A subsequent meta-analysis of the effects of within class grouping (Lou *et al.*, 1996) concludes that on average this form of grouping produces significant gains in attainment.

Affective Outcomes

One of the concerns of those who argue against grouping by ability is that placement in the bottom groups has an adverse impact on pupils' self-esteem, self-concept and on their attitudes towards school and schoolwork (Lacey, 1974; Oakes, 1985; Gamoran and Berends, 1987). The research findings regarding the relationship between pupil self-esteem and ability grouping practices are complex and difficult to interpret, particularly as a variety of measures have been used, both in questionnaire form and interviews. Gamoran and Berends (1987), reviewing the international literature, suggested that there was a negative impact of ability grouping on the motivation and self-esteem of students assigned to low ability groups. Further longitudinal studies are needed to establish a causal relationship.

Students in high tracks or streams tend to have higher educational aspirations and more positive academic and personal self-concepts (Rudd, 1956; Oakes, 1985). Oakes suggests that for low-track students the self-concept becomes more and more negative as years go by and students tend to be critical of their own abilities. Some comparisons of academic self-esteem in mixed-ability or streamed groups indicated that lower-ability pupils tended to have lower academic self-esteem regardless of the way in which they were grouped (Newbold, 1977; Essen, Fogelmann and Tibbenham, 1978).

Ethnographic accounts of individual pupils' views demonstrate that placement in a low set or stream can be viewed negatively (e.g., Lacey, 1974; Boaler, 1997), but it is not clear how many pupils are affected in this way or for how long. In their meta-analysis of 13 studies of the effects of ability grouping on self-esteem, Kulik and Kulik (1992) found no overall effect, but ability grouping tended to raise the self-esteem scores of lower aptitude students and reduce the self-esteem of higher aptitude students.

Pupils' reference groups may be an important influence on their academic self-concepts, but the strength of this relationship may depend on the extent to which teachers emphasize group placement as limiting pupils' chances of success. It seems likely that the effects on self-esteem are mediated by the behaviour of teachers and peers and that these in turn are affected by school ethos.

Attitudes Towards School, Relationships and Alienation

Ethnographic research in this country during the heyday of streaming and in American tracked systems demonstrates that streaming can lead to anti-school attitudes and alienation from school. Where whole peer groups feel alienated anti-school cultures can develop. Streaming, it is argued, can play a major role in polarising students' attitudes into pro- and anti-school camps (Hargreaves, 1967; Lacey, 1970; Ball, 1981; Schwartz, 1981; Gamoran and Berends, 1987). High-ability pupils in high streams tend to accept the school's demands as the normative definition of behaviour, whereas low-stream students resist the school's rules and may even attempt to subvert them. Over time, streaming fosters friendship groups (Hallinan and Sorensen, 1985), which may contribute to polarized stream-related attitudes, the high-stream pupils tending to be more enthusiastic, while those in the low stream are more alienated (Oakes, Samoran and Page, 1991). Pupils also tend to be labelled and stereotyped by teachers according to the stream that they are in (Hargreaves, 1967; Lacey, 1970; Keddie, 1971; Ball, 1981; Schwartz, 1981; Burgess, 1983). Schwartz (1981), for example, reports teachers' stereotyped descriptions of pupils as thick, bright, slow, difficult, etc., and pupils' own stereotypical labels such as teacher's pet, brain, dumb, stupid. At primary level, the research suggests that children in unstreamed classes have healthier and more positive attitudes towards school than children in streamed classes and that this is particularly true for those of lower ability (Barker Lunn, 1970). Where the teachers favoured streaming, children of lower ability tended to be bullied and friendless, reflecting the teachers' attitudes towards lower-ability children. As the Elton Report suggested, bad behaviour can occur in lower streams because of pupils' recognition of their place in the scheme of things – at the bottom (DES, 1989). Research considering the social climate within the classroom indicates that peer relationships are more supportive in high-ability groups, although these classes also tend to be more competitive.

Overall, the evidence relating to alienation and pupils' attitudes towards schools is mixed. Both probably depend to a large extent on the individual school ethos and staff attitudes. One question, as yet unresolved, is whether negative school attitudes result from streaming, banding or setting, or whether grouping procedures merely reflect existing attitudes. What appears to be an outcome of streaming may in fact be a reflection of social alienation, which is reinforced in the school context.

Social Implications

The most serious criticisms of selection, streaming, banding and setting derive from their perceived social consequences. There is clear evidence that low-ability groups tend to include disproportionate numbers of pupils of low socio-economic status (Douglas, 1964; Sandven, 1971; Winn and Wilson, 1983; Oakes, 1985; Burgess, 1986; Vanfossen, Jones and Spade, 1987; Peak and Morrison, 1988), ethnic minorities (Winn and Wilson, 1983; Oakes, 1985; Burgess, 1986; Tomlinson, 1987; Commission for Racial Equality, 1992; Troyna and Siraj-Blatchford, 1993), boys, and those born in the summer (Douglas, 1964; Barker Lunn, 1970). Recent supporting evidence comes from Northern Ireland, where selective education continues and schools are denominationally based. A report for the Northern Ireland Economic Council (McAdam, 1995) recorded concern about the disparities in attainment between social classes and denominations, with middle-class children 2.6 times as likely to enter grammar schools, and Catholic students more likely than Protestants to leave school with no qualifications. There is now considerable hostility towards the grammar schools system (Benn and Chitty, 1996).

Other Aspects of School that Mediate Grouping Practices

The organization of pupils into groups is likely to reflect and impact on many of the factors outlined as important in effective schooling, namely shared vision and goals, the learning environment, concentration on teaching and learning, purposeful teaching, high expectations, positive reinforcement, monitoring progress, pupil rights and responsibilities, and home–school partnerships. These may all mediate the effects of grouping pupils by ability. Streaming, setting or banding policies within a school also seem to be related to school ethos and values, although whether they determine or reflect school ethos is not clear. For example, there is some evidence that both primary and secondary headteachers who favour ability grouping and separate classes for pupils with difficulties in learning do so on pragmatic grounds, whereas those who favour mixed-ability teaching and the integration of pupils into mainstream classrooms tended to hold egalitarian values (Ireson *et al.*, 1992). In the past, rigid systems of pupil grouping were more likely to be found where there were more pupils of lower socio-economic status, larger classes, greater discipline, tighter controls on school uniform, more authoritarian teachers, more testing and a greater concentration on the 3Rs (Fogelman, 1983). This situation in the UK appears to have changed, with many inner city schools currently adopting mixed-ability policies.

Placement of Pupils in Groups

The research evidence indicates a number of practical difficulties relating to the grouping of pupils by ability, with the result that children of similar ability are often placed in different streams. Standardized tests of general cognitive or verbal ability are frequently used to allocate pupils to schools or streams. The use of such tests bases the allocation on an assumption that general intelligence is a single entity which predicts achievement at school. This view has been challenged by recent theories of intelligence, such as multiple intelligences (Gardner, 1983). It is also clear that the environment plays an important role in achievement, and correlations of IQ with school grades, whilst being significant, still leave much variation unexplained. Placement of pupils into groups on the basis of general tests is therefore at best inexact and can lead to the incorrect placement of children (Jackson, 1964). Within a school, pupil behaviour may influence placement, leading to a badly behaved bottom set. Pupils who remain in too high a stream tend to improve but those in too low a stream tend to deteriorate (Barker Lunn, 1970; Peak and Morrison, 1988). The former tended to be the older pupils and the latter the younger pupils in the year group.

In the UK, with the introduction of the National Curriculum and standard assessments at the end of Key Stage 2 (year 6), some secondary schools are now using the Key Stage test scores to allocate pupils to groups in English, mathematics and science. This should mean that pupils will be more easily placed into groups on the basis of progress within the curriculum at least in those subjects. The problems of incorrect placement and lack of movement between groups will nevertheless remain. Once placed in too low a group, movement to a higher group will remain difficult, because of the increasing gap in curriculum covered.

Teachers' preferences for ability grouping are perhaps a reflection of the immense complexity of the task of responding to the differing needs of a class of 30 learners. Ability grouping is seen as one way of reducing the range of needs, thus making the teacher's job easier. In fact, recent inspection reports suggest that teachers frequently underestimate the range of needs in ability grouped classes (OFSTED, 1995). This may be one reason why better results are not achieved in such classes.

Classroom Practices

A substantial literature now indicates the tendency for instruction in lower ability groups to be of different quality to that provided for high-ability groups (Evertson, 1982; Oakes, 1985; Gamoran, 1986). While some differences are to be expected, such as a slower pace, the concern is that instruction in low-ability groups is conceptually simplified with more structured written work, which leaves work fragmented (Hargreaves, 1967; Schwartz, 1981; Burgess, 1983; Page, 1984; Oakes, 1985). Higher-ability classes tend to include more analytic, critical thinking tasks (Hargreaves, 1967; Oakes, 1985). Pupils in high-ability groups are also allowed more independence and choice, opportunities are provided for discussion, and pupils are allowed to take responsibility for their own work. Low streams tend to undertake work that is more tightly structured. There is a concentration on basic skills, worksheets and repetition with fewer opportunities for independent learning, discussion and activities that promote critique, analysis and creativity (Hargreaves, 1967; Burgess, 1983; Oakes, 1985; Page, 1992). Schwartz (1981) also found that when high-track students gave incorrect answers, teachers coaxed them to develop correct answers, while low-track students who were incorrect were ignored. Page (1984) suggested that streaming or tracking sets in motion a vicious cycle. Based on stereotypes and past experience, teachers hold low expectations for low-ability students. Perceiving these views, the students lower expectations for themselves, confirming and further reducing expectations. Some researchers have suggested that there is a hidden agenda for the low-ability students concerned with conformity, getting along with others, working quietly, improving study habits, punctuality, co-operation, and conforming to rules and expectations (Oakes, 1985). Conversely, top sets may be highly competitive with a rapid pace in lessons allowing little time for consolidation and understanding (Boaler, 1997).

On the other hand, mixed-ability teaching is not without its problems. There appears to be a mismatch between the underlying philosophy of mixed ability teaching and its practice (HMI, 1978; Kerry and Sands, 1984). In classrooms, whole-class teaching predominates and there is little evidence of genuine mixed-ability group work. The cognitive demands made on students tend to be low, as are the cognitive levels of verbal transactions between pupils (Kerry, 1982b, 1982c; Kerry and Sands, 1984). Few group tasks make sufficient cognitive demands on the more able and in many cases do not even stretch average pupils. Few teachers seem to advocate individualized learning programmes to satisfy the needs of their pupils (Kerry, 1982a; Kerry and Sands, 1984), except in mathematics where workcards or textbooks are used. These studies predate the introduction of the National Curriculum in this country and it may well be that greater cognitive demands are now being made on pupils.

The evidence to date suggests that successful mixed-ability teaching relies heavily on teacher skills (Reid *et al.*, 1982). Successful teachers of mixed-ability classes are flexible, use a variety of teaching modes in one lesson, vary the pace and style of approach, use a range of audiovisual media and encourage a variety of pupil activities. They have informal relationships with their pupils, involve pupils in decision making and engage them in their learning activities (Kerry and Sands, 1984). To support mixed-ability teaching schools need good backup facilities and resources (Ingleson, 1982).

Alternatives to Ability Grouping

For many years, it has been recognized that a major problem of the UK education system has been the low attainment of a large proportion of school pupils. International comparisons in mathematics and science still demonstrate a 'long tail' of poor attainment among English pupils (Keys, Harris and Fernandes, 1996; Reynolds and Farrell, 1996; Prais, 1998). It is clear from this review that a return to selective schooling is unlikely to solve this problem. Instead, the emphasis should be on developing alternative forms of grouping and improving pedagogy.

One option is to adopt structured ability grouping procedures but attempt to minimize their negative effects according to the principles outlined by Slavin (1987). First, a student's main point of identification should be with a mixed-ability class and regrouping by ability should occur only in subjects in which reducing the spread of attainment in the group is particularly important. Second, the grouping plan must reduce student variability in the specific skill being taught, not just in general ability or achievement. Third, grouping plans should frequently reassess pupils' group assignment and should be flexible enough to allow for easy movement between groups. Fourth, within the groups teachers must actually vary their pace and level of instruction to correspond to students' levels of readiness and learning rates. These principles can also be applied to groups formed across or within year groups or within classes. Within this framework schools might also explore the formation of flexible groups for specific purposes, e.g., to improve language usage, attendance, literacy or the achievement of particular groups.

A second option is to place less emphasis on ability and more on effort. Research comparing the education systems in the Far East, the USA and Europe suggest that the Western concern with differential ability minimizes the importance of student, teacher and parental effort. The concept of differential ability sets a ceiling on what can be expected from a child, whereas in Japan and Taiwan, pupils, with support from parents and teachers, are expected to put in additional effort if they are not successful (Stevenson and Lee, 1990). Similarly in many European countries, the teacher's role is to ensure that the class moves forward together and that learning is consolidated by pupils before moving on. This approach assumes that all pupils will attain similar specified levels of achievement and implies that the teacher will adopt a whole-class approach to instruction.

Another alternative is to modularize the curriculum, allowing greater flexibility in the ways in which students can progress through school. Pupils, with advice and support from their teachers, take greater responsibility for their own learning, selecting modules or levels of work within modules, and evaluating their progress. This might be done for some or all curriculum subjects, while maintaining a core of compulsory subjects. Extension and support modules in core subjects could also be included. Such an approach would facilitate the broadening of access to learning. It could be accomplished within the normal school day but a more radical option would require a longer school day, with classes taking place in the evenings and at weekends in addition to 'normal' school times. Timetabling would become more flexible and there would be more stress on independent study and improved library and computer facilities. Schools would become centres of learning for the whole community with classes including adults and school-aged children. Such a scenario would enable schools to play a central role in the development of a learning society.

Apart from grouping procedures, there are further possibilities that might be considered. One is to improve methods for teaching mixed-ability classes by studying effective mixed ability teaching both in this country and overseas. In this country there has been a tendency to play down the science of pedagogy and to consider teaching as an art (Simon, 1984). This view, coupled with the emphasis on the differential abilities of pupils, has tended to focus attention and debate on the individual development of teachers and pupils. Other countries, such as Germany, France, Switzerland and Japan, have placed more importance on the development of pedagogy with the specific goal of ensuring that all pupils in a class attain a certain standard.

Although there is now a large international literature on ability grouping, there has been very little research in this country in recent years. The current intense debate in the USA and Canada, where there is considerable pressure to discontinue tracking because of its undesirable social consequences, suggests that a return to a national system of selection and structured grouping is, in the long term, no more likely to succeed in the UK now than it did earlier this century. Educators and researchers, in collaboration with parents and other interested parties in the wider community, need to develop alternatives which will carry us forward into the twenty-first century and will encourage the development of the skills and expertise of today's young people for the future, not for the past.

References

Ball, S. J. (1981) *Beachside Comprehensive: A Case-Study of Secondary Schooling*, Cambridge: Cambridge University Press.
Barker Lunn, J. C. (1970) *Streaming in the Primary School*, Slough, NFER.

Benn, C. and Chitty, C. (1996) *Thirty Years On: Is Comprehensive Education Alive and Well or Struggling to Survive?* London: David Fulton.

Boaler, J. (1997) *Experiencing School Mathematics: Teaching Styles, Sex and Setting*, Buckingham: Open University Press.

Burgess, R. G. (1983) *Experiencing Comprehensive Education: A Study of Bishop McGregor School*, London: Methuen.

Burgess, R. G. (1986) *Education, Schools and Society*, London: Batsford.

Commission for Racial Equality (1992) *Set to Fail? Setting and Banding in Secondary Schools*, London: Commission for Racial Equality.

Department for Education and Science (DES) (1989) *Discipline in Schools: Report of the Committee of Enquiry Chaired by Lord Elton*, London: HMSO.

Douglas, J. W. B. (1964) *The Home and the School*, London: MacGibbon and Kee.

Essen, J., Fogelman, K. and Tibbenham, A. (1978) Some non-academic developmental correlates of ability-grouping in secondary schools, *Educational Studies*, **5**(1), pp. 83–93.

Evertson, C. M. (1982) Differences in instructional activities in higher and lower achieving junior high English and math classes, *Elementary School Journal*, **82**, pp. 219–32.

Fogelman, K. (1983) Ability grouping in the secondary school, in K. Fogelman (ed.), *Growing up in Great Britain, Papers from the National Child Development Study*, London: Macmillan for NCB.

Gamoran, A. (1986) Instructional and institutional effects of ability grouping, *Sociology of Education*, **59**, pp. 185–98.

Gamoran, A. Berends, M. (1987) The effects of stratification in secondary schools: synthesis of survey and ethnographic research, *Review of Educational Research*, **57**, pp. 415–35.

Gardner, H. (1983) *Frames of Mind: The Theory of Multiple Intelligences*, New York: Basic.

Goldberg, M. L., Passow, A. H. and Justman, J. (1966) *The Effects of Ability Grouping*, New York: Teachers College Press.

Gray, J., McPherson, A. F. and Raffe, D. (1983) *Reconstructions of Secondary Education: Theory, Myth and Practice since the War*, London: Routledge and Kegan Paul.

Hallinan, M. and Sorensen, A. (1985) Ability grouping and student friendships, *American Educational Research Journal*, **22**, pp. 485–99.

Hargreaves, D. H. (1967) *Social Relations in a Secondary School*, London: Tinling.

HMI (1978) (Department of Education and Science) *Mixed Ability Work in Comprehensive Schools*, London: HMSO.

Ingleson, S. (1982) Creating conditions for success with mixed ability classes, in M. K. Sands and T. Kerry (eds), *Mixed Ability Teaching*, London: Croom Helm.

Ireson J., Evans, P., Redmond, P. and Wedell, K. (1992) Developing the curriculum for pupils experiencing difficulties in learning in the ordinary school: a systematic comparative analysis, *British Educational Research Journal*, **18**(2), pp. 155–73.

Jackson, B. (1964) *Streaming: An Education System in Miniature*, London: Routledge and Kegan Paul.

Keddie, N. (1971) Classroom knowledge, in M. F. D. Young (ed.) *Knowledge and Control*, London: Collier-Macmillan.

Kerry, T. (1982a) Providing for slow learners, *Special Education: Foreward Trends*, **8**(4), p. 911.

Kerry, T. (1982b) The demands made by RE on pupils' thinking, in J. Hull (ed.) *New Directions in Religious Education*, Lewes: Falmer Press.

Kerry, T. (1982c) Teachers' identification of exceptional pupils and the strategies for coping with them, PhD thesis, University of Nottingham.

Kerry, T. and Sands, M. K. (1984) Classroom organisation and learning, in E. C. Wragg (ed.) *Classroom Teaching Skills: The Research Findings of the Teacher Education Project*, London: Routledge.

Keys, W., Harris, S. and Fernandes, C. (1996) *Third International Mathematics and Science Study: first national report. Part 1 and appendices*, Slough: NFER.

Kulik, J. A. and Kulik, C-L. C. (1992) Meta-analytic findings on grouping programs, *Gifted Child Quarterly*, **36**(2), pp. 73–7.

Laarhoven, P. van and de Vries, A. (1987) Effects of heterogeneous groupings in secondary schools, in J. Scheerends and W. Stoel (eds) *Effectiveness of School Organisations*, Lisse: Swets and Zeitlinger.

Lacey, C. (1970) *Hightown Grammar*, Manchester: Manchester University Press.

Lacey, C. (1974) Destreaming in a 'pressured' academic environment, in J. Eggleston (ed.) *Contemporary Research in the Sociology of Education*, London: Methuen.

Lou, Y., Abrami, P. C., Spence, J. C., Poulson, C., Chambers, B. and D'Apollonia, S. (1996) Within-class grouping: a meta-analysis, *Review of Educational Research*, **66**(4), pp. 423–58.

Lughart, E., Roeders, P. J. B., Bosker, R. J. and Bos, K. T. (1989) *Effective school kenmerken in het voortgezet onderwijs. Deel 1: Literatuurstudic* (Effective Schools Characteristics in Secondary Education. Part I: Literature Review), Groningen: RION.

Marks, J., Cox, C. and Pomian-Srednicki, M. (1983) *Standards in English Schools: An Analysis of Examination Results in England for 1981*, London: National Council for Educational Standards.

McAdam, N. (1995) Religious divide costs £35 m, *Times Educational Supplement*, 10 February.

Newbold, D. (1977) *Ability Grouping: the Banbury Enquiry*, Slough: National Foundation for Educational Research.

Oakes, J. (1985) *Keeping Track: How Schools Structure Inequality*, New Haven, CT: Yale University Press.

Oakes, J., Gamoran, A. and Page, R. (1991) Curriculum differentiation: opportunities, consequences and meanings, in P. Jackson (ed.) *Handbook of Research on Curriculum*, New York: Macmillan.

OFSTED (1995) *Standards and Quality in Education. Annual Report of Her Majesty's Chief Inspector of Schools, 1993/94, Part I*, London: Office for Standards in Education.

Page, R N. (1984) Perspectives and processes: the negotiation of educational meaning in high school classes for academically unsuccessful students, unpublished PhD dissertation, University of Wisconsin.

Page, R. (1992) *Lower Track Classrooms: A Curricular and Cultural Perspective*, New York: Teachers College Press.

Peak, B. and Morrison, K. (1988) Investigating banding origins and destinations in a comprehensive school, *School Organisation*, **8**(3), pp. 339–49.

Prais, S. J. (1998) How did English schools and pupils really perform in the 1995 international comparisons in mathematics? *National Institute Economic Review*, **165**, pp. 83–8.

Reid, M. E., Clunies-Ross, L. R., Goachier, B. and Vile, D. (1982) *Mixed Ability Teaching: Problems and Possibilities*, Windsor: NFER-Nelson.

Reynolds, D. and Farrell, S. (1996) *Worlds Apart? A Review of International Surveys of Educational Achievement Involving England*, London: HMSO.

Rudd, W. G. A. (1956) The psychological effects of streaming by attainment with special reference to a group of selected children, *British Journal of Educational Psychology*, **28**, pp. 47–60.

Rutter, M., Maughan, B., Mortimore, P. and Ouston, J. (1979) *Fifteen Thousand Hours: Secondary Schools and their Effects on Children*, London: Open Books.

Sandven, J. I. (1971) Causes of lacking a sense of well-being in school, *Scandinavian Journal of Educational Research*, **15**(1), pp. 21–60.

Scheerens, J., Nanninga, H. C. R. and Pellgrum, W. J. (1989) Generalizability of instructional and school effectiveness indicators across nations; preliminary results of a secondary analysis of the IEA Second Mathematics Study, in B. P. M. Creemers, T. Peters and D. Reynolds (eds) *School Effectiveness and School Improvement, Proceedings of the Second International Congress*, Rotterdam: Lisse, Swets and Zeitlinger.

Schwartz, F. (1981) Supporting or subverting learning: peer groups patterns in four tracked schools, *Anthropology and Education Quarterly*, **12**, pp. 99–121.

Simon, B. (1984) *Does Education Matter?* London: Lawrence and Wishart.

Slavin, R. E. (1987) Ability grouping and student achievement in elementary schools: a best evidence synthesis, *Review of Educational Research*, **57**(3), pp. 293–336.

Steedman, J. (1980) *Progress in Secondary Schools*, London: National Children's Bureau.

Stevenson, H. and Lee, S. (1990) Contexts of achievement: a study of American, Chinese and Japanese children, *Monographs of the Society for Research in Child Development*, **221**(55), pp. 1–2 (University of Chicago).

Tomlinson, S. (1987) Curriculum option choices in multi-ethnic schools, in B. Troyna (ed.) *Racial Inequality in Education*, London: Tavistock.

Troyna, B. and Siraj-Blatchford, I. (1993) Providing support or denying access? The experiences of students designated as ESL and SN in a multi-ethnic secondary school, *Educational Review*, **45**(1), pp. 3–11.

Vanfossen, B. E., Jones, J. D. and Spade, J. Z. (1987) Curriculum tracking and status maintenance, *Sociology of Education*, **60**, April, pp. 104–22.

Winn, W. and Wilson, A. P. (1983) The affect and effect of ability grouping, *Contemporary Education*, **54**, pp. 119–25.

11

Wide Eyes and Open Minds: Observing, Assessing and Respecting Children's Early Achievements

Cathy Nutbrown

This chapter will consider, in three sections, how educators might demonstrate their respect for young children through their observations and assessments. First, I will use some stories about children and their parents to discuss aspects of observation. Second, I focus on assessment, what it might mean and issues leading to the notion of respectful assessment. Finally, I conclude with some ideas that educators may wish to consider if they are further to respect children's achievements.

Observing Children

Children seeing with wide eyes

Children have an awesome capacity to observe in fine detail and they learn from what they see. Parents and other early childhood educators who watch young children know that they have learned so much from watching those close to them and paying attention to things they see. They learn about the uses of keys, how to pour tea from a play teapot, use a knife and fork, use computers, turn on the television, choose a favourite video, operate the video or audio tape recorder, read books, get dressed, hold conversations, hypothesize about how things work or why they have become, resolve conflicts, seek help when they need it. There is so much to learn in the early years, and learning is so complex, that perhaps it would be true to say that only young children are capable of it! Such a capacity for uninterrupted, unthwartable, multidisciplinary learning deserves enormous respect from adults.

Seeing, understanding, acting

Children approach their learning with wide eyes and open minds, so their educators too need wide eyes and open minds to see clearly and to understand what they see. If educators are blinkered, having tunnel vision, they may not have the full picture – so it's not simply a case of understanding what is seen but it is first crucial to *see* what is *really happening* and not what adults sometimes suppose to be happening. Children and the things they do need to be seen in the whole context and adults working with them must be open to seeing what *exists* not what their professional mind tells them they *should* see. Educators need wide eyes too, to guard against stereotypes and to combat prejudices about capabilities of children based on such factors as their gender, race, language, culture or disability. Watching children thinking is one of the greatest privileges of any educator, and there is wide agreement that close observation is an essential process of working with young children (PPA, 1991; Drummond, Rouse and Pugh, 1992; Pugh, 1992; Drummond, 1993; Nutbrown, 1994a).

Educators need to watch the children they work with, keeping open minds and responding with sensitivity and respect to what they see. Children need well-educated educators with knowledge at their fingertips, adults working with them who:

- *see* what is happening,
- *understand* what they see, and
- *act* on what they understand.

Just seeing, just understanding, is not enough. The next essential stage is to take children further along their own learning pathways. This is a marker of quality in any early education provision.

The notion that young children's learning is linked with developmental patterns, or schemas, has been explored by Chris Athey (1990). Educators can provide a more appropriate curriculum which matches the developmental levels and interests of children by using their knowledge of schemas and their skills as observers to develop greater awareness of patterns of learning and understand more about children's predominant interests. The following example shows how adults' knowledge of one child's schema supported her learning and development. The educators (at her group provision and her mother at home) were seeing, understanding and acting upon what they saw.

Belinda

Belinda was 3 years old and she seemed to be tuned in to spotting or seeking out opportunities to enclose or be enclosed, and objects which enclosed. At home she enjoyed emptying and filling the washing machine, and in the garden and the bath she filled numerous containers with water to the point that they overflowed. She and her mother built up a collection of tins and boxes that she enjoyed fitting inside one another in different combinations and she often enjoyed sitting inside cardboard boxes used to carry the shopping from the supermarket, sometimes pretending that it was a car, bus, boat or rocket. Some of Belinda's favourite books contained stories of hiding or enclosing in one way or another; stories like *Boxed In* (Williams, 1991) and *Where's Spot?* (Hill, 1980). At her sessional group Belinda particularly enjoyed playing in the house and hiding the farm animals inside the little wooden farm buildings. She dressed up and liked to play in the tunnel and hidey boxes outside.

Exploring her enveloping/containing schema, Belinda encountered much learning which linked with different areas of learning and experience. She learned about being with others and being apart, co-operating when equipment needed to be shared and dealing with her emotions when she wanted to be the only person in the house and was told to allow other children to play too. Opportunities at home and in the group enabled Belinda to explore her schema and develop her knowledge. The adults around her, sensitized to her interests, provided encouragement where a lack of knowledge may have led adults to stop Belinda doing some of the things she found interesting.

All the adults who lived or worked with Belinda were able to support and extend her learning. She encountered mathematical experiences of collecting, sorting, selecting, counting, ordering, reordering, grading, categorizing, placing. She puzzled ideas of shape and size and how things fitted together. She asked questions such as 'Why does the washing have to get covered in water before it is clean?' and 'Why do we have to wrap the potatoes before they go in the oven?', 'Why won't this one [big tin] fit inside this one here [small tin]?' Her mother extended her interest and in doing so provided more linked experiences such as involving her in baking, washing, writing letters and posting them. They looked at holes and hiding places, talked about being inside a lift and packed the shopping into boxes in the supermarket. She began to learn more about space and place relationships, finding out about relative size. Belinda's mother acted on what she saw and what she understood.

Vygotsky (1978) stressed the crucial role of the adult. Believing that adults with expertise, who were well 'tuned in' to the child they were working with, could bridge the gap (the zone of proximal development) between what a child can do with help 'today' and what – with sensitive and well-timed support – she can do 'tomorrow'. Much of Belinda's learning became possible through interaction.

Children have a right to educators with good observation skills, and the ability to match learning opportunities to a child's prevailing interest. Practice must be underpinned by theories of how children learn, and all the adults involved need to work together and make sense of what they see. Children are denied this right when they spend time with adults who are poorly trained and inadequately supported.

Communication between parents and educators and continuity of experience between home and group settings is all-important. Learning experiences at home can be reinforced at the group when adults working alongside children make time to observe and understand and are able to define their own role more clearly in relation to the children.

Time must be made for ongoing, co-operative and informed dialogue between parents and educators in home or group settings if children's efforts are to be noticed and understood. This makes for a partnership of the highest order and it is an all-important factor in supporting, extending and challenging children as they learn and nurturing them through the emotional struggles that go alongside that learning. Respectful observation can occur where the climate is such that educators and parents – together – watch, listen to and talk with children.

Adults seeing with wide eyes and open minds

Adults need to make detailed and sensitive observations really to 'see' what children are doing, to make sense of their actions, to recognize their achievements and to create further learning opportunities.

> Nadia (7 months) was sitting in her high chair eating a plate of pasta and peas. Using her left hand she carefully picked up each piece of pasta with her fingers and ate them until only peas were left on the plate. Then she ate the peas, one at a time, picking up each one with her fingers, looking at it closely before putting it in her mouth.

Nadia showed any interested and attentive adult that she knew what she wanted to eat first, how she wanted to eat it, which hand she preferred to use and that she could sort different things, in this case two types of food. Young children seize everyday experiences such as eating to develop and then to apply their newly acquired abilities, and adults who watch carefully then have the opportunity to understand a little more of what they know and can do. Adults who persist in teaching children of 2 and 3 to sort coloured counters, bricks or specially purchased plastic toys need first to observe the children to see if it is a skill they already possess and use in real-life situations and therefore do not need to practise in specially created situations of dubious purpose.

As well as observing children to support their learning and understand their development adults have a role to play in protecting children and a responsibility in relation to healthy development, for as Brierley (1980, p. 17) wrote: 'Progress in education and health go hand in hand, for a sick, tired and hungry child will not learn properly.'

Charlotte

Charlotte was just 4 years old. She was admitted to the nursery when she was 3 years and 10 months old, after her mother applied for a place. Initially, Charlotte attended part-time as pressure on places in the nursery class made it difficult to offer more than a part-day place to any child other than those with special educational needs or who needed priority for some other recognized reason. Both the nursery teacher and the nursery nurse felt uneasy about this little girl; they felt that her initial attitude to them as unknown adults was wary and she seemed, even as time went on, to find it difficult to trust them. At first they put this down to natural apprehension of a new situation, but observed carefully and felt that her timidness and general lack of confidence were a cause for concern. One morning Charlotte arrived later than normal and her grandmother, who brought her, explained that the child had stayed with her the night before. That day she was very distressed and spent much of the time putting the dolls to bed and then getting them out, smacking them and telling them to be quiet. The staff observed carefully and later, during a quiet moment in the home corner, she said something in an almost inaudible voice that made the teacher think there was reason to suspect that Charlotte might have suffered some form of abuse. Events moved swiftly, bringing Charlotte, her mother and the teacher into contact with social workers, police, medical personnel, the child psychologist and the child protection liaison teacher, to name but a few. Charlotte's mother, a single parent, was most distressed, she had two other children under 5 at home and always wanted what was best for all her children. Alerted to Charlotte's behaviour and comments in the nursery, she recognized other signs that something might be happening at home and suspected a young male baby-sitter of violence towards Charlotte. This led to court proceedings and eventually a conviction. A home start volunteer offered friendship and support to Charlotte's mother to help her to cope through the distressing time, and counselling and appropriate medical treatment were arranged for Charlotte.

Parents seeing with open minds – partnership

As the story of Belinda illustrates, parents can often see things others do not see, and through working in partnership, parents and educators can see, understand and act together.

Sean

Sean was 3½ years old. He attended a nursery class each morning, where he spent much of his time playing outdoors, on bikes, in tents, climbing, gardening and running. His nursery teacher was concerned that he did not benefit from the other things available indoors – painting, writing, drawing, construction, sharing books, jigsaws, and so on. Even when some of these opportunities were placed outside, Sean still seemed to avoid them. The nursery teacher spoke with Sean's mother, who said: 'We don't have a garden and there's nowhere for Sean to play outside – he hasn't got a bike and there's no park for climbing, or swings around here, or a space to do outside things, but we have lots of books and jigsaws, Lego, play people, we draw and make things.' Sean was balancing his own curriculum – but the adults involved needed to observe and discuss in order to understand what he was doing.

The Sheffield Early Literacy Development Project (Hannon, Weinberger and Nutbrown, 1991) worked with parents to explore how *together* parents and the project team could promote children's early literacy. After home visits and group meetings the parents *saw* more of their children's capabilities and they *understood* more of what they saw. Children's homes and members of their families can offer powerful learning encounters. It makes sense for professional educators and families to work in collaboration, sharing their knowledge, insights and questions.

Views of Assessment

Drummond and Nutbrown (1992, pp. 87–97) discussed four questions in relation to observing and assessing young children:

Why assess and observe young children?
Observation and assessment are the processes by which we can both establish the progress that has already been made, and explore the future, the learning that is yet to come.

Which children should be assessed?
Every child in every form of early years provision is a learner with a right to equality of learning opportunities. Every child's educators, therefore, have the responsibility of observing, assessing, understanding, and so extending that learning.

What do we observe and assess?
Children, and everything they do: exploring, discovering, puzzling, dreaming, struggling with the world, taking their place in it, and making their mark on it.

How do we set about observing and assessing young children?
All early childhood educators already use observation as an integral part of their daily work. The implicit, covert skills of these acts of observing can be developed, and made more explicit: the fruits of observation can be stated more confidently as we learn to record, examine, reflect and act upon the knowledge we gain through observation and assessment.

The UK government requires that all children are assessed from the age of 5. Decisions have been made about 'what counts' as 'worthwhile' assessment and, in the process, what learning is worthy of assessment. Assessment must go further than this, it must incorporate some underpinning principles that guide educators in their assessment of children. The principles of assessment underpinning the work of Drummond and Nutbrown (1992, adapted from pp. 102–3) are summarized below.

- *Respect*: Assessment must be carried out with proper respect for the children themselves, for their parents, carers and educators.
- *Care and education ('educaré')*: The care and education of young children are inseparable. Quality care is educational and quality education is caring. In our assessment practice we will recognize little children learning to love one another, as well as learning to count.

- *The power of the educator*: Early years educators must first acknowledge their awesome power and, second, use it lovingly. The 'loving use of power' (Smail, 1984) in the assessment of young children is a central principle.
- *In the interests of children*: Assessment is a process that must enhance children's lives, their learning and development. Assessment must work for children.

Views of assessment depend upon decisions about what to assess, why it is assessed, who assesses and how and when to assess. Every educator needs to consider what a respectful assessment process might look like and how to assess young children's learning and development repectfully. Wolfendale's (1993) review of baseline assessment instruments is useful in this process of consideration and decision-making. The pack, *Making Assessment Work* (Drummond, Rouse and Pugh, 1992), helps educators to attend to emotional dimensions of assessment as well as philosophical, pedagogical and practical issues. The introduction to the section 'About Feelings' states (*ibid.*, p. 21):

> Helping children to have a sense of their own self worth, encouraging them to believe that they are special, capable, unique individuals, helping them to recognize and accept the importance of their feelings about themselves and other people; these are some of the most difficult and challenging tasks all early years educators undertake. And if we are to do these things effectively, we need to think carefully about children's emotional development, and about how their feelings are affected by our words and deeds – and feelings.

In making observations and assessments of children's development – cognitive, physical and affective educators make numerous decisions. If early education is, in the terms of the UN Convention, to enable every child to fulfil his or her potential, ways need to be found to identify strengths and to support developmental needs. Key questions need to be addressed: Whose knowledge is of most worth? Is it what adults know or can assessment value what children know and the sense they make of situations they encounter? Decisions about what counts as valid goals and outcomes need to be made, and along with this goes the question of who decides: educators, governments, employers, local education authorities, children, parents? The UK Prime Minister's decision to include responsibility for employment within the Department for Education in July 1995 suggested a policy position that education is for training and training is for work. It also indicated that education is about training to do a job, a narrower focus than a view of 'education for life' might suggest, or the broader notion of 'lifelong learning' debated by the Commission on Social Justice (1994). Such decisions can influence ideas of 'what counts' as learning and therefore what is worthy of assessment.

A language of assessment

Different educators talk in different ways using different words about their work. These discourses employ a variety of terms and assumptions.

Positive discourses about young children can include their abilities and their struggles to include themselves in the worlds of home, centre, community, that adults place them in. Other discourses take place in the media, in government, and where observers of, and participants in, early childhood issues continue their own discourses. Terminology chosen for each discourse can contribute significantly to the debate and may influence the climate in which the discourse takes place. As Michael Rosen (1994, p. 1) notes: 'We use the same word for the educational process as we do for horse racing – a course; a predetermined sequence of obstacles that will be negotiated by all participants; anyone falling will be eliminated; only the first three give returns on bets.'

Some participants in the discourse about education choose (or adopt) the language of battle and competition: 'orders', 'standards', 'levels', 'stages', 'targets', and so on. Others choose a language more fitting to 'cherishing the growth of the young', using terms like support, nurture, cherish, development, facilitation, opportunity. Language and common understanding of the terms we use are so important. Many early childhood teachers are already 'bilingual' in some professional settings where necessary, reading, recording and communicating in the imposed language of the National Curriculum and its assessment. At the same time they may work, think, worry and discuss with colleagues and parents in the language of early childhood, the language of *educaré* (Nutbrown, 1994a, 1994b). Conversations that value children's achievements and positive discourses in early childhood are impossible without words like development, exploration, facilitation, response, support, interest, investigation and growth.

What does respectful assessment look like?

Respectful assessment takes account of a range of factors and achievements, and values the participation of the person being assessed as well as the perspectives of those carrying out the assessment. It includes self-assessment and collaborative assessment as well as assessment of one person by someone else. There are examples of respectful assessment (Wolfendale, 1990; Barrs *et al.*, 1991; Bartholomew and Bruce, 1993; Whalley, 1994) where parents, children and their educators and carers work together to record achievement and progress and where such assessments contribute to planning further opportunities for learning.

Respecting Children's Early Achievements

If educators observe children carefully and thoughtfully with wide eyes and open minds they will be showing children the respect they deserve, both as people and as learners. A 6-month-old baby amazes her parents with the

tenacity with which she explores, how she uses every single second to find
out, enjoy, request, repeat, seek. She is learning, as any 6-month-old will
learn – demanding opportunities, challenging (noisily) some of the situations she finds herself in, seizing every moment – thinking about each
experience, concentrating on simple things: a toy, a finger, a collar of a silky
dressing gown, a spoon, a piece of banana, a reflection in a mirror, a sound,
an expression. Adults who respect children's early achievements make the
best educators, for they know that showing respect means accepting some
responsibility.

Responsibilities

The responsibilities which early child educators and carers must shoulder
in order to show respect for children's early achievements are considerable
(Drummond, 1993; Nutbrown, 1994a). People who work with young children must themselves continue to learn. If they do not continue to read,
discuss and to think, to keep up to date with current issues, with theory and
practice, they show a disrespect for the people they work with, the children
and their parents. Systems of funding and management that do not support
early childhood educators in furthering their own learning perpetuate
a disrespect for young children. There must be consideration of the
principles of observation and assessment and serious and continuous
efforts to put them into practice. In carrying out all these responsibilities,
wherever children are living and learning, ways need to be found to allow
children the time they need.

Allowing children time

Time is a precious and important commodity for all human beings and
most of us feel that time is remorselessly short. Technology developed to
enable us to accomplish things more quickly seems to have the effect of
requiring us to do more in a shorter time, and adults at home and at work
try to fit so many tasks into their day. But children have their own pace and
while, as adults, we pursue our own (and others') timescales and agendas
we need to be mindful of the need young children have to take *their* time.
Pausing to listen to an aeroplane in the sky, stopping to watch a ladybird on
a plant, sitting on a rock to watch the waves crash over the quayside –
children have their own agendas and timescales, as they find out more
about their world and make their place in it: they work hard not to let
adults hurry them and we need to heed their message.

Seizing the day and biding one's time

Gardeners don't plant runner beans in January to get an earlier harvest than
their neighbours; if they tried, they would probably get shrivelled and stunted

beans. They fertilise the ground in the early months of the year, so that when the beans are planted – at the right time – they will flourish.

(Oxfordshire County Council, 1991)

There is a sense of urgency about childhood – of hastening progress, of accelerating development. Is this born out of wanting the best for children or from some belief or value base which says the state of childhood is worth less than the state of adulthood and so we must do all we can to reach the day when childhood is over? Gabriela Mistral said:

> We are guilty of many errors and many faults, but our worse crime is abandoning the children, neglecting the fountain of life. Many of the things we need can wait. The child cannot. Right now is the time his bones are being formed, his blood is being made and his senses are being developed. To him we cannot answer 'Tomorrow'. His name is 'Today'.

This sense of urgency, the need to pay attention to children when they need it, can often become confused or be misinterpreted as the need to hasten progress. This is seen in the statutory age of schooling in the UK, where children must begin school at 5, and, even more worrying, in the current trend to admit 4-year-olds into school, endorsed by the decision of the UK government in July 1995 to issue vouchers to parents of 4-year-old children that can be used for a variety of forms of 'nursery education', including early entry into primary schools. To what extent is this plan made out of respect for children? Are its roots more securely embedded in financial and political motivations? These are questions which respectful educators – parents and professionals – would do well to ponder.

There is much truth in Mistral's words – for children it is *today* here, now, this minute that matters, but what we give them today must be made of the things *they need* today. Early intervention of the right kind at the right time bears dividends, but inappropriate intervention can cause harm. There is a mischievous mistruth in the belief that doing certain things early helps children to get ready for the next stage. The best way to help a child to get ready to be 5 is to let her be 3 when she is 3 and let him be 4 when he is 4, and to hold high expectations of what children in their first 48 months of life might achieve. The quality of experiences offered to children in their formative years are most important.

The Children Act 1989 (Department of Health, 1989) focused attention mainly on health and safety of premises and child protection, but it is equally important to nurture healthy minds, secure emotions, grounded personalities and build on children's capacity for quality thinking. Providing opportunities for healthy living and learning from birth to 5 is a way of seizing the day and biding one's time simultaneously – making the most of every moment as well as having patience and respect for the pace of childhood.

Respectful educators will strive to afford every child equality of opportunity. Not just children who are easy to work with, obliging, endearing, clean, pretty, articulate, capable, but *every* child – respecting them for who they are, respecting their language, their culture, their history, their family, their abilities, their needs, their name, their ways and their very essence. This means understanding children's needs and building on their abilities.

To build on children's abilities, adults with knowledge and expertise are needed

Adult knowledge is crucial to extending children's learning and essential if children's early achievements are to be recognized and respected. Gura (1992) demonstrated how being able to discuss children's brick constructions with the correct technical language – language of mathematics, architecture, art and aesthetics – was essential in building on children's abilities. The importance of assessing children's progress is acknowledged by the School Curriculum and Assessment Authority, which describes the following as a feature of good practice (1996, p. 6): 'Children's progress and future learning needs are assessed and recorded through frequent observation and are shared regularly with parents.' Adults' knowledge about children's learning must be derived from their informed observation of them and dialogue with them and their parents.

The UN Convention on the Rights of the Child and the assessment of children

With proper respect for children and childhood we can construct a curriculum for young children which, in the words of the UN Convention on the Rights of the Child, ensures that:

> Every child shall have the right to freedom of expression: this right shall include freedom to seek, receive and impart information and ideas of all kinds, regardless of frontiers, either orally, in writing or in print, in the form of art, or through any other media of the child's choice.
>
> (article 13)

We can then find effective ways of assessing children's progress within such a curriculum.

The assessment of children in their early years must also find ways to enact the rights of children to 'the development of the child's personality, talents and mental and physical abilities to their fullest potential' (article 29).

Our view of childhood, of education, and hence the ways we observe and assess their development, can be one which respects children and their early achievements if childhood is viewed as a time of growth to be valued for itself. As Hepworth said: 'Perhaps what one wants to say is formed in childhood and the rest of one's life is spent in trying to say it.'[1] Adults with expertise who respectfully watch children engaged in their process of living, learning, loving and being are in a better position to understand what it is these youngest citizens are trying to say and find ways of helping them to say it.

References

Athey, C. (1990) *Extending Thought in Young Children: A Parent–Teacher Partnership*, London: Paul Chapman Publishing.

Barrs, M., Ellis, S., Hester, H. and Thomas, A. (1991) *Pattern of Learning: The Primary Language Record and the National Curriculum*, London: Centre for Language in Primary Education.

Bartholomew, L. and Bruce, T. (1993) *Getting to Know You: A Guide to Record-Keeping in Early Childhood Education and Care*, London: Hodder and Stoughton.

Brierley, J. (1980) *Children's Well-Being: Growth, Development and Learning from Conception to Adolescence*, Slough: NFER.

Commission on Social Justice/Institute for Public Policy Research (1994) *Social Justice: Strategies for National Renewal*, London: Vintage.

Committee on the Rights of the Child (1995) *Consideration of Reports of State Parties: United Kingdom of Great Britain and Northern Ireland*, CRC/C/SR.205, January.

Department of Health (1989) *The Children Act*, London: HMSO.

Drummond, M. J. (1993) *Assessing Children's Learning*, London: David Fulton.

Drummond, M. J. and Nutbrown, C. (1992) Observing and assessing young children, in G. Pugh (ed.) *Contemporary Issues in the Early Years: Working Collaboratively for Children*, London: NCB/Paul Chapman Publishing.

Drummond, M. J., Rouse, D. and Pugh, G. (1992) *Making Assessment Work*, London: NCB/NES Arnold.

Gura, P. (ed.) (1992) *Exploring Learning: Young Children and Block-Play*, London: Paul Chapman Publishing.

Hannon, P., Weinberger, J. and Nutbrown, C. (1991) A study of ways of working with parents to promote early literacy development, *Research Papers in Education*, **6**(2), pp. 77–97.

Hill, E. (1980) *Where's Spot?*, London: Heinemann.

Newell, P. (1991) The UN Convention and Children's Rights in the UK, National Children's Bureau, London.

Nutbrown, C. (1994a) *Threads of Thinking: Young Children Learning and the Role of Early Education*, London: Paul Chapman Publishing.

Nutbrown, C. (1994b) Young children in educational establishments, in T. David (ed.) *Working Together for Young Children*, London: Routledge.

Oxfordshire County Council (1991) *Quality in Learning for Under Fives*, Oxford: Oxfordshire County Council.

Pugh, G. (ed.) (1992) *Contemporary Issues in the Early Years: Working Collaboratively for Children*, London: NCB/Paul Chapman Publishing.

Preschool Playgroups Associated (PPA) (1991) *What Children Learn in Playgroup: A PPA Curriculum*, London: PPA.

Rosen, M. (ed.) (1994) *The Penguin Book of Childhood*, London: Penguin.

School Curriculum and Assessment Authority (SCAA) (1996) *Nursery Education: Desirable Outcomes for Children's Learning on Entering Compulsory Education*, London: SCAA and DFEE.

Vygotsky, L. S. (1978) *Mind in Society: The Development of Higher Level Psychological Processes*, Cambridge, MA: Harvard University Press.
Whalley, M. (1994) *Learning to be Strong*, London: Hodder and Stoughton.
Williams, V. (1991) *Boxed In*, London: Red Fox.
Wolfendale, S. (1990) *All About Me*, London: NES, Arnold.

Section 4: Cultural Capital and Learning

The final part of this reader returns to the earlier discussion about democratic participation in education. In particular this section highlights the importance of pupils and parents contributing to, and having a voice in, debates about education. Parental rights and choices are a consideration in the measurement of school and teacher accountability. It is through parents' perceptions of a school's effectiveness that popular schools remain competitive and others decline. On the other hand the significance of parental roles to the successful learning of their children is increasingly being recognized. This would encompass learning in school and out; in cognitive, social, cultural and emotional domains. Moreover, as other chapters have indicated, within constructivist views of learning children's perceptions are an essential part of the learning and assessment process.

The ideological clashes which could occur in linking home and school can only be avoided by giving due consideration to the complex and controversial dimensions of what partnership is, what purposes it serves and how it is to be established and maintained. Positive but unquestioning and uncritical assumptions about the 'right relationship' between the partners in this relationship will not serve either party well. Schools are the crucible in which children's personalities are forged and identities confirmed. What this means for us as educators is that issues of politics, social class, gender, sexuality and racism as well as achievement should all form part of the agenda.

Taken together the chapters in this section:

- examine the effect of a testing regime on the learners' self-perceptions
- consider the formation of academic and social identity of learners
- explore the notion of home–school partnerships
- examine issues of cultural capital within home–school relationships
- consider the ways in which the interests of certain groups work against the interests of others.

In Chapter 12, Diane Reay and Dylan Wiliam examine a dimension of assessment which is often overlooked, namely, the effect of assessment on the learners in terms of their experience of the assessment process, of the judgements made about them and their perceptions of themselves as learners. Drawing on interviews and observations, Reay and Wiliam identify how the processes of categorization and consignment affect not only the children at an immediate and personal level, but also the pedagogical decision-making of teachers and the curriculum that is offered to children. In this chapter the links between testing, teaching and driving up standards are clearly visible, exposing the extent of the pressure not only on the belief systems of the teachers but on the children's perceptions of themselves. For the children and their teachers, as their voices testify, these are testing times.

In Chapter 13, Andrew Pollard and Ann Filer also highlight the need to consider the views of children and to pay heed to the factors which influence self-perception and identity. Developing a recurring theme in this book, Pollard and Filer emphasize the importance of social relationships in both learning and in the formation of identity. Drawing on longitudinal case study data of one child, they show how William shaped, maintained and changed his social and academic identity through changing structures, expectations and teacher perceptions of successive classroom contexts. It is important to remember that the models of 'learning, identity and social setting' and 'dynamics of strategic action' presented in this chapter were originally constructed as part of a much larger longitudinal studies.

In Chapter 14, Sally Tomlinson turns her attention to issues related to home–school partnerships. She begins her chapter with an overview of the history of home–school contacts. This reveals that up until the 1970s home–school contacts were never a large priority in English education. Moreover, discrimination and repression of some parent groups have always featured as part of the debate. For example, the literature discussing the relationship between school attainment, personal and social behaviour has, Tomlinson would argue, always worked to the disadvantage of working-class homes and parents. The four stages of progression in the growth of home–school partnerships provides a useful framework for those wishing to establish and maintain more equitable and democratic links between home and school.

In Chapter 15, Carol Vincent develops and expands issues raised in the previous chapter by giving further consideration to the way in which relationships between parents and teachers, homes and schools are presented in the literature. She argues that much of the home–school literature lacks a critical appproach particularly with regard to class, gender or ethnic-based differences. The aim of this chapter is to rectify this omission by highlighting, with reference to two schools, some of the salient ways in which ethnicity, class and gender affect home–school relationships. The chapter concludes that a focus on such issues is an integral part of an analytical approach to researching and debating home–school relations.

12

'I'll Be A Nothing': Structure, Agency and the Construction of Identity through Assessment

Diane Reay and Dylan Wiliam

The primary purpose of the 1988 Education Reform Act was to create an educational 'market' that, it was assumed by its proponents, would increase standards of performance in schools. Freeing schools from the homogenizing effects that local education authorities were believed to exert would create a diversity of provision, allowing parents, who were generally viewed as the 'consumers' of education (rather than, say, students, or the wider community), to choose schools that reflected their aspirations and wishes. Popular schools would expand, and those that were not, would have to improve or, if they could not, would close. However, in order to allow the market to function 'efficiently', it was necessary to create an index of performance. The national school-leaving examination (the General Certificate of Secondary Education) provided such an index for students at age 16, but of course would provide no information about the performance of students in primary schools. The solution enacted in the Education Reform Act was the creation of a National Curriculum for all students of compulsory school age in England and Wales, with national assessments for all 7-, 11- and 14-year-olds, the results of which, at least for 11- and 14-year-olds, were to be published for each school.

Although it was claimed that these results would also be useful for informing parents of the academic progress of their children, the information on the attainment of 7-, 11- and 14-year-olds is not available until June or July, and is therefore far too late to influence choices of junior or secondary schools, or of subject options in upper secondary school. The primary purpose of National Curriculum assessment is to provide information on the performance of schools, rather than individuals, in order to inform parental choice (Daugherty, 1995).

Since the development and implementation of the National Curriculum, however, it has become clear that parents and students have not relied exclusively, or even primarily, on aggregate measures of the academic achievement of students in selecting schools, as might have been hoped for by the proponents of the Education Reform Act (see, for example, Gewirtz, Ball and Bowe, 1995). A range of other factors, such as the appropriateness of the school for the individual child, are also taken into account.

More recently, however, the pressure on schools to improve their students' performance on National Curriculum tests and in national examinations has been increased by the use of aggregate measures of student performance in the national system of school inspections. The original report of the National Curriculum Task Group on Assessment and Testing (1988) proposed a system of reporting National Curriculum assessment results that would allow the *increase* in students' attainment over a period of schooling (the so-called 'value added') to be reported alongside any absolute measures of achievement. Despite the considerable technical difficulties in agreeing an operational definition of 'value added' (Wiliam, 1992; Jesson, 1996), it is government policy that such value-added measures of achievement should be published alongside absolute measures of students' academic performance.

In view of this, the insistence of Her Majesty's Chief Inspector of Schools (Office for Standards in Education, 1997) that inspections of schools take into account absolute levels of achievement in schools, irrespective of the students' prior attainment, seems rather perverse. While it cannot be denied that there are considerable variations in the academic success of schools drawing students from similar cultural and socio-economic backgrounds, to subject a school to 'special measures' (the preliminary stage of a process that can result in the school being closed) because its students arrive at the school with lower attainment than might be expected for their age is clearly unjust. More importantly for the purpose of the present study, it creates a situation in which schools, particularly those in socio-economically disadvantaged areas, are under pressure to increase the *indices* of performance (e.g., the proportion of students achieving a given level in the National Curriculum tests) at almost any price.

The effects of such 'top-down' attempts to improve educational provision on teachers and on school communities have been the subject of extensive studies (see, for example, Corbett and Wilson, 1991), but apart from the work of Rudduck, Chaplain and Wallance (1995) with secondary school students and that of Andrew Pollard and his colleagues with primary pupils (Pollard with Filer, 1996; Pollard, Thiessen and Filer, 1997), there is virtually no literature which engages with students' perspectives. Rather, it is in the silences in relation to children's perspectives that it is assumed either that National Curriculum assessments have minimal impact on children's subjectivities or that children's concerns and attitudes are merely a backdrop to the assessment process; simply part of the social context. On the one hand the interplay between the assessment process and children's identities and identifications is not considered an important area for research and theoretical consideration, while on the other hand children are subsumed as a means to an end within a process which is primarily an exercise in evaluating schools and teachers. However, despite the former assumption that their agency is unaffected by the assessments and the latter assumption that they are passively caught up in a process where the main focus is teachers and the institution, children are simultaneously active in the assessment process and profoundly affected by it.

The research study

Patricia Broadfoot describes the assessment arrangements for National Curriculum assessment as an example of the ways in which apparently benign and rational techniques of assessment are currently being used to impose norms by reducing value debates to technical questions (Broadfoot, 1996). However, the consequences of the new assessment system for pupils have been overlooked in much of the research which examines changes in assessment. This small-scale study attempts to highlight the importance of considering children's perspectives on assessment if we are to glimpse the extent to which new subjectivities are being constructed in the primary classroom. Although the research project extended over the full school year from September 1997 until July 1998, this chapter draws on empirical data gathered over the Easter term 1998 to provide some preliminary indications of the impact of National Curriculum assessment on year 6 (age 10–11) students' self-definitions as learners.

The focus of this chapter is a class of 20 students in Windermere School – a south London primary school serving a predominantly working-class, ethnically mixed community, and whose students typically achieve levels slightly below the national average. Initially, all the students were interviewed in focus groups and half the class were then interviewed individually about their attitudes towards, and feelings about, impending National Curriculum tests. Additionally, both the children and their class teacher were observed over the term as increasing amounts of time were devoted to test preparation. The themes generated through focus group discussions were strongly supported both in individual interviews and by the data collected through participant observation.

The SATs: Shifting Identifications as Learners

Hannah: I'm really scared about the SATs [standard assessment tasks]. Mrs O'Brien [a teacher at the school] came and talked to us about our spelling and I'm no good at spelling and David [the class teacher] is giving us times tables tests every morning and I'm hopeless at times tables so I'm frightened I'll do the SATs and I'll be a nothing.

Diane: I don't understand Hannah. You can't be a nothing.

Hannah: Yes, you can 'cause you have to get a level like a level 4 or a level 5 and if you're no good at spellings and times tables you don't get those levels and so you're a nothing.

Diane: I'm sure that's not right.
Hannah: Yes it is 'cause that's what Mrs O'Brien was saying.

This is a particularly stark example but it exemplifies some of the ways in which children's identifications as learners (Skeggs, 1997) are constructed through the assessment process. For Hannah what constitutes academic success is correct spelling and knowing your times tables. She is an accomplished writer, a gifted dancer and artist and good at problem-solving yet none of those skills makes her somebody in her own eyes. Instead she constructs herself as a failure, an academic non-person, by a metonymic shift in which she comes to see herself entirely in terms of the level to which her performance in the SATs is ascribed. Although Windermere School had a general policy of playing down the importance of SATs, Hannah's teacher, in his second year of teaching, was still feeling under intense external pressure to ensure his pupils do well. As is apparent in the following quotation, the fever pitch in the classroom surrounding the impending SATs is generated in no small part by his anxieties:

> I was appalled by how most of you did on the science test. You don't know anything. I want to say that you are judged at the end of the day by what you get in the SATs and some of you won't even get level 2.

Some children resist and challenge such all-embracing assignments; for example, Terry was outraged by his teacher's comment and shouted out, 'Hold on we're not that bad'. However, others, like Hannah, appear to accept and internalize its strictures.

Hannah's account underscores the extent to which SATs have set in motion a new set of tensions with which year 6 students are expected to cope. As the quotations presented later indicate, all the children, apart from Terry, expressed varying degrees of anxiety about failure. While there is a gender dimension to this anxiety in that girls expressed higher degrees of anxiety than boys (see also Shaw, 1995), the overall impression from the year 6 interviews was that most pupils of both sexes took the SATs very seriously. They wanted to do well. At the same time, children expressed a great deal of concern about the narrow focus of the SATs and not being able to produce their best under strict (and unfamiliar) test conditions. Their concerns seem to be borne out by research into the validity of the Key Stage 2 English SATs:

> Nicely rounded handwriting and reasonable spelling of fairly simple words seemed to impress some markers favourably. In contrast, idiosyncratic or jerky handwriting with insecure spellings seemed to prejudice some markers against the content.

> (Close, Furlong and Simon, 1997, p. 4.30)

The students also seemed very aware of the (not-so) hidden agenda surrounding SATs:

Mary: SATs are about how good the teachers have been teaching you and if everybody gets really low marks they think the teachers haven't been teaching you properly.

and:

> *Diane*:   So what are the SATs for?
> *Jackie*: To see if the teachers have taught us anything.
> *Terry*:   If we don't know nothing then the teacher will get all the blame.
> *Jackie*: Yeah. It's the teacher's fault.
> *Tunde*:   Yeah. They get blamed.

Yet, despite frequent rationalizations that SATs were primarily judgements of teaching, nearly all the children indicated a sense of unease and feelings of discomfort about what SATs might reveal about themselves as learners. Some of the children seemed to be indicating far-reaching consequences in which good SATs results were linked to positive life prospects and, concomitantly, poor results meant future failures and hardships:

> *Sharon*: I think I'll get a two, only Stuart will get a six.
> *Diane*:   So if Stuart gets a six what will that say about him?
> *Sharon*: He's heading for a good job and a good life and it shows he's not gonna be living on the streets and stuff like that.
> *Diane*:   And if you get a level two what will that say about you?
> *Sharon*: Um, I might not have a good life in front of me and I might grow up and do something naughty or something like that.

In three of the focus group sessions the children drew on an apocalyptic tale of 'the boy who ruined his chances'. There follows an excerpt from the girls' focus group, but both the boys' and the mixed group referred to the same example in order to exemplify how things can go terribly wrong in the SATs if you don't make the right choices:

> *Norma*:   There was someone so good at writing stories . . .
> *Mary*:   Yeah, and he wrote a leaflet . . .
> *Norma*:   He picked to write a leaflet and then when he wrote the leaflet he blew it.
> *Lily*:   He just ruined his whole SAT. He ruined it. If he'd written the story he would have got a really good mark. He was the best at writing stories. And he thought he wanted to try it out . . . and he just ruined it for himself.
> *Norma*:   Mrs O'Brien said that he was . . . what was the word, kind of scared thing . . . ?
> *Diane*:   Got in a panic.
> *Norma*:   Yeah, and he didn't do the story because he thought he would get that wrong.
> *Mary*:   So he did the leaflet and he just ruined his chances, totally ruined his chances.

In this excerpt and the others, performance in SATs is about far more than simply getting a test right or wrong, it is conflated in the children's minds with future prospects. To perform badly is 'to ruin one's chances'. At other times there was far more disputation and contention about the importance of SATs for future prospects:

> *Diane*:   So are they important, SATs?
> *Lily*:   Depends.
> *Tunde*:   Yes.

Terry: No, definitely not.
Lewis: It does affect your life.
Ayse: Yeah, it does affect your life.
Terry: No, as if it means you know I do badly then that means I'm gonna be a road sweeper.

However, while Terry is clear that SATs have no impact on future prospects, other students lack his certainty:

Diane: You mean, you think that if you do badly in SATs then you won't be able to do well or get good jobs?
Jackie: Yeah, 'cause that's what David's saying.
Diane: What is he saying?
Jackie: He's saying if we don't like, get good things, in our SATS, when we grow up we are not gonna get good jobs and . . .
Terry: Be plumbers and road-sweepers . . .
Tunde: But what if you wanted to do that?
Diane: Instead of what?
Terry: Footballers, singers, vets, archaeologists. We ain't gonna be nothing like that if we don't get high levels.
Diane: And does that worry you about your future?
Jackie: Yeah.
Lewis: Yeah.
Ayse: Yeah it worries me a lot.
Terry: No, because he's telling fibs.

Assessment in English schooling in the late 1990s is surrounded by controversy and disputation (Black, 1998). It has become a political football. Yet, despite heavily contested changes there are enduring continuities. Students have always informally assessed their own academic performance and that of their peers. Class 6S is no different. There is unanimous agreement among the children that Stuart is the cleverest child in the class and almost unanimous agreement that Peter is the second cleverest:

Norma: Stuart is the cleverest child in the whole school. He'll get level 6 for everything.

In this short excerpt cleverness is very clearly conflated with doing well in the SATs. There is an assumption of causation; being clever automatically leads to good SAT results. Yet, later on Norma talks about her own nervousness and how that might affect her own performance in the same tests:

Norma: I'm no good at tests. I get too nervous so I know I won't do very well.

Patricia Broadfoot writes of the elements of panoptic surveillance embedded in assessment processes whereby pupils learn to judge themselves 'as if some external eye was constantly monitoring their performance' (Broadfoot, 1996, p. 68), encouraging the internalization of the evaluative criteria of those in power.

> Because the commitment to technical efficiency is increasingly being incorporated at the level of meaning and volition, as well as that of practice, this provides pressure for the non-bureaucratic, potentially contradictory languages of professionalism and democratic participation to define their own criteria of value and, hence, personal accountability in the same terms.
>
> (Broadfoot, 1996, pp. 239–40).

One result is a strong pressure on both pupils and teachers to assume that value can be quantified.

> Belief systems concerning the individual should not be construed as inhabiting a diffuse field of 'culture', but as embodied in institutional and technical practices – through which forms of individuality are specified and governed. The history of the self should be written at this 'technological' level, in terms of the techniques and evaluations for developing, evaluating, perfecting, managing the self, the way it is rendered into words, made visible, inspected, judged and reformed.
>
> (Rose, 1989, p. 218).

The battle over assessment and the triumph of publishable, measurement-based, competitive, pencil and paper tests over diagnostic, open-ended, process-oriented assessments has resulted in the establishment of assessment procedures which operate primarily 'as performance indicators of teacher effectivity' (Ball, 1994, p. 41). At the macro-level SATs can be seen as regulatory mechanisms that link the conduct of individuals and organizations to political objectives; the assumption being that they will impact powerfully on teachers' subjectivities and practices. However, as the children's discussions quoted earlier illustrate, at the micro-level of the classroom there are regular glimpses of the normalizing and regulatory function of the SATs on children.

Perhaps Tracey provides the best example of 'the governance of the soul' (Rose, 1989).

> *Tracey*: I think even now, at night times I think about it and I think I'm going to get them.
> *Diane*: You think about your SATs at night time?
> *Tracey*: Yeah, lots. When I'm in bed, because I've got stars on my ceiling, I'm hoping and I look up and I go, 'I know I'm gonna get there'. And my mum goes, 'Who's talking in there?' And I goes, 'Nothing mum'.
> *Diane*: So what are you hoping?
> *Tracey*: Um, I think about a three. I dunno. I don't think I'll get a five. I'm hoping to get a five. When I look at the stars I hope I'll get a five.

Allan Hanson writes about the increasing disposition of American students to define themselves in terms of test scores, citing an example of college students who displayed their scores on the Scholastic Aptitude Test on their T-shirts (Hanson, 1993). While we are not suggesting that processes of quantifying academic ability were anything like as extreme as Hanson found in some American colleges, there were disturbing shifts in how children viewed themselves and others, which could be attributed to the assessment process and the ways in which the classroom pedagogy transformed in response to the imminence of the SATs.

Assessment procedures are implicated in technologies of the self and the struggle to gain 'intimate and secure' social relations – intimate because they feed into the ordering of subjectivity, and secure because of the apparent naturalness of the categories they generate (Donald, 1985). As the term progressed children increasingly referred to the levels they expected themselves and others to achieve. Their talk raises concerns about the crudeness of the assessments to which pupils have access. The SATs levels constitute very simplistic judgements purged of any subtlety and complexity about the sort of learners pupils are judged to be.

Children's Emotional Responses to Assessment

As is evident throughout the children's texts cited earlier, there are strong currents of fear and anxiety permeating children's relationships to the SATs process:

> *Tunde*: Because if you get too scared or something, or paranoid, or something it kind of stops you from doing it, because you just think you are going to get everything wrong and it's easy to get paranoid about the SATs.

and:

> *Diane*: Norma, why are you worried about SATs now?
> *Norma*: Well, it seems like I'll get no points or I won't be able to do it, too hard or something.
> *Diane*: What would it mean to get no points?
> *Norma*: Well instead of being level three I'll be a nothing and do badly – very badly.
> *Diane*: What makes you think that? Have you been practising?
> *Norma*: No, like I analyse . . . I know I worry about loads of things.
> *Diane*: Like what?
> *Norma*: I don't know, I just worry about things and my mum is going to take me to a special aromatherapy lady, or something like that. I don't know, but she said something about that because I am always panicking and I've been worrying about when it's SATs.
> *Diane*: But no one was mentioning SATs last term, were they? What's made everybody start worrying about it now?
> *Norma*: Mrs O'Brien came in today and she was doing language and she said loads of things, well not language, but dictionaries and she said loads of things about SATs.
> *Diane*: And you got in a panic.
> *Norma*: [Laughing] Well, not in a big panic, it was just like, what if I get stuck here and I don't finish the story and I don't get any points or things like that.

and:

> *Stuart*: What if I get level one?
> *Diane*: You won't get level one. Honestly, I'm quite positive you won't get level one.
> *Stuart*: I might in English, since Mrs O'Brien told us about that boy messing up his chances I've been worried about it 'cause it's the sort of thing I could do.

After children have marked each others' practice mathematics SATs there is the ritual recounting of marks. Nadia, Mary, Jessica, Terry, Peter and Lewis have all got 20 but a big commotion breaks out when the others realize Stuart has only got 16. Peter says, 'God did you really only get 16?' Simon tells him, 'Your brain must have stopped working', while Lewis comments, 'He's lost his genius man'. Stuart rather forlornly comments, 'At this rate I'm only going to get level one for maths'. As these excerpts indicate, the negative emotions generated by the impending SATs and a changing classroom curriculum affected all the children, regardless of ability levels.

Impact on Pedagogy and the Curriculum on Offer

Many studies have examined the consequences of high-stakes assessment systems on the breadth of curriculum that students experience (see, for example, Kellaghan, Madaus and Airasian, 1982). However, almost all of these studies have taken an 'outsider's' perspective on curricular changes. Even where studies have attempted to work from an 'insider's' perspective, it has been assumed that the students themselves have little to contribute on this aspect of the social consequences of test use (Messick, 1980). However, the evidence from the current study is that students as young as 11 have very clear perceptions about the influence of external assessment on the curriculum:

> *Jackie*:   We've already had SATs. We've been doing them for so long, all the old papers we must have done, we must have done three SATs already.

A narrowing of the curriculum was very evident in 6S over the spring term and was a cause of both complaint and regret among the children:

> *Lewis*:   I wish we did technology.
> *Jackie*:   Yeah, that would be good.
> *Tunde*:   We should do more dance. We should have dance in the SATs.
> *Terry*:   And they never teach you anything about cavemen either.
> *Ayse*:   And we don't do history any more.
> *Terry*   All I know is because I've read about it on my own.
> *Ayse*:   And we don't do geography. Only science, language and maths. Just over and over again.
> *Diane*:   So is the curriculum very different this term to what it was last term?
> *Terry*:   Yeah.
> *Jackie*:   Last year we done music and dance, interesting things.
> *Terry*:   The best thing we did is PE. And last week was the best session we've had in ages 'cause it was something different. And I hate football and it was football but it was the best session we done in ages.

But it was the emphasis on more individualized, competitive ways of working, which were increasingly displacing the mutually supportive, collaborative group work to which the children were accustomed – a shift from a 'communitarian climate' to 'academic press' (Phillips, 1997) – that caused the most disquiet:

> *Tunde*:   Peter helped me, Peter and Lewis.
> *Terry*:   But we're not allowed to help, to help anyone, they're all on your own.

Jackie: Yeah, but we're used to helping each other.
Lewis: I still help people.
Jackie: So do I.
Ayse: I didn't get no help.
Terry: We're not allowed to help any more. It's cheating.

Progressive primary schools like Windermere have not traditionally been subject to processes of overt differentiation and polarization (Lacey, 1970). Such processes have normally been found in selective secondary schools where streaming and setting are common practice. However, there were indications of both increasing differentiation and polarization in the class under study (6S), with negative repercussions for both teacher–pupil and pupil–pupil interaction. Webb (1993) suggests that the Key Stage 2 teachers in her study appeared to be altering both their curriculum and pedagogic strategies as a result of the pressures exerted by OFSTED and the new assessment regimes and this also seemed to be the case in 6S.

Over the course of the spring term 1998 the researcher spent 60 hours observing teaching and learning processes in the classroom and also amassed extensive field notes documenting both changing pedagogic approaches and the children's responses to them. During this period there were innumerable mundane examples of overt academic differentiation as a direct consequence of the teacher's increasing preoccupation with SATs. Concomitantly, there were many examples within the peer group of the deepening of existing divisions, as well as the opening up of new divisions based on academic rather than social criteria as a direct result of SATs and SATs practice, of which the two examples described next are only the most stark.

In March 1998 the children were working their way individually through an old science SATs paper. Fumi had protested at the beginning of the session when told the children were expected to work on their own, telling the teacher, 'But we're used to working together'. Every few minutes she would sigh audibly until eventually the teacher came across to where she was sitting and proceeded to put lines through a number of the SATs questions, commenting, 'Don't try and do these. They'll be too difficult for you. Answer the easy ones.' Fumi struggled on for a few more minutes. It was clear to the researcher and the children sitting near her that she was crying. After a few more minutes she got to her feet, pushing her chair out of the way and stormed out the classroom, sobbing. Out in the corridor she kept on repeating over and over again 'He thinks I'm thick. He thinks I'm thick. He wants all the others to think I'm thick.' As we have discussed earlier, children did engage in informal assessments of each others' academic ability, but prior to the SATs such processes had a benign air and had never resulted in confrontations between either the teacher and a student or between students. Even when Fumi was eventually coaxed back into the classroom she was openly rebellious, scribbling all over the SATs paper and muttering 'I hate you' under her breath at the teacher – behaviour which resulted in her missing her playtime.

Equally worrying was the consequence of regular SATs practice for Stuart's positioning within the peer group. In earlier interview sessions, carried out over the autumn term, children often compared themselves academically to Stuart, citing him as the cleverest child in the class. Such comments were presented simply as statements of fact and there was no malice or ill-feeling expressed. However, towards the end of the Easter term, with a programme of daily mathematics tests and regular science and English SATs practice, Stuart's situation among the peer group, particularly with the other boys, was becoming increasingly vulnerable. On one occasion, after the teacher had pointed out that Stuart was the only child to get 20 out of 20 for the mathematics test and that everybody else must try to do better, Terry leaned over and thumped him hard in the back. Twice Stuart came back from playtime with scratches either to his cheek or the back of his neck. He was not sure 'exactly who was responsible' but complained that the other boys had started to 'gang up' on him. The language other children used to describe him shifted discernibly. Before he had simply been recognized as clever; now he was increasingly labelled as 'a swot' by both girls and boys. There are frequent entries in the field notes which testify to a growing climate of hostility towards Stuart. For example:

Jolene: I hate Stuart, he's just a teacher's pet – a spotty swotty . . .

and:

Alice: Stuart's such a clever clogs that's why no one likes him.
Diane: But you said you liked him.
Alice: That's before he started showing off.

But Stuart had not started to show off. Rather, the classroom practices in 6S over the spring term had dramatically increased processes of differentiation, which in turn had led to a growing polarization among the peer group. In particular, the relationship between Stuart and the rest of 6S noticeably worsened.

Conclusion

While we make no claims that the shifts in both the children's self-perceptions and the teaching regime in 6S over the course of the term are representative of all year 6 classrooms, we would argue that what our evidence does indicate is a need for further investigation to map out the extent to which both pupil and teacher identities and practices are being modified through new assessment processes. We believe that the data that we have presented here provide convincing evidence that students as young as 10 or 11 are well aware of the effects of National Curriculum assessments, and their voices are an important part of any picture of the social consequences of the use of test results as measures of educational effectiveness.

The threat to the continued existence of a school posed by poor SATs results creates a situation in which individual teachers are under increasing pressure to improve the scores achieved by the students, *irrespective of the consequences for students' achievement in wider terms*. For some, this may be exactly what was intended. By asserting that National Curriculum assessments embody all that is valid, the narrowing of the experiences of students to just those aspects that can be assessed in a one-hour written test represent a return to the certainties of the 'curriculum of the dead' (Ball, 1993). However, it seems to us far more likely that for most observers, this narrowing of the focus of assessment, together with an emphasis on achieving the highest scores possible, produces a situation in which unjustifiable educational practices are not only possible, but encouraged. Whether 'teaching to the test' in this way is regarded as cheating or not is open to question (Smith, 1991), but there is no doubt that such activities rob National Curriculum assessments of the power to say anything useful about what the students have learnt. The more specific the government is about what it is that schools are to achieve, the more likely it is to get it, but the less likely it is to mean anything.

The teacher of the class we have been describing is relatively inexperienced, and therefore, perhaps, less able to resist the pressure to concentrate on the narrow range of achievements assessed in the SATs. However, as the government's new requirements on schools to set targets for aggregate school and individual achievement increases pressure on schools to improve measured performance, it seems more than likely that students will be inscribed into school practices entirely in terms of their ability to contribute to the school's target for the proportion of students achieving specified levels in the national curriculum assessments.

References

Ball, S. J. (1993) Education, Majorism and the 'curriculum of the dead', *Curriculum Studies*, **1**, pp. 195–214.

Ball, S. J. (1994) *Education Reform: A Critical and Post-Structural Approach*, Buckingham: Open University Press.

Black, P. J. (1998) *Testing: Friend or Foe? The Theory and Practice of Assessment and Testing*, London: Falmer Press.

Broadfoot, P. M. (1996) *Education, Assessment and Society: A Sociological Analysis*, Buckingham: Open University Press.

Close, G. S., Furlong, T. and Simon, S. A. (1997) *The Validity of the 1996 Key Stage 2 Tests in English, Mathematics and Science*, report prepared for Association of Teachers and Lecturers, London: King's College, London School of Education.

Corbett, H. D. and Wilson, B. L. (1991) *Testing, Reform and Rebellion*, Hillsdale, NJ: Ablex.

Daugherty, R. (1995) *National Curriculum Assessment: A Review of Policy 1987–1994*, London: Falmer Press.

Donald, J. (1985) Beacons of the future: schooling, subjection and subjectification, in V. Beechey and J. Donald (eds) *Subjectivity and Social Relations*, Milton Keynes: Open University Press.

Gewirtz, S., Ball, S. J. and Bowe, R. (1995) *Markets, Choice and Equity in Education*, Buckingham: Open University Press.

Hanson, F. A. (1993) *Testing Testing: Social Consequences of the Examined Life*, Berkeley, CA: University of California Press.

Jesson, D. (1996) *Value Added Measures of School Performance*, London: Department for Education and Employment.

Kellaghan, T., Madaus, G. F. and Airasian, P. W. (1982) *The Effects of Standardized Testing*, Boston, MA: Kluwer.

Lacey, C. (1970) *Hightown Grammar: The School as a Social System*, Manchester: Manchester University Press.

Messick, S. (1980) Test validity and the ethics of assessment. *American Psychologist*, **35**, pp. 1012–27.

National Curriculum Task Group on Assessment and Testing (1988) *A Report*, London: Department of Education and Science.

Office for Standards in Education (1997) *Annual Report of Her Majesty's Chief Inspector of Schools*, London: Her Majesty's Stationery Office.

Phillips, M. (1997) What makes a school effective? A comparison of the relationship of communitarian climate and academic climate to mathematics achievement and attendance during middle school, *American Educational Research Journal*, **34**, pp. 633–62.

Pollard, A. with Filer, A. (1996) *The Social World of Children's Learning: Case Studies of Pupils from Four to Seven*, London: Cassell.

Pollard, A., Thiessen, D. and Filer, A. (eds) (1997) *Children and their Curriculum: The Perspectives of Primary and Elementary School Pupils*, London: Falmer Press.

Rose, N. (1989) *Governing the Soul: The Shaping of the Private Self*, London: Routledge.

Rudduck, J., Chaplain, R. and Wallance, G. (1995) *School Improvement: What Can Pupils Tell Us?* London: David Fulton.

Shaw, J. (1995) *Education, Gender and Anxiety*, London: Taylor and Francis.

Skeggs, B. (1997) *Formations of Class and Gender: Becoming Respectable*, London: Sage.

Smith, M. L. (1991) Meanings of test preparation, *American Educational Research Journal*, **28**, pp. 521–42.

Webb, R. (1993) *Eating the Elephant Bit by Bit: The National Curriculum at Key Stage 2*, final report of research commissioned by the Association of Teachers and Lecturers (ATL), London: ATL Publishers.

Wiliam, D. (1992) Value-added attacks? Technical issues in publishing National Curriculum assessments, *British Educational Research Journal*, **18**, pp. 329–41.

13

Learning and Pupil Career in a Primary School: the Case of William

Andrew Pollard and Ann Filer

This chapter draws on a pair of longitudinal ethnographies known as the Identity and Learning Programme (ILP) (Pollard and Filer, 1987–2001). The ILP is concerned with tracking the learning, identity and pupil careers of two cohorts of children, from very different socio-economic communities, through their primary and secondary schools. This chapter relates to the primary phase of the project and to Greenside School, situated in the more affluent and middle class of our two sample communities. It presents theoretical models which illustrate the recursive and dynamic nature of pupils' learning and strategic action in response to successive classroom contexts. Drawing on case study data relating to the home, classroom and playground life of one child, William, this account shows how he shaped and maintained his academic and social identity through changing structures, expectations and teacher perceptions of successive classroom contexts. We use this case to illustrate the analytic models we have constructed. Unavoidably, the account is highly condensed and a more complete account can be found in Pollard and Filer (1999).

Social Relationships, Learning and the Case of William

Figures 13.1, 13.2 and 13.3 are matrices compiled from data collected for William. The matrices enable an overview of his career, assisting the process of analysis and the creation of William's story. Data relating to the contexts of home and family relationships, the playground and peer relationships and the classroom and teacher relationships, for each year of the study, are organized in the first three columns respectively. A summary analysis for each year can be found under the headings of 'Identity' and 'Career' in the right-hand columns.

In the following we use the case of William to illustrate a simplified representation of a model of learning, identity and social setting (Figure 13.4). Clearly this model (and the more complex one from which it derives) was constructed from a huge amount of data relating to other children as well as to William.

Relationships	Peer group relationships	Teacher relationships	Identity	Career
		Reception: Mrs Powell		
William has a sister Abigail who is three years younger. His parents have strong Christian convictions. Parents try to avoid putting pressure to succeed on children. Mother taught William to read before school. He sometimes withdraws from situations he does not grasp immediately.	William's parents worry that he may be vulnerable to peer pressure. He is popular and willing to lead or follow others. Some clashes with best friend Richard. Both are 'strong personalities' their teacher says. Picks up definite ideas about appropriate gender behaviour at school. Likes to get the class laughing.	Structural position: among the oldest few. Ma & Eng, ½ way down class. Entered school full of confidence. 'Played' for the first term with no concentration on work. Minimalist approach to writing and rushes through artistic-creative tasks. 'Doesn't see why anyone should tell him what to do'.	Confidence high, though not predictably so. Popular with adults and children. Teacher sees him as 'Nice' 'Silly' 'A bit tough' 'Strong willed'. Difficult to discipline. Liked to create laughter in the classroom. Consciously beginning to shape and articulate a positive self-image as a pupil.	Considerable ability and enthusiasms contrasted with frequently minimalistic approach to tasks and withdrawal. Strives for autonomy in teacher–pupil relationship. Concerned to avoid trouble with his teacher. Attains status in the peer group.
		Year 1: Miss Scott		
Parents concerned over William's progress. Reassured by Miss Scott. Some complaints from William about school and his teacher shouting. Mother explains teacher's 'moods' and is satisfied he can handle the relationship. Showing increased 'stickability' at home. Occasional 'flare ups' between William and Abigail.	Richard and Stephen are his best friends. Complaints at home about girls at school being 'bossy', but he relates well to them. William's friends are not so astute at disengaging from trouble as he is.	Structural position: age, ½ way down class. Ma & Eng, about ½ way down. William says writing is 'boring' but maths is 'brilliant' because of trying to get onto different stages. Often distracted in class. Claims to hate construction equipment 'because there is nothing for Mum and Dad to see when they come into school'.	Seen as confident and outward-going by his teacher. Seen by his teacher as 'a bit devious'. Dominant with peers. Socially astute. His social identity is seen as a hindrance to learning. Confident in his approach to teachers.	Began to show a tendency to be motivated by extrinsic rewards and develop a 'product' orientation to school tasks. Willingness to strive for status with peers and within the family becoming apparent. Able to read social situations to protect his own interests. Despite problems, William continues to enjoy school.

Figure 13.1: *William, early years, a summary matrix*

Family relationships	Peer group relationships	Teacher relationships	Identity	Career
		Year 2: Miss Sage		
William is creative and entertaining at home. Mother says she knows nothing of the school's methods but likes the atmosphere there. Difficult to handle, verbally aggressive to mother sometimes. Gets on well with sister but sometimes belittles her still.	At home and in interview William is scathing about girls – their achievements do not count. Continues to be an active participant in 'kiss chase'. Best friend Richard leaves the school at the end of Year 2. William says he will be best friends with Oliver next year.	Structural position: age ⅔ from top. Eng & Ma ⅓ from top. Miss Sage says he has lots of ideas and shares them. Develops a rapport with Miss Sage who encourages him to give more time to his writing. Also enjoys 'filling books' and formal expectations of a supply teacher.	Seen by his teacher as friendly and sensitive. Seen by himself as clever and hard-working. Does not like to be told what to do. 'Showman' at home.	Develops a rapport with his teacher. Writing now rapidly develops. Had experienced two broadly different motivational systems and could operate either successfully. William develops a relaxed, informal approach to teachers around the school.
		Year 3: Mr Brown		
At home, can be critical of school organization and teacher strategies. Some concern and loss of sleep over tests. Parents coach to reduce anxiety. Likes to relate to older boys as a matter of status. Style conscious. Abigail starts school.	William openly acknowledges girls as friends again. William and friends describe selves as 'The Terrible Two' and 'Jesters'. Has a reputation for being exclusive in his friendships. Peers say '. . . they think they are the Smart Guys'.	Structural position: age ½ way down class. Ma Sci Eng, in top ⅓ of class. Mr Brown enjoys his company and sees him as lively and enthusiastic. Works with Daniel noisily, likes to articulate problems. Challenges teacher with ideas – 'Why don't we . . .'	William is seen as 'ideas man' by teacher. *Social* identity enhances his academic identity. Says his teacher regards him as 'best working boy'. 'Jesters' William's group '. . . think they are the Smart Guys'.	William's communicator, negotiator identity seen by his teacher as integral to the learning process. Thus, as in Year 2, social skills were harnessed for the benefit of learning. Ready to challenge authority. Has a strong sense of his future.
		Year 4: Miss King		
William is resourceful in imaginative play with sister Abigail. Begins private violin lessons. Parents report 'delusions of grandeur'. High aspirations generally.	William and friends mix with high status girls, though boys resent girls as 'swots' and 'teacher's pets'. Daniel has left. He works with Stephen to 'have a laugh'. Later, Stephen moves seat to get more work done.	Structural position: among the oldest. MA Sci Eng, among the top few. Has a very good relationship with his teacher. Devotes time to careful work, though seen as noisy and gets his name on the board.	Teacher sees him as funny and sarcastic. 'Gets a joke'. 'Stroppy' when told off, 'On a pedestal' with peers. His group described as 'the sexy ones'. Has an image of himself as successful.	William's jokey identity appreciated and he is allowed to convert it into enthusiasm for tasks. Joins school orchestra a year early. Associated with high status girls.

Figure 13.2:   *William, the middle years, a summary matrix*

Family relationships	Peer group relationships	Teacher relationships	Identity	Career
		Year 5: Mr Brown		
William mentions school assessment from time to time. Parents say it matters to him what level he has reached. Auditions for city youth orchestra. Enjoys swimming and tennis. Likes to win but is not desperately competitive at sport. With friends, less focused in play. Continues to be image and style conscious.	William is not selected for sports teams. Status of friends Stephen and Ian raised by getting in teams. William is marginalized by them sometimes. Continues to enjoy the company of friends, not isolated. Mr Brown says William has mocked, teased those pupils in class who tend to be 'rejects'. William is mortified that Mr Brown noticed. Friends in Sally's group of high status girls are not in this class.	Structural position: among the youngest few. Ma Sci & Eng, within the bottom ⅓. William perceives that much teacher esteem accorded to high achieving, socially mature Y6 girls and sporting boys. Retreats into a search for structure. Delivers a standard run-of-the-mill presentation of tasks as a result. William flourishes when Y6 pupils go to camp and his status is restored.	Seen by his teacher as more conforming and less confident in relation to him. Some 'deviant' behaviour in relation to peers. Loss of group identities of exclusive and 'the sexy ones' formerly accorded by peers in earlier classes. Very low structural position means that the identity developed of being at the cutting edge of teacher expectations and peer group norms no longer viable.	Some loss of teacher esteem experienced. Loss of high social and academic status within this classroom. Somewhat floundering in relationships and approach to learning. Retreat into conformity with some anti-conformity, the latter teacher and parents collaborate to curb. William still enjoys school.
		Year 6: Mrs Chard		
Takes part in youth orchestra concert but expected to give up the violin. Challenges fairness of school rules at home. Pushing hard at the boundaries at home. Mother says William is friends oriented more than family oriented. Being his parents has always entailed constant negotiation.	William is back with his familiar year group. Long-standing rivalries and resentments among high achieving competitive pupils become publicly aired in classroom. William and friends think Mrs Chard favours girls and is sexist. William's group dub themselves 'The Rebels'.	Structural position: age ½ way down class. Ma & Sci ⅓ down the class, Eng well within top ⅓. Has an 'abrasive' relationship with Mrs Chard who thinks he talks too much, lacks concentration and does not like not being noticed. William withdraws co-operation from teacher when feels unjustly treated. 'Gives of his best when he feels like it.'	Seen by his teacher as something of a noisy nuisance, 'likes to come out as one of the top dogs'. Also 'fun' 'popular' and talented in the use of language and in his writing. Social identity no longer enhances his academic identity. William and friends redefine their group as 'The Rebels'.	William could not achieve teacher esteem through either of his customary strategies in this class. Easy, negotiative relationships with teachers gradually degenerate into critical opposition. William and friends condemn 'mismanagement' of school systems of reward, to which they still look for prestige.

Figure 13.3: *William, the later years, a summary matrix*

Five deceptively simple questions were posed in the analysis of *The Social World of Children's Learning* (Pollard with Filer, 1996) and these are represented in Figure 13.4. The first question, 'When and where is learning taking place?', asserts the significance of the socio-historical context. Throughout our longitudinal studies, children's case studies are contextualized within the broad socio-cultural, economic and political circumstances of the country, region, city, community, families and school over the period concerned. For instance, some of this wider socio-historical context concerned the rising prosperity among the predominantly middle-class families of Greenside during much of the life of the Thatcher government of the late 1980s and into the 1990s. This contrasted with the increase in unemployment and the reduced lifestyle of some of the poorer citizens of Easthampton (Filer, 1997; Filer and Pollard, 2000) and in the United Kingdom generally. During William's primary school years, momentous changes to the nation's education system in the form of, for example, the National Curriculum, national assessment and local management of schools had a profound impact upon Greenside School, as in schools across the country. At the same time, other changes in expectations for teachers and pupils were being introduced into Greenside School by a new headteacher, Mrs Davison. Traditional and somewhat formal approaches supporting exam success and cultural expectations of the independent sector gave way to a complete change of ethos in the school. Expectations were increasingly for children to be active in planning, negotiating and reviewing their curricular learning. Throughout the period of the study, many Greenside parents opposed such changes, their position fuelled by continuing political and public debate surrounding teaching methods and standards in primary schools.

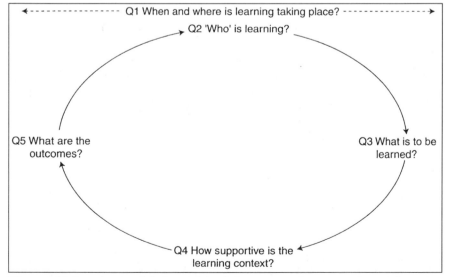

Figure 13.4: *A simplified model of learning, identity and social setting (from Pollard with Filer 1996, p. 14).*

'Who is learning?' is a reference to the key issue of identity – or 'self'. In *The Social World of Children's Learning* each child's sense of self is seen primarily as a product of their relationships with significant others. However, the influence of biological endowment and social circumstances are recognized as considerable. Thus interpersonal factors in the development of identity are conditioned by both intellectual and physical potentialities as they are realized, and by the opportunities or constraints afforded by the material, cultural and linguistic resources available to each family. Thus, for example, William's matrix for his Reception year alludes to the strong Christian convictions of his parents, that he was taught early reading skills before he went to school and something of his early learning strategies at home. The matrix cell relating to his home life also gives an indication of early social competence and the degree of confidence with which he embarked upon school life:

> He had a playgroup he went to three times a week . . . It wouldn't be unfair or whatever, to say that he was very popular at playgroup, both to the helpers and to the other children. He was very well liked. He was very outgoing . . .

> His very first day at Greenside, he was positively excited about it before he started and he ran in and his exact words to me were 'Bye Mummy. I don't need you any more.'   (Mrs Patterson, parent interview, March 1988, Reception)

The third question, 'What has to be learned?', draws attention to the form and content of new learning challenges and to the learning stance and strategies which each child adopts. New learning challenges arrive in the form of experiences and relationships as well as in the form of curricular tasks. In each case, the content of the particular learning challenge will affect each child's motivation, self-confidence and degree of control which they are able to exert in particular social settings. In turn, this will affect the range of strategic resources on which they draw. We can take William's data matrix relating to Year 1 as an example to illustrate these factors in relation to the model. As indicated above, during the early years of the cohort's primary experience, despite changes under way in the school, a fairly traditional, teacher-structured and, for William, relatively undemanding set of curriculum expectations were in place. The matrix summarizes what the data for that year tells us about his learning strategies at that time. Thus we see that, although William was beginning to make a bid for academic status in the classroom that year, this tended to be motivated by extrinsic rewards such as parental approval and the classroom status of grades. However, the culture of the peer group, his status within it and the pursuit of his own interests were strong counter attractions:

> Yes, he is very assured, very noisy, will think up the ideas and get everyone else doing them . . . William I think is quite devious. I think he is very attuned. (Last year) he probably thought he was quite a laugh, quite a character.
> (Miss Scott, teacher interview, November 1988, Year 1)

> He is often at the centre of some distracting activity. Confident and outward going, friendly with relationships well established. He can be quite a strong willed

child, insisting on his own innocence even when obviously at the centre of some argument. A leader of his own group of boys. Apt to do his own thing.

(Miss Scott, teacher records, November 1988, Year 1)

From data such as this we can begin to perceive William as having a social identity in the classroom that was characterized by autonomy and challenge, communicative competence and exuberance. The data also indicates William's socially astute nature, which allowed him to operate on a knife-edge of asserting his own interests and staying out of trouble with his teacher. However, as this and the summary matrix (Figure 13.1) suggest, William's social identity did not enhance his academic identity in the eyes of his Reception and Year 1 teachers. His classroom social relations were seen as a threat to teacher control and authority and as a source of distraction for others as well as for himself.

'How supportive is the learning context?' takes us to questions about the quality of classroom relationships and assistance in learning. For example, we can ask 'How is power used in the classroom?' and 'Is instruction well matched to the child's cognitive and motivational needs?' The question concerns how these factors affect children's willingness to take risks as they engage in learning, and the issue is as apposite in homes as it is in schools. To illustrate the way in which this question relates to William's learning we can draw on a comparison between the different expectations of teachers in William's Year 3 of primary school (Figure 13.2). His teacher in that year experienced and interpreted his social identity in different ways than had been the case in his early years. A new school ethos had brought a corresponding complete change of teaching staff at Greenside School. From William's Year 2 onwards, the expectation was that pupils should be active and interactive learners, taking some responsibility for their own learning. The data cell relating to teacher relationships in Year 3 (Figure 13.2) is again indicative of high levels of interaction with friends in the classroom, of autonomy and challenge to teachers and of exuberance. Now however, these same characteristics were positively valued as integral to the learning process and to good teacher–pupil relationships:

> William is very loud, that's the biggest thing, it's trying to quieten him down but he's an ideas man and thinks hard about things. He's buzzing with ideas, they come shooting out at all times. Wrong times! But very much an original thinker I'd say. He's always saying, 'Why can't we do this? Why don't we do that?', which is nice. If I throw things back at the class and say 'How are we going to solve this problem?', those are the two who I would expect to come up with the answer first.
>
> (Teacher interview, October 1990, Year 3)

In his later years at Greenside, William and his cohort met still different teacher expectations. In Year 5, for example, although William again had Mr Brown for his teacher, he was now among the youngest in a class of predominantly Year 6 pupils. The data box relating to his relationship with Mr Brown that year (Figure 13.3) indicates that the highest teacher esteem and classroom status seemed to be accorded to Year 6 pupils with greater social maturity and academic and sporting prowess than William was capable of at that time. The following descriptions of William given by Mr

Brown can be compared with those he gave in Year 3, and are indicative of the loss of confidence and retreat from risk in both his relationships with his teacher and in his approach to learning.

> He's still *fairly* familiar with teachers but at the same time he's afraid to go too far. William will only chat when everyone else is, when we're having a joke, and he'll *dive* in then. And again it's Year 6 that have that maturity. A lot of the girls can certainly come in and have quite a mature conversation and that shows a big difference really that you find you can't have with many of them.

> He has all the skills there to take things on and get on with it but he isn't quite as confident to go for it. As I've said before he tends to conform. He's a bit more frightened that I'll come along and say 'What are you doing?' But more often than not he'll think of how he's going to approach something, then check with me before he takes the plunge. So you'll find his topic book is fairly sort of standard in the way he presents his findings or whatever. It's fairly sort of run of the mill. He doesn't kind of think of a really exciting way of doing it very often.
>
> (Mr Brown, teacher interview, July 1993, Year 5)

A change in William's structural position in Year 5 thus had implications for the competent management of his relationships with his teacher and with his peers as well as for his competent management of classroom tasks.

The fifth question, 'What are the outcomes?', draws attention both to formal and informal outcomes. In formal terms, the learner achieves a new capability, attainment or standard, and may even be tested and certified for it. In terms of identity formation, however, there are perhaps even more significant informal processes, as friends, family and teachers affirm, mediate and interpret those achievements. The consequence is that social status, self-esteem and perception of one self as a learner are affected, and their influence rolls round to contribute once more to the question of identity – 'Who is learning?' The longitudinal tracking of William's learning outcomes enables us to analyse this recursive process of development. Indeed, as we show in the above data samples, we cannot discuss questions one to four in relation to William without also discussing outcomes. Thus social and academic outcomes reflect continuities and change in family and school expectations, in William's sense of self as a learner, in his motivation and social strategies in relation to particular classroom contexts, tasks, status and power relations, etc. In fact, in his case, his involvement in learning, responses to tasks, achievement of potential and co-operation with teachers changed with the different contexts. His classwork could show individuality and flair – but it could also become low-risk, minimalist and conformist. His usual easy, negotiative relationships with teachers could degenerate and flounder into critical opposition or withdrawal of effort. Teacher and peer perceptions of his academic and social identity were fluid and dynamic. The classroom and peer status for which he strove was not always achievable.

The model of learning, identity and social setting therefore describes a *recursive* process. From the small amount of data that we have been able to reproduce from William's story and from the summary matrices, we hope to have shown something of that continuous dynamic and thus something of the evolution of his primary school learning and identity as a pupil. Our full 20,000 word narrative of William's career is told in *The Social World of Pupil Careers* (Pollard and Filer 1999), together with the stories of three other children from the cohort.

We can thus conceptualize the dynamic and recursive aspects of pupil career in terms of a spiralling through successive classroom and other school learning and social contexts, year on year. As we spiral the 'learning and identity' model (Figure 13.4) on through the years, 'pupil career' is constituted from the patterns of a pupil's coping strategies and of the learning and social outcomes they achieve. The process is one of continuous shaping and developing one's identity and status as a pupil.

The concept of a spiral focuses our attention on the longitudinal aspects of the study, and of William's story in particular, as we move on to discuss learning and identity at the further analytic level of 'pupil career'.

Pupil Identity, Pupil Career and the Case of William

'Pupil identity': the background and development

The 'learning and identity' model in Figure 13.4 poses the question of identity in terms of 'Who is learning?' The learner in the model has certain resources and potential, relationships and experiences to draw on and which are brought to successive learning contexts. Recursively it is also what she or he becomes through interaction with significant others and the quality of learning experiences. We can see this process at work through the 'identity' column of William's matrices. There, in his reception year, we indicate that the data shows William beginning to shape and articulate a positive image of himself as a learner. In Year 2 he sees himself as 'clever and hard-working'. In Year 3 his teacher sees him as an 'ideas man', and so on.

In *The Social World of Pupil Careers* 'identity' is developed more specifically in relation to 'pupil identity'. We were able to see children's school experience in terms of *patterns* which were coherent across their relationships with teachers and peers, their motivation and learning stance, their learning outcomes and status outcomes. As the children got older, we also saw them moving into school-wide social and learning contexts in addition to those of classroom and playground as important sites for shaping and maintaining their identities in primary schools. We can see this in William's matrices with references, for instance, to the school orchestra (Year 4) and sports teams (Year 5). Thus the spiral of career progression must be refined to incorporate distinct but interrelated areas of experience, through which pupil identity and career are constructed. We distinguish four main elements of this, with associated questions:

- *Academic identity*: how is the child seen as a learner in terms of the school curriculum, and what is the child's own perception?

- *Official social identity*: how is the child seen in terms of school behaviour and social relationships, and what is the child's own perception?
- *Extracurricular identity*: how is the child seen as a participant in extracurricular activities, and what is the child's own perception?
- *Unofficial social identity*: how is the child seen by his or her friends and by other pupils, and what is the child's own perception?

We have identified these particular aspects as constituting what it means to be a pupil. They represent aspects of school experience which are assessed and evaluated, both formally and informally, by teachers, peers, and parents (see Filer and Pollard, 2000) and therefore through which pupils shape, maintain and *experience* their status and sense of self as a pupil. As well as aspects of pupil identity, therefore, they can, analytically, also be regarded as aspects of pupil career: aspects of school within which pupils interact, work and compete (or not as the case may be) for what is valued by their significant others; peers, parents and teachers, as well as by pupils themselves.

They are thus the *aspects of career* through which pupil identity is expressed and through which it is reflected (i.e. evaluated by others). In this therefore, as in the 'identity and learning' model (Figure 13.4), we continue to see reflected the symbolic interactionist view whereby identity is constructed from how individuals see themselves as well as how others see them.

Patterns and dimensions of strategic action

Sociologist have studied pupil cultures and adaptations to school life for many years, with the result that we are not short of analytic models and representations. These range from the relatively simple bi-polar opposition of 'pro-school and 'anti-school' (e.g., Hargreaves, 1967; Willis, 1977; Turner, 1983) to more sophisticated typologies of strategies (e.g., Woods, 1979; Ball, 1981). Such classifications are usually empirically derived and often take on local colour through the naming of groups. The 'Goodie, Joker and Gang' classification developed by Pollard (1985) is a case in point. Like many other typologies, it achieves its object in conveying something of the social organization of pupil groups at the time at which they were studied. The same occurs at the level of empirical illustration. Thus Pollard (1985) offers us 'Janine's Terrors' and 'The Scorpion Gang'; Mac an Ghaill (1989) 'Black Sisters' and the 'Black Brotherhood'; and Aggleton (1987) 'Rebels'.

This rich accumulation of studies provides excellent resources for understanding pupil cultures, though almost all of it derives from relatively short, cross-sectional studies based on one or two years of fieldwork. A resulting strength is that such work is often thoroughly contextualized. A concomitant weakness is that it has tended to yield relatively static analytic models.

We have found these to be unsuitable for tracking processes of strategic adaptation and change over seven years of primary school education, and on into the further five years of secondary education to which we are committed in the *Identity and Learning Programme* as a whole.

As well as being static, existing studies are also partial. None of them extends across the range of academic, extracurricular official and unofficial social experience that this longitudinal study has enabled us to identify as sites for strategic action, and hence for shaping and maintaining one's identity as a pupil.

We have therefore attempted to develop an analytic structure which is relatively timeless and more contextually portable than previous work on pupil cultures. We also wanted it to be conceptually parsimonious, whilst also, of course, being capable of representing the complexities and dynamics of strategic adaptation as they occurred.

In considering the detail of the analytic progression of the concept of strategic action, we can return to the 'learning and identity' model (Figure 13.4). From that, just as we develop 'identity' in patterned ways as 'learners' become 'pupils', so we develop 'strategy' as pupils' coping strategies are seen to evolve into *patterns of strategic action*. In fact, a major concern for us has been the development of a model through which we could present data relating to seven years' work in a dynamic way.

The *dimensions* illustrated in the typology in Figure 13.5 indicate patterned ways in which pupils relate to and negotiate the structures and expectations which are enbedded in the major aspects of pupil career: academic, extra curricular, official and unofficial aspects of career. At the core of this representation is the concept of *conformity*, and the conventional counterpoint to this is *anti-conformity*. However, our models also introduce the dimensions of *non-conformity* and *redefinition*. In a little more detail, the dimensions can be described as follows:

- *Conformity*: reification of academic and social structures, expectations and norms; low-risk conformity to others' learning and social agendas, characterized as 'adaptation'.
- *Anti-conformity*: rejection of academic and social structures, expectation and norms; oppositional learning and social agendas, characterized as 'deviance'.
- *Non-conformity*: some indifference and lack of awareness of academic and social structures, expectations and norms; little perception of risk because pupils have own learning and social agendas, characterized as 'independence'.
- *Redefining*: personal identification with academic and social structures, expectations and norms; high-risk strategies for influencing learning and social agendas, characterized by 'negotiation and challenge'.

Referring again to William's data, it can be seen that we constructed the dimension concerned with *redefining* in relation to coherent collections of strategies which he, and a number of other pupils, fairly consistently

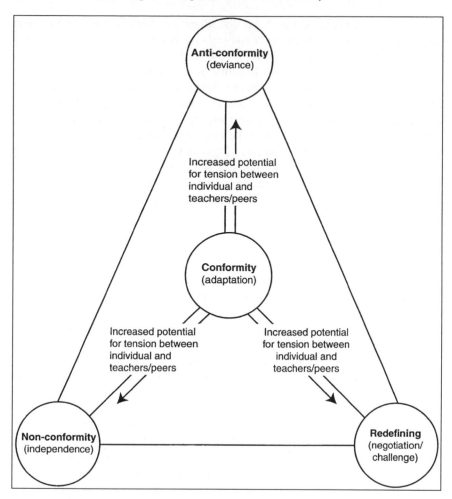

Figure 13.5:   *Dynamics of strategic action*

deployed. Pupils using *redefining* strategies are certainly *associated* with the mainstream patterns of expectations, achievement and cultural norms as the majority of their peers. However, they are not so much operating within them and *conforming* to them as at the cutting edge of them and *shaping* them. They are pushing at the boundaries of teacher and peer group expectations, negotiating, challenging and leading their peers. We examine further William's strategies in this light below in considering the 'dynamics of strategic action'. It is, however, important at this point to stress the difference between this typology and those constructed in the past by sociologists of edcuation. That is, unlike the sorts of typologies derived from cross-sectional studies described above, the 'dimensions of strategic action' *do not describe pupils or groups of pupils*. Similarly, unlike traditional psychological taxonomies of conformity, neither do they represent psychological 'types'. Rather the typology describes coherent collections of strategies which pupils adopt in shaping and maintaining their sense of self as a pupil, as a girl or boy, as a member of a peer group and friendship group and so on. Our longitudinal tracking of pupils, in the contexts of both schools in the Identity and Learning Programme, shows pupils using particular dimensions consistently, in so far as the *meaning* of the context remains the same for them. However, pupils can change their patterned responses. This can happen where accustomed status, identity, or preferred ways of working become subject to disruption or change, becoming no longer appropriate or viable. This, as we have shown in the case of William, can happen through changed teacher expectations or structural position vis-à-vis a class of peers. We can now use William's career story to illustrate how we conceptualize the nature of this dynamic, and to present a model of it.

The dynamics of strategic action

The model in Figure 13.5 is designed to show the dynamics of pupil strategy. Pupils may, as we saw in William's case, move towards greater or lesser *conformity* in response to a particular pedagogy or structural position in the learning context. For similar reasons, as again we saw in William's career, a switch from, for example, a *redefining* position of negotiation and challenge towards *anti-conformity* (deviance) may occur. Let us examine some of the dynamics of William's career in more detail in order to illustrate the model.

With respect to his relationships with teachers and curricular expectations, William was cue-conscious. He was also socially adept, especially with regard to testing the boundaries of rules and expectations. In his early school years he strove for autonomy and operated at the boundary of the permissible while retaining reasonably good teacher relationships. In his middle years he developed special, easy, negotiative relationships that won him some indulgences to operate, and develop, his own interactive and humorous identity within the classroom. In his later years, however, negotiation turned to challenging the rights of others to academic status and teacher esteem when it seemed to William that teachers withheld them from him. During these years he displayed strategies of deviancy or *anti-conformity*, withdrawing co-operation from one teacher and critically opposing structures and reward systems of school. These forays into deviancy were brief. Though William and his like-thinking friends dubbed themselves 'The Rebels' during this time, none of them set up the alternative status systems that would have been indicative of true rebelliousness (*anti-conformity*). Teacher and parental pressure put William back on track and understandably so, for it was always in relation to the existing academic and social structures that William struggled for recognition and esteem.

In relation to other pupils, William was a leader within the mainstream peer cultures of the playground and classroom. He was popular though often seen by his peers as the 'smart guy' who was exclusive in his friendship choices, and at the forefront of the sorts of 'sophisticated' social and sexual behaviour associated with the dominant, higher-status friendship group to which he belonged.

It was clear, however, that William's *redefiner* status was only viable where and when his structural position was sufficiently high to enable him to operate at the cutting edge of classroom and peer group culture. This was not a realistic option for him when he was matching himself against the skills and maturity of much older Year 6 children in his Year 5. In that circumstance, as well as retreating into a pattern of *conformity* to teacher expectations he showed some aspects of *anti-conformity* in his peer relations. This took the form of periods of 'hitting out' at other, more successful peers, challenging their right to success and denigrating others in the class of low achievement and status.

Thus William negotiated a career at the cutting edge of classroom, playground and school life generally. *Redefining*, for the autonomous William, was in many respects a risky operation, frequently carried out on a knife-edge of social approval. It was a matter of a socially astute, highly interactive and competitive bid for status; a collection of strategies not open to all his peers by any means and only altogether manageable or viable even for the socially astute William within some classroom contexts and expectations that he met.

To return to Figure 13.5, the model of the 'dynamics of strategic action' is also designed to depict the way in which the gaps between *conformity* and the other strategic actions of *anti-conformity*, *non-conformity* and *redefining* are potentially sites of tension. Such tension may occur between an individual pupil and a teacher or between individual pupils and their peers as a result of a learning stance or an expression of identity which contravenes the norms and expectations of classroom or playground.

Some of this potential for tension has been demonstrated in William's data and in his career 'story' above. As we have seen, as William encountered different teacher expectations and learning contexts, so his communicative, exuberant, autonomous and challenging identity was liable to be experienced and interpreted differently by different teachers. Thus, in relation to 'identity' we have focused on the way in which William's *social* identity was in some years seen as a hindrance to his *academic* identity and was a threat to the teacher–pupil relationship. In other years it enhanced his academic identity, indeed was seen as integral to the learning process, and promoted rapport in his relationships with teachers. From the point of view of William himself, perhaps the difference between 'best working boy' and a 'Jester' (Year 3) and a 'Rebel' (Year 6) also reflects some of the ebb and flow of tension in relation to successive teachers.

The Relevance of Longitudinal Ethnography

Perhaps the most powerful benefit of longitudinal ethnography lies in the fact that it adds the dimension of time to the holistic and multi-perspective research design of classic ethnography. In so doing it is more able to distinguish the enduring from the transient in social action, to track conditions for change together with the ways in which change is differentially experienced and acted upon by individuals and groups. Below, we present a summarized account of the cumulative arguments which continue to be developed through the Identity and Learning Programme. Three key issues are fundamental:

- Children are active in constructing and negotiating their experience in coherent and patterned ways.
- Children are influential in shaping the experiences and strategies of others.
- Children's actions are context related and are responsive to changing circumstances.

The analysis and models relating to learning (Figure 13.4) and career (Figure 13.5) have developed these propositions in the following ways.

Figure 13.4 encapsulates the early learning experience concerned with the influence of interpersonal processes on learning, social outcomes and the development of one's identity as a learner. In the analytic development of that model, and building on questions 1–3 in Figure 13.4, the following insights were gained.

- Children's development of their identity as learners can be conceptualized as a recursive process. Through their encounters with successive learning challenges in particular social contexts, children are influenced by informal as well as formal outcomes in the development of their sense of self as a learner.
- Relationships with parents (or carers) and siblings are major formative influences on a very young child's sense of self as a learner. As children progressively engage with the world beyond the family, parents, and increasingly peers, act as *mediators* – interpreting new experiences and acting as a significant reference point with regard to engagement with learning and the meaning and valuation of outcomes.
- There are two major social influences on pupils' classroom learning. First, pupils become effective if they are able to manage their coping strategies and presentation of self in ways which are viable in relation to different teachers' expectations, changing structural positions and peer group contexts. Second, pupils become effective when they have sufficient self-confidence and trust in their teacher to manage risk and task ambiguity in classrooms. They are then, of course, dependent on teachers providing them with appropriate intellectual challenge and support.

While we have illustrated some of these insights in relation to William's data, the matrices provide further instances of others.

Figure 13.5 is a formal representation of the dimensions and dynamics of pupil identities and careers through their primary school. Extending the longitudinal development of children's case studies has enabled us to advance the conceptions of 'identity' developed through *The Social World of Children's Learning*. Through documenting continuity and change within and between cases, we have been able to advance those earlier conceptions of children's 'sense of self as learner'. In so doing we have formalized the concept of 'pupil identity' in terms of the *dimensions of strategic action* and the *dynamics of strategic action*. By way of major conclusions therefore, we suggest the following:

1. For analytical purposes, it is helpful to distinguish four major *dimensions* of strategic orientation: *conformity, anti-conformity, non-conformity* and *redefining*. These are not 'pupil types' or 'psychological types' but rather reflect characteristic orientations and *coherent* patterns of response to school life.

2. Children's strategic orientations are coherent with (which is not to say they are necessarily the same as) patterns of action formed within the family, including siblings, the wider family and community. Children's strategic orientations reflect the mediating influence of parents. However, by the same token, parents' strategies and responses are shaped by those of their children through challenge, negotiation and compromise. Similarly children's strategic responses articulate with peer social systems. They are mutually influential with regard to stability and change within the microcultures of pupil friendship groups.

3. While pupils exhibit relatively continuous patterns of strategic orientation through their primary school, there is nothing fixed or inevitable in this, nor in the way their strategies are perceived or responded to by teachers and schools. Individuals continuously shape, maintain and actively evolve their pupil identities as they move through successive classroom contexts. A child's sense of self as a pupil may be enhanced or threatened by successive changes in their relative success, failure or structural position in their classrooms, and similarly by teacher expectations, pedagogic strategies, classroom organisation, criteria of evaluation, modes of interpretation, etc. In such circumstances, existing strategies are liable to modification or change, if they become no longer viable, appropriate or comfortable for a pupil to maintain. Strategic action is therefore *dynamic* as children actively negotiate a path through successive teacher and classroom settings, shaping and maintaining their identity and career as a pupil.

These models and conclusions represent our analytic insights regarding pupils' strategic orientations and adaptations to school and regarding the interrelation of classroom, home and peer group contexts and their effect on learning and career.

In terms of the generalizability of this analysis, we certainly claim the capacity of ethnography to generate grounded, valid and holistic insights that are not available through other forms of enquiry. We are also aware of the many readers who continue to find a resonance between school ethnography and their own experiences as pupils, teachers and parents. While this gives credence to the work, it is up to each reader to judge the applicability of our analysis to situations with which he or she is concerned. We would argue that this process can promote reflection, particularly in relation to the practices of teachers and parents.

References

Aggleton, P. (1987) *Rebels Without a Cause*, Lewes: Falmer Press.

Ball, S. (1981) *Beachside Comprehensive*, Cambridge: Cambridge University Press.

Filer. A. (1997) At least they were laughing: assessment and the functions of children's language in their news session, in A. Pollard, D. Thiessen and A. Filer (eds), *Children and their curriculum, A New Challenge*, London: Falmer.

Filer, A. and Pollard, A. (2000) *The Social World of Primary School Assessment*, London: Continuum.

Hargreaves, D. H. (1967) *Social Relations in a Secondary School*, London: Routledge and Kegan Paul.

Mac an Ghaill, M. (1989) *Young, Gifted and Black*, Buckingham: Open University Press.

Pollard, A. (1985) *The Social World of the Primary School*, London: Cassell.

Pollard, A. with Filer, A. (1996). *The Social World of Children's Learning*, London: Cassell.

Pollard, A. and Filer, A. (1999) *The Social World of Pupil Careers*, London: Cassell.

Turner, G. (1983) *The Social World of the Comprehensive School*, Beckenham: Croom Helm.

Willis, P. (1977) *Learning to Labour: How Working Class Kids Get Working Class Jobs*, Aldershot: Saxon House.

Woods, P. (1979) *The Divided School*, London: Routledge and Kegan Paul.

14

Home–School Links

Sally Tomlinson

This chapter is largely about the development of links between homes and schools which create a partnership. For most of the twentieth century education has been equated with schooling, teachers have defended their professional territory and there has been a separation of home and school. Now, there are increasingly moves to reverse this situation and to recognize that children's school performance and their personal and social development are most successful when a partnership is established between home and school. Home–school relations figure prominently on the agendas of politicians, professionals and parents, although from different perspectives, but there is a widespread acceptance that 'good' relations include effective communication and information-giving, accountability of school to parents, encouraging parents to support children's learning and development, and creating a sense of shared purpose and identity between parents, pupils and teachers. However, there is currently a political divide as to the form parental involvement should take. The 1986, 1988 and 1993 Education Acts have encouraged parents to regard themselves as consumers in an educational market and as managers via representation on governing bodies. Parental choices of schools are intended to promote competition between schools and to help close ineffective ones. Whether the role of parent as consumer and agent of competition will actually improve children's educational performance and enhance their personal and social development is debatable.

This chapter briefly reviews home–school contacts in Britain up to the present, noting that much of the literature on home–school relations has used a simplistic social class model in which 'working-class' homes have been regarded as deficient and less likely to care about children's achievements or pastoral needs. The chapter also covers problems inherent in creating partnerships and the experiences of other European countries.

Home–School Contacts

Home–school contacts have never figured large as a priority in English education, and up to the 1970s talk of partnership in education usually referred to that between central and local education authorities.

Literature discussing the relationship between school attainments, personal and social behaviour and homes has always worked to the disadvantage of working-class homes and parents. On measures of achievement, children from manual workers' homes and those with unemployed parents have tended on average to do less well, and it has usually been children from the lower socio-economic groups who have acquired the labels and reputation for being 'troublesome'. Explanations for this have, over the past hundred years, run a gamut from Victorian beliefs in the genetic inferiority of the 'lower classes' (Tredgold, 1908) through material and social disadvantage, cultural and linguistic deprivation, apathetic parenting and ineffective homes (Rutter and Mage, 1976). The misuse of Basil Bernstein's 1960s work on language codes (Bernstein, 1973) reinforced teachers' views that working-class speech was 'deficient'. Many teachers came to believe that school influence was marginal when set against a 'poor' home background, and held low expectations of large groups of children. This included, from the 1960s, pupils from ethnic minorities who were also subject to stereotyped beliefs about their culture, language and potentialities.

The middle–working class divide appearing in much of the literature undoubtedly led some teachers to underestimate the ambitions and capabilities of working-class and minority parents and their children, and many of the perceived problems in home–school contacts do have a class and a racial dimension. Research during the 1980s demonstrated that working-class and minority parents actually have very positive attitudes to education but lack the knowledge and information about the education system, and how to 'manage' it, that middle-class parents usually have (Roberts, 1984; Tomlinson, 1984; 1991; Gewirtz, Ball and Bowe, 1992). It has become a truism that it has always been the more informed and articulate parents who can obtain most from the education system.

Home–School Links

The Plowden Report (1967) proved to be a watershed in helping schools to understand why closer home–school links were desirable.

It set out a minimum programme by which schools could inform parents and encourage home–school links. This included welcome to school, open days, regular reports and written information, and meetings with teachers. By the 1980s the extent of home–school links in a majority of schools had gone beyond this minimum programme. Visits of teachers to homes, and parents to school, letters, circulars, pupil reports and records of achievement, governors' reports, school prospectuses and education–employer–parent compacts all constituted very direct forms of communication and linkage. Parental involvement in day-to-day activities as classroom helpers, translators, materials-makers, assistants on outings, and in home–school reading, maths and homework schemes, and involvement via parent–teacher and other associations had also become more commonplace.

Parental partnerships and home–school links have been furthered, to some extent, by the existence of parents' voluntary organizations. The Home–School Council, founded in 1930, and the National Confederation of Parent–Teacher Associations, founded in 1956, have acted as pressure groups on government to improve home–school links, as have more radical groups such as the Campaign for State Education (1962), The National Association for Governors and Managers (1970) and local groups such as the All London Parents Action Group, and the Haringey and Brent Black Parents Associations. The only national parental advisory service, ACE (Advisory Centre for Education, 1962), is currently encouraging the creation of local advisory services, to help give parents a local power base from which to influence schools and government policies.

Legislation in the 1980s gave parents far more rights to information about schools, access to curriculum documents, governors and HMI reports, and equal representation on governing bodies. From 1988 parents were, however, encouraged to 'choose' between schools rather than opt for a local neighbourhood school, and to vote in ballots for their children's school to opt out of local authority control and become grant maintained by central government. A Parents' Charter, published in 1991, set out existing parental rights and promised a variety of new rights but devoted only a short section to the notion of parents as partners. While this legislation and approach placed a premium on home–school links best described as customer–provider, and actively *discouraged* parents from supporting local schools in their local community, there has also been, during the 1990s particularly, a countervailing movement. There has in practice been an expansion of many different kinds of home–school links which indicate an increasing desire on the part of teachers and parents to work together.

A project exploring expanded partnerships in education, was set up in 1989 by the Royal Society of Arts and the National Association of Headteachers. This project was initially based in 20 schools around Britain, the schools being selected on the basis of an interest in developing home–school relations. The essence of the project was that it set out to:

- consider changing legal and contractual requirements to develop effective partnerships between schools and homes. This means that partnership will be not an optional extra but an essential requirement, and will include all parents, not just the 'active and unrepresentative' ones.
- develop whole-school approaches to policy and practice – reviewing existing home–school relations, developing home–school contracts or signed understandings, and planning, organizing and evaluating home–school activities.

This project, which included a strong European dimension, is described in Tomlinson (1991) and Jones *et al.* (1992).

Parents as Partners

Whatever the political context and desires of government, home–school links cannot be forced. Contacts take different forms and are at different levels, most parents initially becoming involved in school activities to improve the progress and well-being of their own child. From this point parents may become involved at whole-class and whole-school level, but only a few go on to influence school policies via governance and management. A major obstacle to the creation of partnerships has been that many teachers have embraced a notion of professionalism that excluded parents, and needed to be persuaded that professional teaching does recognize the integral role of parents in education. Macbeth (1989) suggested that there were four stages of progression in the growth of home–school partnerships which depended on a developing teacher and school acceptance of a new professionalism:

- *The self-contained school* is characterized by teacher autonomy, limited and formalized contacts with parents, little parental choice or consultation, a denial of access to school records, and with curriculum and teaching methods regarded as the teacher's domain.
- *Professional uncertainty* is characterized by tentative experiment with home–school liaison and participation but teachers still restricting consultation and blaming homes for low pupil attainment.
- *Growing commitment* is the stage at which the school leadership encourages liaison and consultation with parents, recognizes the value of home teaching, encourages parents on to governing bodies, and generally begins to adapt the school system to include parents.
- *The school and family concordat* represents the ultimate stage in the attempt to involve all families in formal schooling, recognizing that home learning is part of education and the role of parents is crucial in this, and emphasizing the obligation of parents to be involved and to co-operate with schools.

Schools in Britain could certainly be rated along this continuum, with many being at stages one or two. On the parental side, many parents are still reluctant to become involved in their children's formal education, lacking confidence and knowledge, or regarding classroom affairs as the teacher's domain.

Asking teachers to incorporate a 'practice' of home–school contacts into their professional activity, to accept criticism of their practice and to accept parents as equal partners, requires justification. Teachers must be convinced that it is in their interests, as well as the interests of parents and children, to regard parents as integral to the whole process of education and training from preschool to post-16. They will also have to work out the different kinds of partnership required as children progress through school. New requirements for teacher-training, however, do not encourage student-teachers to think of parents as partners, but as consumers to be informed of their children's comparative achievements vis-à-vis other children's.

There are other problems inherent in the notion of partnership – particularly from the parents' side. Parents, for example, have no distinctive power base. There is a plethora of local and national groups but no single group that the government could negotiate with or fund. Parents' organizations may influence policy on single issues but are not regarded at national, local or school level as integral to decision-making. Parent governors still have limited influence, especially given the historically dominant position of headteachers in England.

Parents often find the language of education difficult, particularly as the educational reforms have introduced a whole new curriculum and assessment language, and initials and acronyms abound. In addition, many aspects of school are beyond actual parental influence. Inadequate resourcing and poor teachers are two issues which worry parents but which are difficult to address, particularly if parents are regarded simply as clients and consumers.

European Policies

It is useful to consider some other European home–school policies and learn from positive developments. A European Economic Community (EEC)-funded project in the early 1980s, The School and Family in the European Community, suggested that politicians, educators and parents themselves often assumed that home–school partnerships could be achieved by simple strategies (Macbeth, 1989). An EEC conference held in Luxembourg in 1983 noted that 'there is widespread recognition that parents and teachers should be partners in educating children but there are difficulties in putting this ideal into practice'. However, it is possible that Europe-wide parental initiatives are now in advance of governmental or educationalists' thinking. The European Parents Association – and a more recent French initiative, the Centre Européen des Parents d'Ecole Publique (CEPEP) – aim to work out joint goals for the future of publicly funded education in Europe which will include parental partnership. CEPEP has representation from parents' organizations in France, England (via Parents Initiative), Eire, Italy, Germany, Spain, Portugal and Belgium and interest expressed by groups in Holland, Denmark, Greece, Austria and Luxembourg. This group has set in train discussion of a common educational philosophy for EEC countries and has suggested that national education systems should all include a home–school association in every school, government-funded parent associations, home–school links to be compulsory study in teacher training, and parents to be represented at all local and national levels where educational policies are formulated.

In *France* the schooling is secular and centralized, teachers are civil servants and there is a national curriculum. However, dialogue with parents has been a feature of the education system for some time. The Ministry of Education publishes material explaining the education system and a bulletin, 'A letter to parents'. All French primary schools are required by law to have a joint committee of teachers and parents and parents are consulted over the choice of books and materials for schools.

In *Italy* co-operation with parents has been included in Ministerial decrees since 1955, and a *decreti delagati* in 1974 introduced an elaborate system of councils which were intended to involve parents and local communities in all aspects and levels of education. The complexity of the pyramid of councils – school class, school, district, provincial and a national council – and the elaborate system of representation has not notably included parents in actual decision-making but the councils have reduced mutual mistrust between parents and teachers, given parents better information and encouraged parents to regard education as a joint home–school process.

In *Germany* the post-war Federal Basic Law laid down broad guidelines for the control and administration of education in (West) Germany, which is undertaken by the eleven provinces (*Länder*). The Basic Law incorporated principles of parental rights and responsibilities for their children's education and all the provincial constitutions require co-operation between schools and families, although each province varies in the details of its written requirements. The Bavarian constitution, for example, notes that 'The common educational task which confronts school and parents requires co-operation carried out in mutual trust'. In Rhineland-Palatinate, 'parents have the right and duty to co-operate with school in the education of their children'.

All provinces have legal requirements for parents' councils at different levels of education. In Baden-Württemberg, for example, there are school class councils chaired by a parent, school, district and provincial councils. The provisional parents' council offers advice to the Ministry of Education and must be kept informed by the Ministry.

The *Danish* school system is rooted in the notion of community education and gives more legal recognition and informed support to partnership between the family and the school than any other country. The Danish Basic School Law of 1975 reads: 'The task of the Basic School is, in co-operation with parents, to offer possibilities for pupils to acquire knowledge, skills, working methods and forms of expression which will contribute to each individual's development' (Macbeth, 1989, p. 174). The Danish approach recognizes that schools can do no more than make facilities available; they cannot, unaided, educate the 'whole child' and make no claims to this. Pupils attend the basic school (*Folkeskole*) for a minimum of nine years, and the class teacher moves with the pupils accentuating the possibilities of partnership with families. Municipal committees oversee the *folkeskoles* and there is parental representation on these committees. Each school board comprises parents with voting rights, teachers and pupils in its participants. Within schools, class associations of parents, teachers and pupils have developed, and the Education Ministry publishes a guide to co-operation between homes and schools. The national parents' organization, Skole og Samfund, incorporates all school boards and voluntary parental associations. Danish parents are recognized in law and in practice as sharing partnership rights and responsibilities at all levels of schooling.

In *Spain* one approach to parental involvement has been to recognize that parental involvement means educating parents in school and educational matters in ways not hitherto envisaged. At the University of Navarro 'schools for parents' have been devised, working on a modular basis with university staff and parent co-ordinators. Sexton, who learned about this development at a European Parents Association Conference in Italy, was so impressed by the way such courses improved parental participation in education that he has introduced pilot 'schools for parents' in the UK (Sexton, 1992).

Conclusion

This chapter started from the premise that improving children's educational performance, enhancing their personal and social development and creating genuine home–school links could happen only if the current stress on parents as consumers of education and agents of competition gave way to a belief that parents must be partners in the educative process.

If we are really concerned to raise educational standards and improve the quality of education, a *convergence* of home and school and a partnership between parents and teachers is a necessity. Policies must be geared to the understanding that schools and homes are *joint producers of education* and that in future parents will need to be more centrally involved in the process of schooling.

Any government which is seriously concerned about raising standards and offering an improved education to all pupils will concentrate on enhancing parental support, involvement and obligation to participate in formal education. It will also recognize that a more equal relationship between parents and teachers will require a different legislative framework to the present one. The legal framework will need to include more right to information, for parent education, for parents to be involved in their children's day-to-day schooling, to be automatically members of a home–school association and to make an educational agreement whith the school.

Home–school partnerships can remain empty rhetoric, be a cover for enhancing professional powers or become another mechanism for 'policing' pupils. We need open and equal relationships between schools and homes to contribute to better understandings, higher standards and an improved quality of education.

References

Bernstein, B. (1973) *Class Codes and Control*, vol. 1, London: Routledge.

Gewirtz, S., Ball, S. and Bowe, R. (1992) Parents, privilege and the education market place, paper to the British Educational Research Association, Stirling, Scotland, August.

Jones, G., Bastiani, J., Bell, G. and Chapman, C. (1992) *A Willing Partnership: Project Study of the Home–School Contract of Partnership*, London: Royal Society of Arts.

Macbeth, A. (1989) *Involving Parents*, Oxford: Heinemann.

Parent's Charter (1991) *You and Your Child's Education*, London: DES.

Plowden Report (1967) *Children and Their Primary Schools*, London: HMSO (2 vols).

Roberts, K. (1984) *School Leavers and Their Prospects*, Milton Keynes: Open University Press.

Rutter, M. and Madge, N. (1976) *Cycles of Disadvantage*, London: Heinemann.

Sexton, S. (1992) Parents can be teachers too, *The Times*, 3 November.

Tomlinson, S. (1984) *Home and School in Multicultural Britain*, London: Batsford.

Tomlinson, S. (1991) Home–school partnerships, *Teachers and Parents*, Education and Training paper no. 7, Institute for Public Policy Research. London, pp. 1–18.

Tredgold, A. E. (1908) *Mental Deficiency*, London: Balliere, Tindal and Cox.

15

Researching Home–School Relations:
a Critical Approach

Carol Vincent

Introduction

This chapter gives further consideration to the way in which relationships between parents and teachers, homes and schools are presented in the literature. The first section of this chapter argues that much of the home–school debate lacks a critical approach, and advances three illustrations to support this. The typology is expressed in terms of 'parents', and lacks detailed references to class, gender or ethnic-based differences. Therefore the second task of this chapter is to rectify that omission, by highlighting, with reference to Hill St and Low Rd, some of the salient ways in which ethnicity, class and gender affect home–school relationships. The chapter concludes by suggesting that a focus on structural dimensions, such as social class, is an integral part of an analytical approach to researching and debating home–school relations.

Problematizing Home–School Relationships

A closer look at the literature

Before focusing on class, ethnicity and gender, three illustrations can be advanced to illustrate and support the contention that discussions around home–school issues are often perfunctory and superficial. The first example is the reliance on consensual language, such as 'partnership', 'dialogue', 'involvement', 'sharing', which feature strongly in the home–school literature, thus editing tension and conflict out of the relationship. Such terms encourage easy agreement, but may also serve to obscure difficulties in interpretation and emphasis. These differences may not be articulated, but can nevertheless result in increasing tensions, capable of significantly disrupting an initiative. Consensual words and phrases, although vague and lacking specificity, can also be powerful in constructing norms for home–school relations. The terms suggest a warm 'community spirit'; if this is not achieved both teacher and parents are vulnerable to feelings of disillusionment and inadequacy, and the initiatives may lapse. However, in the recounting of projects, a cheery, unfailingly positive tone seems *de rigueur*, which means that pitfalls, problems or failures get edited out of the 'story' being told. This manner of dissemination means that it is difficult to get beneath the rhetoric and critically assess projects. Thus an article in the Royal Society of Arts' (RSA) 'Parents in a Learning Society' newsletter purports to evaluate home–school activities in 15 schools in East London (Wolfendale, 1994). This, admittedly short, article categorizes parental responses into six groups. All the categories and illustrative quotes from parents are positive. Yet even the most successful project surely runs into some problems, fails to reach some groups, tries, perhaps successfully, to broaden its scope. All these considerations are absent. Dissemination in this manner fails to inform or aid others trying to develop practice in this area, and instead cloaks the possibility or actuality of conflict, non-participation, apathy or hostility with a rosy glow. This is being addressed to some extent by the increasing degree of contact between small, local projects.

The second factor illustrating the occasionally superficial nature of home–school discussions is the assumption of a positive correlation between parental involvement and children's educational achievement (for example, Epstein, 1994; Jowett, Baginsky and MacDonald MacNeil, 1991; Stacey, 1991; Lareau, 1989; ILEA, 1985). On closer examination, the exact relationship is unclear. What kind of involvement triggers such improvement, and how is that improvement defined? There are two main claims in this area. Some projects argue that their results reveal a quantifiable increase after a period of close parental intervention in the curriculum (Epstein and Herrick, 1991; Dye, 1989; Hewison and Tizard, 1980). Others claim a more general improvement. For instance, frequent, positive home–school contact is assumed to result in the child feeling happier in the classroom, and thus achieving a higher standard (Stacey, 1991; Edwards and Redfern, 1988). With reference to the first group, Peter Hannon (1989) examines several home-reading initiatives and the evidence supporting their claim for higher achievement. He identifies several problems with reading tests. Do they test recognizable reading behaviour, or do they ask the child to decode out-of-context words? Are they prone to cultural bias? Other variables can also affect results, such as levels of existing parental involvement, and the attitudes of staff (*ibid.*; Boland and Simons, 1987). Hannon (1989) concludes, 'we know . . . that in some circumstances, parental involvement improves scores, whereas in other circumstances there may be virtually no improvement' (p. 39). He adds that at least there does not appear to be any evidence that parental involvement decreases achievement levels! Awareness of such problems leads advocates to make more general assertions concerning the value of parental involvement for children's learning. In theory, positive parent–teacher relationships will result in trust and congruence between home and school, which will then help the children progress further and faster. However, improvements in parent and teachers' social relationships do not necessarily increase the amount of interaction over educational issues (Smith, 1988; Tizard, Mortimore and Burchell, 1981). Second, increasing the congruence of home and school often means in practice that the home is required to change to match the school, a task which many parents will be unable or unwilling to undertake. Therefore, conclusive evidence of the direct link between parental improvement and achievement is difficult to obtain because of the many variables involved (David, 1993).

A third illustration of the home–school debate's somewhat superficial nature is its vulnerability to trends (Torkington, 1986). This results in one particular innovation being seen as sufficient to 'solve' the 'problem' of home–school relationships. One such example, particularly prevalent in City in the mid-1980s, was the establishment of parents' rooms in primary schools. A more recent example is home–school contracts. As single strategies however, such initiatives can have only limited and temporary effects.

Social class, ethnicity, and gender in home–school relations

Over the last 50 years, educationists' approaches to home–school relationships have undergone considerable change both in style and emphasis. Parental roles, once confined to ensuring that children attended school, have expanded to include the provision of ancillary help within the school, and even a role as educator in conjunction with teaching staff. Once the potential of parental influence upon the child's attitudes, behaviour, and perhaps abilities, entered the professional consciousness, educators sought to induct parents into school norms (see the Haddow Report, Consultative Committee, 1931, and the Plowden Report, CACE, 1967). Ideas of 'appropriate' parental behaviour were, of course, influenced by dominant social discourses concerning social class, gender and ethnicity. The *Plowden Report*, for instance, is pervaded by middle-class conceptions of ideal parent–child interaction. Hewison (1985) comments,

> Parents were seen as essentially passive 'supporters' of the activities of schools: a 'supportive' home provided a child with appropriate language skills, an appropriate interest in books and learning, and even appropriate role models . . . children from supportive homes arrived at school well-equipped to learn from their teachers; children from 'unsupportive' homes provided teachers with much less satisfactory educational raw material.
>
> (p. 45)

'Norms' of child development evolved from the experiences of middle- and upper-class children in the late 1800s and early 1900s. Yet it was against this 'norm' that working class children were also measured and often found lacking (Steedman, 1985). Therefore, mothers (the term 'parent', despite its gender neutrality, often applies primarily to women) required careful guidance to ensure that they exercised their influence in pursuit of the correct goals (David, 1993). As teachers are predominantly white, middle-class individuals (Musgrave, 1979), their relationships with working-class parents are shaped by in imbalance of structural power (in class terms at least). Teachers also have recourse to their professional identity, which may enable them to remain dominant in a relationship with parents with whom they share a social class position. New teachers are introduced to particular values, attitudes, and language, as part of their socialization into the profession. Values and attitudes are also refined locally, through staff-room conversations which reflects both the school's general ethos on home–school relations, and the reputations of particular families. Many parents lack access to an equivalent forum. Andrew Brown (1992) comments:

> Through actual interactions, spoken or written, an image of 'what parents are' is built up within teacher discourse. This acts to build up a 'normalizing' image of parents and parenting practice, which in turn provides . . . a standard against which to judge 'actual' parents. This is however, at a high level of generality, although the inscribed qualities might be highly specific . . . placed in relation to this 'general', 'normal' or even 'natural' parent, are specific groups of parents who may diverge in some way.
>
> (p. 197)

One identifiable, though heterogeneous group of parents who may be seen to diverge from the norm are ethnic minority families, particularly non-white groups. Research has consistently found evidence of stereotypical and negative attitudes towards black pupils, (Tomlinson, 1984; Wright, 1987; 1992; Mac an Ghaill, 1988; Gee, 1989; Gillborn, 1990; 1995). The same attitudes extend to their families. When Barbara Tizard and her colleagues (1988) asked white teachers about their experience of black parents, 70 per cent mentioned a negative attribute in reply (see also Townsend and Brittan, 1972; Smith, 1988; Howard and Hollingsworth, 1985). Heidi Mirza (1992) argues that the neo-conservative discourse of 'dysfunctional' families, often applied to African/Caribbean families, em-phasizes 'family composition' (for example, one-parent families) over 'fam-ily disposition' (for example, attitudes and values). Unsurprisingly, black groups and individuals often respond with disillusionment and suspicion of the white-dominated education system. Participants at an ACER (Afro-Caribbean Educational Resource Centre) conference in the late 1980s re-vealed considerable wariness of home visiting, for instance. One is reported as asking, 'are they coming with a set of values and assumptions that imply our way of life is inferior?' (ACER, 1986, p. 17). Indeed the tone employed by 1960s compensatory initiatives lingers on. A project described by Mac-leod (1985), attempted to 'involve' South Asian parents in their young children's education. Home–school liaison teachers (HSLTs) (mainly monolingual) visited parents at home to 'explain school policy and prac-tice' (*ibid.*, p. 2).

Macleod illustrates the 'problem' of 'parents who fail to conform' (*ibid.*, p. 14), by describing a mother who did the ironing throughout the HSLT's visit. 'She showed no sign that she had even the remotest understanding of the value of the . . . intervention programme – or indeed any motivation to understand what was going on' (*ibid.*, p. 30). Macleod continues, not by suggesting any reasons for this reaction – perhaps the woman resented the invasion of her privacy by someone intent on showing her how to interact with her child – but by warning the HSLTs to guard against being treated like childminders (for examples of similar attitudes among education professionals, see Mac an Ghaill, 1988; Mirza, 1992). However, Tizard, Mortimore and Burchell (1988) and Tomlinson and Hutchinson (1991; Tomlinson, 1992) also writing about the involvement of ethnic minority parents, comment on the isolation of schools and teachers from the surrounding locality and its residents. Teachers may spend little time in the area, other than when they are inside the school building. They may be unaware of locally based groups or provision, such as supplementary schools, although, to parents, these may be important sources of education for their children. Such isolation does not help foster teachers' awareness of cultures, religions or languages other than their own (Tomlinson and Hutchinson, 1991). Nor does it foster close parent–teachers links, leaving minority parents, who may have been educated in different, and often more formal, school systems, disenchanted with what can, in contrast, appear as the lax atmosphere characterizing many British primary schools. In schools which are fundamentally monocultural, in terms of curriculum, staffing and ethos, racial prejudice may go unremarked. While equal opportunity policies may be fairly widespread now, in many settings these remain 'paper policies', making little difference to practice (Troyna, 1993; Gillborn, 1995). Certainly, parents are rarely involved in the planning of such policies and may not even know of their existence. Tizard, Mortimore and Burchell (1988) conclude that, faced with this situation, it is hardly surprising that many minority parents view their children's school with a mixture of wariness, bemusement and anger.

Much literature on home–school relations speaks routinely of 'parents'. Yet particularly in primary schools the overwhelming majority of parents, involved with the school, are women. The use of 'parents' can be seen as an advance from the once-common and overtly paternalistic 'mums'. 'Parent' at least includes the possibility of male involvement. However, Bob Burgess and colleagues noted in their recent study, that the slippage from 'parents' to 'mums' persisted and was common among nursery educators (Burgess, Hughes and Moxon, 1991; David, 1990). Furthermore, gender divisions were reinforced as women helpers were assigned tasks traditionally designated as 'female' occupations, such as sewing and cooking.

In recent years, feminist researchers have highlighted the way in which mothers, especially in the early stages of their child's education, are subject to considerable pressures to conform to an idealized image of 'good mothering'. State education has long been seen as a potential remedy for the inadequacies of working-class mothers (David, 1993; Griffith and Smith, 1987). Specific practices (notably a child-centred approach) are normalized through the agencies of (often female) teachers and healthcare 'experts', as well as the media. As many 'school-approved' activities stem from the cultural practices and values of a specific socio-economic group, (the white middle class), white working-class women, or women from ethnic minorities are presented with an image of 'good mothering', which for various economic, cultural or ideological reasons they may be unable or unwilling to fulfil (Duxbury, 1987; Walkerdine, 1985; Finch, 1984b). For example, Valerie Walkerdine (1985) suggests child-centred approaches are less likely to be adopted by those in an economically insecure position. Failure to maintain the correct image can cause feelings of guilt or inadequacy; if the woman rejects or is unaware of the ideal, she risks being branded by professionals as a 'bad mother'.

Walkerdine and Lucey (1989) develop the concept of the 'sensitive mother'. This requires women to educate their preschool children in two ways; first, by giving them experience of early number and language ideas by turning household tasks into 'learning experiences', and second, by teaching them social skills. Walkerdine and Lucey argue that the 'sensitive mother' ideal oppresses women who ascribe to it. Their study suggests that these mothers made little time for themselves because of the pressure of constantly interacting in a 'sensitive' way with their child. Again failure to match the image could provoke severe guilt. Similarly Griffith and Smith (1987) argue that once a child is school aged, her mother has little opportunity, and less power to intervene in the classroom. Yet if a problem arises concerning the child, the likelihood is that the mother, rather than the teacher or any other family member, will assume responsibility for the child's 'deficiency'.

Hill St and Low Rd: Class, Gender, Ethnicity

Class: the experiences of working-class parents

Perceptions of social class distinctions between parents and teachers were particularly noticeable at *Low Rd School*. Although there were many individual exceptions, relationships between parents and teachers were often marked by wariness and in a few occasions, outright hostility. It may be thought that the degree of mutual suspicion which existed suggests that this school is atypical in this respect. However, I would argue that relationships pushed to the limit more easily reveal their underlying assumptions.

Although incidents of physical and verbal abuse were not the determining characteristic of most teacher–parent contacts, there had been a period at the end of the 1980s when there had been a marked increase in such assaults. The legacy of this time was discernible in the attitudes of the present staff. For many teachers, the working-class parents of Low Rd were distinguished by their 'otherness', and were perceived as a potential threat, both to teachers personally and to the smooth running of the school.

There are undeniable pressures upon some families. However, such an emphasis risks ignoring the school's contribution to parent–teacher relationships. Schools are not neutral institutions, and while their effects are undoubtedly more minor than poor housing, or high unemployment rates, they are nevertheless discernible. The period 1988–90, coinciding with the rise in the harassment of staff, was a time of disruption at Low Rd with high levels of teacher turnover and inexperienced staff. The degree to which such organizational disarray affects the standards of learning and behaviour within schools is often not appreciated by those not in daily contact with them.

The headteacher, Ms Court, had attempted to strengthen the school's links with social services, housing departments, police and health service. This is explained by the school's need to know what is going on in other areas of the children and parents' lives in order to understand conflicts that might surface at school; an approach which is common in schools in areas of economic deprivation and has been influenced by the ideology of reformist community education. The rationale is that the school should no longer appear remote from other concerns in everyday life, nor blind to outside influences affecting the children's enthusiasm and willingness to learn. However, this type of contact with other agencies operates over the heads of local families (see also Baron, 1989). The school appears to form part of a 'wall' made up of the 'caring professions', backed up by the police, and designed to 'manage' the local population. The families themselves remain 'cases' or 'clients' and have no entry into the power structure of such institutions. The amount of blank walls some parents met with in an attempt to run their lives was guaranteed to induce a severe sense of frustration. The following quotation gives some sense of this, although the respondent emphasized that she felt herself to be in a more secure financial and personal position than many.

> It's a poor area, housing conditions are bad, it's not just education, there are other social problems. You try and keep the children settled and calm but look at the bad housing, the unemployment. I'm not trying to make excuses for the kids not learning, but parents do try to keep them on a steady keel and present some form of normalcy. My husband was unemployed for almost two years. That's not just a one-off thing, here it's almost normal . . . There's just too many factors. What can you do? . . . I said to the councillor, 'Look at this place, it's not centrally heated, we can't even get our repairs done.' This is just basic living, we're not asking for a swimming pool in the back garden.
>
> (African/Caribbean mother, Low Rd)

This sense of having to battle to improve or just to protect one's position and belonging increases the likelihood of conflicts between parents and teachers starting because the parent is defending his or her child, often on non-educational matters. This individualistic focus did not mean that parents thought their own children were incapable of doing wrong; indeed, several respondents acknowledged how difficult it was for the school, and sometimes themselves, to manage the child. However, they often perceived the school's criticism of their children as an implicit criticism of their parenting ability, and in self-defence would turn the complaints back against the school. One mother finally responded to what she perceived as constant disparagement of her child with the words: 'You deal with it, you're the teacher. You never say nothing good about him.' For many parents the school was another institution seeking to exert control over their families, but over which they apparently had no control. The school made demands of them (send your children to school regularly and punctually, make sure their behaviour is good, read to them at home and so on), but there seemed to be no effective channel through which parents could present their demands. Anger grew from frustration; but it also served another function, motivating parents into tackling those who worked in the school, who understood how it operated, and who could (seemingly) determine their children's future (see also Grace, 1978; Carspecken, 1990). The teachers, however, perceived the situation quite differently, feeling themselves vulnerable as potential victims of parents' often misdirected anger. Experience of a very few abusive parents had contributed to some teachers' seeing parents' lifestyles and personalities as abnormal, which helped to legitimize their exclusion from school.

However, some teachers at Low Rd, especially the (all female) senior management team (SMT), stressed the severe social and economic pressures which prevented parents becoming more closely involved with the school.

> The parents are all interested, if it's your child, you're interested. It's either pressure of work, or they think you're the teacher they'll let you get on with it, or possibly language differences. A couple of children in the class, their families have got so many pressures, home pressures, emotional pressures, social pressures, they're just glad that someone's looking after the children during the day.
>
> (White, female teacher)

It should be remembered, however, that Low Rd parents were not offered many opportunities to display their interest in their child's education or the school. When I asked one woman if there had been school social events for parents, she laughed,

> Ms Castle: People do that way out [in the suburbs]. This is [City], they wouldn't do that here.
> CV: Is that because the teachers wouldn't do it, or the parents wouldn't be interested?
> Ms C: (pause) I don't know. If they did discos even for the kids . . . we could come in and help. They could give something a try.

Ms Castle had regular contact with the school, concerning her son's behaviour. She was aware that home–school communication on issues other than discipline was limited, and disliked this minimal relationship. However, she accepted it as the norm for an inner-city school. She discerned quite clearly the social class differences that characterized the two 'sides'. However, she was unaware that she, and parents like her, were seen by the teachers as responsible for this situation through their apparent lack of support for the school.

Gender: the experiences of mothers

The negative views held by many of the *Low Rd* teachers of their pupils' parents were also gendered, and did not impact equally upon the children's mothers and fathers. An example of this is the casual derogatory comments both male and female teachers made about the sexual morality of particular women.

> Her children have all got different fathers, she's not 'Mrs.' at all!

> Some of these kids don't even know where their mum spends the night, if you see what I mean.

> Oh, he's terrible [the child] and she's awful! . . . Of course, she's not the mother really, she's his dad's girlfriend.

Two mothers who met at a battered women's refuge and now shared a flat commented, 'We tell everyone we are sisters, otherwise they'll think we're gay . . . they don't like us round here anyway'. The implications of such remarks is that women who do not live within a traditional nuclear family are inadequate as mothers; they are deemed so for disrupting conventional notions of sexual morality. These constraints do no apply to men. Similarly, not all women are subject to the same degree of prurience. Middle-class women (with the possible exception of lesbian mothers) are less likely to have their ability to be a parent measured in terms of who they are having a relationship with. With limits on welfare state spending, unorthodox families who cannot provide for themselves economically are seen as likely to be suffering moral poverty too (Isaac, 1990). Such value systems are pervasive. Gender, sexuality and class discrimination interact. For the working-class women of the Low Road area, sexual behaviour is one characteristic that contributes towards the picture of them as the 'undeserving poor' (Golding and Middleton, 1982). Such comments were not made about mothers at Hill St. It is arguable that Low Road mothers, because of the greater degree of poverty in the area, were seen as living less 'normal' lifestyles than their Hill St counterparts. Golding and Middleton (*ibid.*) conclude that explanations for poverty that focus on individuals' failings – 'blaming the victim' – are widespread and coexist with a persistent belief in the existence of an irresponsible welfare 'scrounger' figure (also Taylor-Gooby, 1985). The prevalence of such ideas within society has the potential to affect all its members, including teachers. Certainly, more casual comments made by some teachers – for instance, 'The parents were all in the pubs, instead of doing PACT' [the home-reading scheme] – suggested that they employed such stereotypes.

Ethnicity: the experiences of black and bilingual parents

On paper, Hill St and Low Rd both had anti-racist policies. In practice, however, the two schools reacted to particular racial incidents rather than proactively trying to create an environment in which racism was deemed unacceptable (see Troyna and Carrington, 1990; Gillborn, 1993). Low Rd provides an example of this point. While there were instances of stereotyping and ethnocentric remarks made to me by white parents at both schools, it was at Low Rd that a significant minority of white parents and children made overtly racist comments, particularly directed towards children or adults of Bangladeshi origin. The primary complaint of these racist parents (16 per cent of the Low Rd parent-respondents) was that the school favoured the 'Pakis', although no one was able to give any example of this phenomenon. This was unsurprising given that little or no provision existed which was specifically directed to the Bangladeshi population. It might be argued that there is little a school can do to affect parents' attitudes and behaviour. However, Low Rd made few overt attempts to encourage a climate throughout the school, which might mitigate such behaviour on the part of the children, and clearly publicize its non-racist stance to their parents. Indeed, as becomes clear in the following section, the school neglected the experiences and concerns of Bangladeshi families and other minority groups; a neglect which, in effect, compounded the overt racism shown by some parents.

Parent–teacher communication: Bangladeshi parents at Low Rd
The families of approximately one-third of Low Rd's pupils came from Bangladesh. Speaking mainly through Shajna, the interpreter, the parents who took part in this study felt very strongly that the school's ethos was shaped by teachers with whom they shared no common ground, be it in terms of ethnicity, social class, language or religious belief. As evidence, they argued that Low Rd had only one Bengali-speaking member of staff, made no provision for Bengali classes, and had no books in Bengali (teachers claimed the school did actually have a few dual-language books and was ordering more). Several factors combined to make communication between home and school particularly difficult for Bangladeshi parents. The one Bengali/Sylheti speaking teacher, Ms Ali, was a class teacher, and therefore, despite her best efforts, not always available to see parents. This problem was compounded by the absence of any regular parent–teacher meetings at Low Rd. There was widespread parental support for specific invitations to visit the school. Planned parent–teacher meetings with interpreters present were particulary important for those Bangladeshi parents who were monolingual, and found themselves faced with monolingual teachers. Since the primary mode of teacher–parent communication at Low Rd was informal, unscheduled conversations, Bangladeshi parents frequently resorted to using their children as interpreters. This often proved unsatisfactory, particularly as the children themselves were usually the subject of discussion. As Ms Ali was the only person able to translate notes home, she tended to concentrate on individual letters, and the more general notes often went out in English only. Given this situation, it is unsurprising that all of the Bangladeshi parents interviewed during

fieldwork, felt, first of all, that they had no reliable and easily accessible source of information on the progress of their individual child, and second, that they were precluded from knowing about general, organizational developments at Low Rd.

This linguistic isolation was mirrored in the parents' perception of Low Road's attitude towards religion. Little attention seemed to be given to Islam; even obvious opportunities to do so, for example by celebrating Id-ul-Fitr, the festival which marks the end of Ramadan, had not been taken (a similar criticism was made by Muslim parents at Hill St). Later in the year, Low Rd appointed a second Bengali/Sylheti speaker to the staff. This teacher considered that Bangladeshi culture and Islam should be afforded a more visible role in school life. He found that other teachers were not opposed to such developments (they encouraged him as he organized a celebration of Id, for example). Such inaction, he commented, was in itself an action, symbolizing the marginalization of Bangladeshi families at Low Rd.

Community–school relations: South Asian Muslims and Turkish-speaking parents at Hill St

It was not only at Low Rd where ethnic minority parents suggested that they felt the school was unaware of, and uninterested in, their concerns and opinions. At Hill St, many black and bilingual parent-respondents revealed a similar sense of alienation. The combined impact of the incidents and events to which they referred indicates the level of institutional neglect of issues related to ethinicity.

Hill St School had instituted twice-weekly, separate assemblies for Muslim children. The initiative had been prompted by a Muslim governor, and was supported by a nearby mosque. The Muslim parents who participated in this study all welcomed the development, which, however, proved short-lived. The assemblies were soon reduced to a weekly basis; the school apparently found, as one teacher put it, that the logistical requirements for more frequent assemblies were 'intrusive'.

This was not the sole initiative that Hill St undertook, as one member of its staff expended considerable time and energy in building links with local community groups, particularly the two nearby Islamic associations. But the school, as a corporate body, had no clear view of the type of liaison it wished to establish. The issue, in fact, was not discussed, as visiting the centres was seen as an end in itself. Thus the community groups were used as resource centres, places that could provide translations, information and teachers for language lessons. Pressure of work on all those involved meant that such contact remained limited and infrequent. Thus opportunities to establish a more interactive, pervasive link between Hill St School and the community centres were lost.

This is exemplified by the school's arrangements for the Gujerati and Urdu lessons which were offered to South Asian children during the school day. Teachers for these lessons were found through one of the local Islamic community associations. In several respects, however, the programme seemed half-hearted. The lessons were conducted in the shabby room which was nominally the Parents' Room. There was no attempt to integrate these teachers into the main staff body; when they finished their lessons, they left the premises, having had little chance to make contact with other teachers or children (see also Macdonald *et al.*, 1989, for similar examples).

Families recently arrived in England are particularly likely to perceive institutions as remote and distant, unless the institution actively endeavours to present itself otherwise. One of the most recent groups of arrivals in City were Turkish-speaking families. Hill St had a part-time Turkish-speaking teacher, Dideem, who was funded by a local community group to work with children from eight or nine families. All the families had been in England for less than two years (although the issue was not explored, it is likely that most of these families were Kurdish refugees). Through Dideem, I spoke to five parents. On arrival, many had had no information on schools, housing, or jobs, and were almost totally reliant on other community members. They stressed the importance of education for their children, but found the English education system informal and unstructured, compared to Turkey's (see Sonyel, 1987). This contributed to their difficulty in gaining information; there was no timetable, no homework, and the children claimed they mostly did maths and drawing (i.e. simple activities for teachers to arrange for bilingual beginners). The parents wanted opportunities to talk to the teachers, to ask about teaching methods and school routines, and how they could help their children at home. In previous years, and on her own initiative, Dideem had arranged meetings to try and answer these questions. However, the teachers tended to perceive her as a resource, someone to interpret and translate for them. This was important work, but Dideem was able and willing to establish coherent links with Turkish-speaking parents, rather than simply acting as a link between individual teachers and parents.

Discipline and behaviour: Bangladeshi parents at Low Rd and African/ Caribbean parents at Hill St
Bangladeshi parents at Low Rd shared a general parental concern with questions of discipline and behaviour, and this was a frequent topic in interviews. With Shajna interpreting (and contributing her own experiences), we also discussed racial abuse and harassment. Parents had divergent opinions on the issue of racist behaviour at school. Some felt that bullying and name-calling were directed at Bangladeshi children more than at other groups. Others considered that there was a generally high level of indiscipline at Low Rd which involved all children. (It should be noted that children may not always tell their parents about racist incidents; Troyna and Hatcher, 1992.)

Nevertheless, the Bangladeshi parents all agreed that teachers rarely followed up incidents or complaints from children. This criticism was in fact voiced by parent-respondents from all ethnic groups. Low Rd did have a policy for dealing with fighting and name-calling, and all such episodes should have been recorded and the headteacher notified.

Issues of discipline and behaviour are particularly controversial in respect of the disproportionately high rate of exclusions of African/Caribbean children, especially boys. Several studies have explored the interaction between teachers and black children in an attempt to explore the factors which lead to this situation. David Gillborn (1990), for example, focuses on what he terms 'the myth of an Afro-Caribbean challenge to authority' (p. 19). Gillborn argues that much conflict is triggered by teachers' expectations that African/Caribbean boys will engage in disruptive or challenging behaviour, and also by their ethnocentric interpretations of these pupils' preferred clothes, their manner of speech, or even the ways in which they walk (*ibid.*; see also Wright, 1987; 1992; Mac an Ghaill, 1988). Four of the ten Hill St African/Caribbean mothers who took part in this study commented on this syndrome. They felt that they had witnessed examples of their children being labelled as 'troublemakers', as this mother describes.

> They think I think he wears a halo, but I know what kind of kid he can be . . . [But] the child who came to school was not the child who came home . . . Sometimes he's treated quite rightly, sometimes it's just the name of the child, regardless of who did what. It he's involved, he's the culprit . . . He's got a name that goes with him from class to class.

[. . .]

Incidents such as these are not atypical. They may, in isolation, be considered insignificant by the school authorities, and therefore not fully investigated. They may only rarely have such formal consequences as a complaint to the school's governing body. But from a parent's perspective, they may contribute to rapidly cooling home–school relations.

Many black and minority ethnic parents at Low Rd and Hill St harboured an appreciable sense of disaffection with their children's apparently insular, ethnocentric schools. But it cannot be assumed that a particular view of, or approach to, a school can be 'read off' from membership of a particular ethnic group. Although most parent respondents also shared the same gender and class groups, other factors played a integral part in structuring their attitudes. These included such matters as their previous familiarity with the English primary education system, their perceptions of their children's progress, and also their religious affiliation. Similarly, many white working class parents who took part in the study also argued that the schools neglected their particular needs and concerns. As McCarthy (1990) has suggested it is oversimplistic to conclude that the reactions and relations of actors in any school context can be explained simply in terms of ethnicity.

Conclusion

This chapter locates the home–school debate as an illustration of Miriam David's assertion that, a particular framework has been used by policy-makers and social scientists alike to inform and interpret social and educational reforms. This framework has tended to ignore, or not make explicit, questions of gender or race. However despite both the gender-neutral and race-neutral language, reforms and research have been constructed around gender and racial divisions.

(David, 1993, p. 207)

The chapter has supplied empirical examples of the ways in which home–school relationships are framed by the effects of social class, gender and ethnicity. Omitting these, and other structural dimensions, from the debate can result in uncritical and superficial discussions, which assume consensus over key issues such as appropriate teacher–pupil relationships, curriculum issues, or modes of parental involvement. However, a closer analysis of home–school relations may reveal differences and divisions between different social groups concerning all these issues. Understanding this situation is vital if simplistic strategies are to be avoided.

References

ACER (1986) *Parents' Voices in Early Childhood Education*, London: ACER.

Baron, S. (1989) 'Community education: from the Cam to the Rea', in L. Barton and S. Walker (eds), *The Politics and Processes of Schooling*, Milton Keynes: Open University Press.

Boland, N. and Simmons, K. (1987) Attitudes to reading: a parental involvement project, *Education 3–13*, **15**(2), pp. 28–32.

Brown, A. (1992) Mathematics: rhetoric and practice in primary teaching, in J. Riley (ed.), *The National Curriculum and the Primary School: Springboard or Straitjacket?* London: Kogan Paul.

Burgess, R., Hughes, C. and Moxon, S. (1991) Parents are welcome: headteachers' and matrons' perspectives on parental participation in the early years, *Qualitative Studies in Education*, **4**(2), pp. 95–107.

Carspecken, P. (1990) *Community Schooling and the Nature of Power: The Battle for Croxteth Comprehensive*, London: Routledge.

David, M. (1993) *Parents, Gender and Education Reform*, London: Polity Press.

David, T. (1990) *Under Five – Under Educated?* Milton Keynes: Open University Press.

Duxbury, S. (1987) Childcare ideologies and resistance: The manipulative strategies of pre-school children, in A. Pollard (ed.), *Children and Their Primary Schools*, London: Falmer Press.

Edwards, V. and Redfern, A. (1988) *At Home In School*, London: Routledge.

Epstein, J. (1994) Family math that's above average: take home activities for kids and their parents, *Instructor*, **103**(8), pp. 17–18.

Epstein, J. and Herrick, S. (1991) *Implementation and Effects of Summer Home Learning Packets in the Middle Grades*, Baltimore, MD: Centre for Research on Effective Schooling for Disadvantaged Students.

Finch, J. (1984b) A first class environment? Working class playgroups as pre-school experience, *British Educational Research Journal*, **10**(1), pp. 3–17.

Gee, J. (1989) The narratization of experience in the oral style, *Journal of Education*, **7**(1), pp. 75–96.

Gillborn, D. (1990) *Race, Ethnicity and Education*, London: Unwin Hyman.

Gillborn, D. (1993) Racial violence and harassment, in D. Tattum (ed.), *Understanding and Managing Bullying*, London: Heinemann Books.

Gillborn, D. (1995) *Racism and Antiracism in Real Schools*, Buckingham: Open University Press.

Golding, P. and Middleton, S. (1982) *Images of Welfare and Poverty*, Oxford: Martin Robinson.

Grace, G. (1978) *Teachers, Ideology and Control*, London: Routledge and Kegan Paul.

Griffith, A. and Smith D. (1987) Constructing and cultural knowledge: mothering as a discourse, in J. Gaskell and A. McLaren (eds), *Women and Education: A Canadian Perspective*, Alberta: Detselig Enterprises.

Hannon, P. (1989) How should parental involvement in the teaching of reading be evaluated? *British Educational Research Journal*, **15**(1), pp. 33–40.

Hewison, J. (1985) The evidence of case studies of parents' involvement in schools, in C. Cullingford (ed.), *Parents, Teachers and Schools*, London: Robert Royce.

Hewison, J. and Tizard, J. (1980) Parental involvement and reading attainment, *British Journal of Educational Psychology*, **50**, pp. 209–15.

Howard, S. and Hollingsworth, A. (1985) Linking home and school in theory and practice, *Journal of Community Education*, **4**(3), pp. 12–18.

Inner London Education Authority (ILEA) (1985) *Parents and Primary Schools*, London: ILEA.

Isaac, J. (1990) The new right and the moral society, *Parliamentary Affairs*, **43**(2), pp. 209–23.

Jowett, S., Baginsky, M. and MacDonald MacNeil, M. (1991) *Building Bridges: Parental Involvement in School*, Windsor: NFER-Nelson.

Lareau, A. (1989) *Home Advantage: Social Class and Parental Intervention in Elementary Education*, London: Falmer Press.

Mac an Ghaill, M. (1988) *Young, Gifted and Black*, Milton Keynes: Open University Press.

MacDonald, I., Bhavnani, R., Khan, L. and John, G. (1989) *Murder in the Playground* (The Macdonald Report), London: Longsight Press.

Macleod, F. (1985) *Parents in Partnership: Involving Muslim Parents in their Children's Education*, Coventry: Community Education Development Centre.

McCarthy, C. (1990) *Race and Curriculum*, London: Falmer Press.

Mirza, H. (1992) *Young, Female and Black*, London: Routledge.

Musgrave, P. (1979) *The Sociology of Education*, London: Methuen.

Smith, T. (1988) Parents and pre-school, in J. Bastiani (ed.), *Parents and Teachers 2*, Windsor: NFER-Nelson.

Sonyel, S. (1987) The silent minority: Turkish children in British schools, *Multicultural Teaching*, **5**(3), pp. 15–19.

Stacey, M. (1991) *Parents and Teaching Together*, Milton Keynes: Open University Press.

Steedman, C. (1985) Listen how the caged bird sings: Amarjit's song, in C. Steedman, C. Urwin and V. Walkerdine (eds), *Language, Gender and Childhood*, London: Routledge and Kegan Paul.

Taylor-Gooby, P. (1985) *Public Opinion, Ideology, and State Welfare*, London: Routledge and Kegan Paul.

Tizard, B., Blatchford, P., Burke, J., Farquhar, C. and Plewis, I. (1988) *Young Children at School in the Inner City*, London: Lawrence Erlbaum Press.

Tizard, B., Mortimore, J. and Burchell, B. (1981) *Involving Parents in Nursery and Infant Schools*, Oxford: Grant McIntyre.

Tomlinson, S. (1984) *Home and School in Multicultural Britain*, London: Batsford.

Tomlinson, S. (1992) Disadvantaging the disadvantaged: Bangladeshis and education in Tower Hamlets, *British Journal of Sociology of Education*, **13**(4), pp. 437–46.

Tomlinson, S. and Hutchison, S. (1991) *Bangladeshi Parents and Education in Tower Hamlets*, London: Advisory Centre for Education.

Torkington, K. (1986) Involving parents in the primary curriculum, in M. Hughes (ed.), *Involving Parents in the Primary Curriculum, Perspectives 24*, Exeter: University of Exeter, School of Education.

Townsend, H. and Brittan, E. (1972) *Organisation in Multiracial Schools*, London: NFER.

Troyna, B. (1993) *Racism and Education*, Buckingham: Open University Press.

Troyna, B. and Carrington, B. (1990) *Education, Racism and Reform*, London: Routledge.

Troyna, B. and Hatcher, R. (1992) *Racism in Children's Lives: A Study of Mainly-White Primary Schools*, London: Routledge.

Walkerdine, V. (1985) On the regulation of speaking and silence: subjectivity, class and gender in contemporary schooling, in C. Steedman, C. Urwin and V. Walkerdine (eds), *Language, Gender and Childhood*, London: Routledge and Kegan Paul.

Walkerdine, V. and Lucey, H. (1989) *Democracy in the Kitchen*, London: Virago.

Wolfendale, S. (1994) Parents views of home-school links, parents in a learning society, *Royal Society of Arts News*, **4**, p. 5.

Wright, C. (1987) Black students, white teachers, in B. Troyna (ed.), *Racial Inequality in Education*, London: Tavistock.

Wright, C. (1992) *Race Relations within the Primary School*, London: David Fulton.

Index